National Key Book Publishing Planning Project of the 13th Five
"十三五"国家重点图书出版规划项目
International Clinical Medicine Series Based on the Belt and Road Initiative
"一带一路"背景下国际化临床医学丛书

Medical Chinese

医学汉语

Chief Editor　Wang Huamin　Jiang Yaochuan
主编　王华民　　　蒋尧传

郑州大学出版社
ZHENGZHOU UNIVERSITY PRESS

图书在版编目(CIP)数据

医学汉语 = Medical Chinese：英文／王华民，蒋尧传主编. — 郑州：郑州大学出版社，2021.10

("一带一路"背景下国际化临床医学丛书)

ISBN 978-7-5645-6590-9

Ⅰ.①医… Ⅱ.①王…②蒋… Ⅲ.①医学 - 汉语 - 对外汉语教学 - 教材 Ⅳ.①H195.4

中国版本图书馆 CIP 数据核字(2019)第 157863 号

医学汉语 = Medical Chinese：英文

项目负责人	孙保营　杨秦予	策划编辑	孙保营
责任编辑	李龙传　董　珊	装帧设计	苏永生
责任校对	张彦勤	责任监制	凌　青　李瑞卿

出版发行	郑州大学出版社有限公司	地　　址	郑州市大学路 40 号(450052)
出 版 人	孙保营	网　　址	http://www.zzup.cn
经　　销	全国新华书店	发行电话	0371-66966070
印　　刷	河南文华印务有限公司		
开　　本	850 mm×1 168 mm　1／16		
印　　张	18.5	字　　数	714 千字
版　　次	2021 年 10 月第 1 版	印　　次	2021 年 10 月第 1 次印刷

书　　号	ISBN 978-7-5645-6590-9	定　　价	79.00 元

Staff of Expert Steering Committee

Chairmen

Zhong Shizhen Li Sijin Lü Chuanzhu

Vice Chairmen

Bai Yuting	Chen Xu	Cui Wen	Huang Gang	Huang Yuanhua
Jiang Zhisheng	Li Yumin	Liu Zhangsuo	Luo Baojun	Lü Yi
Tang Shiying				

Committee Member

An Dongping	Bai Xiaochun	Cao Shanying	Chen Jun	Chen Yijiu
Chen Zhesheng	Chen Zhihong	Chen Zhiqiao	Ding Yueming	Du Hua
Duan Zhongping	Guan Chengnong	Huang Xufeng	Jian Jie	Jiang Yaochuan
Jiao Xiaomin	Li Cairui	Li Guoxin	Li Guoming	Li Jiabin
Li Ling	Li Zhijie	Liu Hongmin	Liu Huifan	Liu Kangdong
Song Weiqun	Tang Chunzhi	Wang Huamin	Wang Huixin	Wang Jiahong
Wang Jiangang	Wang Wenjun	Wang Yuan	Wei Jia	Wen Xiaojun
Wu Jun	Wu Weidong	Wu Xuedong	Xie Xieju	Xue Qing
Yan Wenhai	Yan Xinming	Yang Donghua	Yu Feng	Yu Xiyong
Zhang Lirong	Zhang Mao	Zhang Ming	Zhang Yu'an	Zhang Junjian
Zhao Song	Zhao Yumin	Zheng Weiyang	Zhu Lin	

专家指导委员会

主 任 委 员

钟世镇　李思进　吕传柱

副主任委员（以姓氏汉语拼音为序）

白育庭　陈　旭　崔　文　黄　钢　黄元华　姜志胜

李玉民　刘章锁　雒保军　吕　毅　唐世英

委　　　员（以姓氏汉语拼音为序）

安东平　白晓春　曹山鹰　陈　君　陈忆九　陈哲生

陈志宏　陈志桥　丁跃明　杜　华　段钟平　官成浓

黄旭枫　简　洁　蒋尧传　焦小民　李才锐　李国新

李果明　李家斌　李　玲　李志杰　刘宏民　刘会范

刘康栋　宋为群　唐纯志　王华民　王慧欣　王家宏

王建刚　王文军　王　渊　韦　嘉　温小军　吴　军

吴卫东　吴学东　谢协驹　薛　青　鄢文海　闫新明

杨冬华　余　峰　余细勇　张莉蓉　张　茂　张　明

张玉安　章军建　赵　松　赵玉敏　郑维扬　朱　林

Staff of Editor Steering Committee

编审委员会

Editorial Staff

作者名单

主　编

王华民　　海南医学院

蒋尧传　　桂林医学院

副主编

姜冬梅　　海南医学院

张　帆　　海南医学院

凌　奕　　海南医学院第一附属医院

吕兆格　　郑州大学

蒋　伟　　桂林医学院

编　委（以姓氏汉语拼音为序）

代　晶　　桂林医学院

金心怡　　海南医学院

刘　畅　　徐州医科大学

马　平　　山东中医药大学

马生元　　桂林医学院

毛　雪　　郑州大学

王　越　　昆明医科大学

尹忠慧　　河北中医学院

张　勇　　昆明医科大学

张均智　　桂林医学院

Preface

At the Second Belt and Road Summit Forum on International Cooperation in 2019 and the Seventy-third World Health Assembly in 2020, General Secretary Xi Jinping stated the importance for promoting the construction of the "Belt and Road" and jointly build a community for human health. Countries and regions along the "Belt and Road" have a large number of overseas Chinese communities, and shared close geographic proximity, similarities in culture, disease profiles and medical habits. They also shared a profound mass base with ample space for cooperation and exchange in Clinical Medicine. The publication of the International Clinical Medicine series for clinical researchers, medical teachers and students in countries along the "Belt and Road" is a concrete measure to promote the exchange of Chinese and foreign medical science and technology with mutual appreciation and reciprocity.

Zhengzhou University Press coordinated more than 600 medical experts from over 160 renowned medical research institutes, medical schools and clinical hospitals across China. It produced this set of medical tools in English to serve the needs for the construction of the "Belt and Road". It comprehensively coversaspects in the theoretical framework and clinical practices in Clinical Medicine, including basic science, multiple clinical specialities and social medicine. It reflects the latest academic and technological developments, and the international frontiers of academic advancements in Clinical Medicine. It shared with the world China's latest diagnosis and therapeutic approaches, clinical techniques, and experiences in prescription and medication. It has an important role in disseminating contemporary Chinese medical science and technology innovations, demonstrating the achievements of modern China's economic and social development, and promoting the unique charm of Chinese culture to the world.

The series is the first set of medical tools written in English by Chinese medical experts to serve the needs of the "Belt and Road" construction. It systematically and comprehensively reflects the Chinese characteristics in Clinical Medicine. Also, it presents a landmark achievement in the implementation of the "Belt and Road" initiative in promoting exchanges in medical science and technology. This series is theoretical in nature, with each volume built on the mainlines in traditional disciplines but at the same time introducing contemporary theories that guide clinical practices, diagnosis and treatment methods, echoing the latest research findings in Clinical Medicine.

As the disciplines in Clinical Medicine rapidly advances, different views on knowledge, inclusiveness, and medical ethics may arise. We hope this work will facilitate the exchange of ideas, build common ground while allowing differences, and contribute to the building of a community for human health in a broad spectrum of disciplines and research focuses.

Nick Lemoine

Foreign Academician of the Chinese Academy of Engineering

Dean, Academy of Medical Sciences of Zhengzhou University

Director, Barts Cancer Institute, London, UK

6th August, 2020

2019 年海南省高等学校教育教学改革研究重点项目(编号:Hnjg2019-54)

前　言

随着我国国际地位不断提升和对外开放程度不断扩大,来华学习医学的留学生迅速增多。2020 年教育部颁布《来华留学生临床医学专业本科教育(英语授课)质量控制标准(试行)》,明确指出汉语及医学汉语须作为必修课程贯穿临床实习前的教学全过程,以满足留学生在华学习、实践和生活需要。

医学汉语(Medical Chinese)也称"特殊用途汉语"即:Chinese for Special Purpose(ESC)或 Subject-related Chinese。就课程性质而言,其目的主要是提高学习者在医院这一特定环境或其他环境下,与患者和医务工作人员就患者的病情或相关疾病,用汉语进行交流的听、说、读、写综合交际能力。与医学专业课程注重医学知识的传授和技能的训练有较大区别。

本教材的编写目的是满足留学生在华学习生活和临床见习、实习接触患者的需要,培养和训练留学生在医院见习、实习时的听说能力,阅读一般病历、检验报告等医院日常文档的能力以及根据与患者及其家属、指导医生等人员的交谈记录患者情况的书写能力。教材内容包含医学专业术语、常用句式及体现医学用语语体风格的对话及短文等。本教材使用对象是汉语能力达到新汉语水平考试四级(新 HSK 4)的来华临床医学本科(英语授课)留学生,也可供具有一定汉语水平的护理专业留学生和对医学汉语感兴趣的外国人使用。

本教材注重突出以下几个特点。

1. 根据留学生汉语学习特点和需求选择编写内容,注重教材的实用性和针对性。

目前国内学习医学汉语的留学生多为学过 1~3 年普通汉语,汉语水平达到 HSK 3~4 级的留学生。大多数医学院校在第 5~9 学期开设医学汉语课程,总课时数为 100~300 学时。在医院见习和实习期间,听说为最常用的沟通方式,其次为阅读,最后为书写。因此,本教材以医学生在医院场景中与患者和医务工作人员的交际为基础,采用对话为主、短文为辅,外加少量病历等应用文形式呈现,突出了教材的实用性和针对性。

2. 遵循一般语言教材的编写规律,融入交际法、任务型和主题式语言教学理念,以医学专业知识为载体培养留学生的专业汉语交际能力。

交际法、任务型教学理念强调在真实的语言情景中培养留学生的语言交际能力。主题式语言教学理念以内容为载体、以文本的内涵为主体,强调内容的多样性和丰富性。本教材以相关科室的常见疾病的真实典型病例为基础编写,尽量再现真实的医学场景,帮助留学生在接近真实的医学场景中习得和培养汉语交际能力。相关单元又采用"关键词+功能+医学知识"相结合的方式编排,帮助留学生在提高医学汉语交际能力的同时,也了解和促进相关的专业知识的学习。

3. 根据医学专业知识的特点,注重教材的系统性和科学性。

本教材根据我国三级综合医院机构设置和医学专业学习的特点,以医院主要临床科室和人体系统为线索,选取各科室和各系统常见病为主题组织编排教学内容,重点教授医院各科室、常用药物、人体结构、常见病的中文名称以及各类常见病主要症状和体征的汉语表达方式等,突出了教材的系统性。整合医学基础知识与临床医学汉语交际对话,突出了教材的科学性。

本教材共 31 个单元,每单元由教学目的、热身、会话、短文和练习 5 个部分组成。热身部分为相应单元涉及到的人体系统或病症症状的关键词,引导留学生回顾所学专业基础课程的汉语表达方式,教师可根据留学生的实际情况做相应的回顾和拓展,为后面的会话及短文学习做铺垫。为引导留学生逐渐适应阅读汉字篇章的能力,前十课课文标注了拼音,后二十一课课文没有标注拼音。因为医学汉语通常是在特定的场景中使用,范围有限,专业性强。因此,本教材的生词部分主要是根据课文内容需要,以实用先行为原则选择编排,没有严格按照汉语水平考试的词汇大纲等级要求进行编排。

本教材也是海南省高等学校教育教学改革研究重点项目——来琼学历国际学生汉语课程体系优化实践与探究(编号:Hnjg2019-54)的阶段性研究成果。由海南医学院牵头组织桂林医学院、郑州大学、昆明医科大学、徐州医科大学、山东中医药大学、河北中医学院等高校的一线医学汉语教师共同完成。从编写大纲、教材编写、审稿到出版,都付出了大量时间精力。在此谨向本教材编写团队表示衷心的感谢。编写过程中,参阅了大量网上资料,参考了部分汉语教材和前辈时贤的论著,在此特别对相关作者表示感谢。本教材的顺利完成,得到了郑州大学出版社的大力支持和帮助,在此表示衷心的感谢。

由于编写时间较短,编写人员水平有限,不足之处在所难免,诚望专家、同仁和使用者批评指正。

编　者

目　录

第一单元

消化内科（一）——慢性胃炎

我肚子痛得很厉害

第一单元
生词、对话、短文

【学习目的】

1.学会用汉语表述胃的解剖结构。

2.学会用汉语问诊慢性胃炎的典型病例。

3.了解慢性胃炎的相关医学常识。

【热身】

一、给下面的词语选择对应的字母。

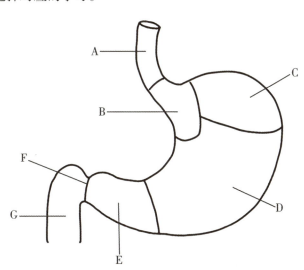

1.食管_____　　2.胃底_____　　3.贲门_____　　4.幽门_____　　5.幽门窦_____

6.胃体_____　　7.十二指肠_____

二、根据汉字写英文。

1.贲门_____

2.幽门窦_____

　　3.十二指肠＿＿＿＿＿＿＿＿＿＿＿＿

　　4.食管＿＿＿＿＿＿＿＿＿＿＿＿

　　5.幽门＿＿＿＿＿＿＿＿＿＿＿＿

【会话】

场景简介:
人物:患者——李可(男,54 岁)
　　　医生——王华(男,47 岁)
　　　实习医生——赛义德(男,25 岁,巴基斯坦人)
地点:消化内科门诊

对话一

生词

序号	词语	词性	拼音	词义
1	呕吐	动	ǒutù	vomit
2	食欲	名	shíyù	appetite
3	吗丁啉	名	Mǎdīnglín	Domperidone
4	胃炎	名	wèiyán	gastritis
5	胃镜	名	wèijìng	gastroscope

李　可:王医生,我肚子痛得很厉害。

王　华:您肚子痛了多久了?

李　可:大概有 1 个星期了,特别是吃完饭以后。

王　华:您吃了什么生、冷、硬、辣的东西没有?

李　可:没有。

王　华:肚子痛的时候有没有恶心、呕吐?

李　可:有时候有,吃的东西都吐出来了。

王　华:呕吐物里面有血吗?

李　可:没有。

王　华:这段时间精神、食欲、大小便怎么样?

李　可:食欲不太好,不太想吃东西。去药店买了吗丁啉吃,但还是很痛。

王　华:根据您的症状,我考虑您得的是慢性胃炎。还需要给您做胃镜检查才能进一步明确诊断。

　　Lǐ Kě:Wáng yīsheng,wǒ dùzi tòng de hěn lìhai。

　　Wáng Huá:Nín dùzi tòng le duōjiǔ le?

　　Lǐ Kě:Dàgài yǒu yí gè xīngqī le,tèbié shì chī wán fàn yǐhòu。

　　Wáng Huá:Nǐ chī le shénme shēng lěng yìng là de dōngxi méiyǒu?

　　Lǐ Kě:Méiyǒu。

　　Wáng Huá:Dùzi tòng de shíhou yǒu méiyǒu ěxin、ǒutù?

　　Lǐ Kě:Yǒu shíhou huì yǒu,chī de dōngxi dōu tǔ chūlái le。

　　Wáng Huá:Ǒutùwù lǐmiàn yǒu xuè ma?

Lǐ Kě：Méiyǒu。

Wáng Huá：Zhè duàn shíjiān jīngshen、shíyù、dàxiǎobiàn zěnmeyàng?

Lǐ Kě：Shíyù bú tài hǎo，bú tài xiǎng chī dōngxi。Qù yàodiàn mǎi le Mǎdīnglín chī，dàn háishì hěn tòng。

Wáng Huá：Gēnjù nín de zhèngzhuàng，wǒ kǎolǜ nín dé de shì mànxìng wèiyán。Hái xūyào gěi nín zuò wèijìng jiǎnchá cái néng jìn yí bù míngquè zhěnduàn。

Li Ke：Doctor Wang，I have a terrible stomachache.

Wang Hua：How long have you had a stomachache?

Li Ke：About one week，especially after dinner.

Wang Hua：Did you eat any cold，spicy or any other food hard to digest?

Li Ke：No.

Wang Hua：Do you have nausea and vomiting during stomachache?

Li Ke：Sometime the eaten foods are spitted out.

Wang Hua：Is there any blood mixed with it?

Li Ke：No.

Wang Hua：During this period do you feel exhaustion，loss of appetite? And how about the recent urinating and defecating?

Li Ke：Appetite is not good. Do not like to eat food. I took Domperidone from nearby drugstore. But it still hurts.

Wang Hua：According to your symptoms it shows chronic gastritis. For definitive diagnosis I suggest you to do a gastroscopy.

对话二

生词

序号	词语	词性	拼音	词义
1	幽门螺杆菌	名	yōumén luógǎnjūn	*Helicobacter pylori*
2	感染	动	gǎnrǎn	infect
3	临床表现	–	línchuáng biǎoxiàn	general clinic manifestation
4	上腹部	名	shàng fùbù	upper abdomen
5	诊断	动	zhěnduàn	diagnose

王　华：慢性胃炎最常见的病因是什么?

赛义德：最常见的病因是幽门螺杆菌感染。

王　华：慢性胃炎一般有什么临床表现?

赛义德：大多数患者无症状。也可表现为恶心、呕吐、反酸、上腹部痛等。查体可有上腹部轻压痛。

王　华：慢性胃炎的诊断方法主要是什么?

赛义德：胃镜及活组织检查，可同时行幽门螺杆菌检查。

Wáng Huá：Mànxìng wèiyán zuì chángjiàn de bìngyīn shì shénme?

Sài Yìdé：Zuì chángjiàn de bìngyīn shì yōumén luógǎnjūn gǎnrǎn。

Wáng Huá：Mànxìng wèiyán yìbān yǒu shénme línchuáng biǎoxiàn？

Sài Yìdé：Dà duōshù huànzhě wú zhèngzhuàng。Yě kě biǎoxiàn wéi ěxin、ǒutù、fǎnsuān、shàng fùbù tòng děng。Chátǐ kě yǒu shàng fùbù qīng yātòng。

Wáng Huá：Mànxìng wèiyán de zhěnduàn fāngfǎ zhǔyào shì shénme？

Sài Yìdé：Wèijìng jí huózǔzhī jiǎnchá，kě tóngshí xíng yōumén luógǎnjūn jiǎnchá。

Wang Hua：What is the most common cause of chronic gastritis？

Sayyid：The most common cause is *Helicobacter pylori* infection.

Wang Hua：What are the general clinic manifestation of chronic gastritis？

Sayyid：Most patients present no symptom. May have nausea，vomiting，acid reflux，epigastric pain etc. Physical examination may have light tenderness in upper abdomen.

Wang Hua：What are the main diagnostic methods of chronic gastritis？

Sayyid：Gastroscopy and biopsy at the same time for detecting *Helicobacter pylori*.

【短文】

生词

序号	词语	词性	拼音	词义
1	慢性	形	mànxìng	chronic
2	萎缩性	形	wěisuōxìng	atrophic
3	动脉硬化	名	dòngmài yìnghuà	arteriosclerosis
4	胃黏膜	名	wèi niánmó	gastric mucosa
5	嗳气	名	àiqì	belching
6	胃纳	名	wèinà	appetite
7	复查	动	fùchá	recheck
8	病变	动	bìngbiàn	lesion
9	癌变	动	áibiàn	canceration

慢性萎缩性胃炎

慢性萎缩性胃炎是消化系统常见的疾病之一，在慢性胃炎中占10％～30％。

引起慢性萎缩性胃炎的原因很多，如动脉硬化，不好的烟、酒、茶、饮食习惯等都容易损害胃黏膜，引起慢性萎缩性胃炎。慢性萎缩性胃炎的临床表现为上腹部饱胀、嗳气、胃纳减退等症状。胃镜检查是目前慢性萎缩性胃炎的主要诊断方法，但是更深入的检查还需要病理组织学检查。

慢性萎缩性胃炎可以用药物治疗，需要积极治疗幽门螺杆菌，还要定期做胃镜复查，这样才能尽量减少病变，避免癌变。

Mànxìng wěisuōxìng wèiyán

Mànxìng wěisuōxìng wèiyán shì xiāohuà xìtǒng chángjiàn de jíbìng zhī yī，zài mànxìng wèiyán zhōng zhàn 10％～30％。

Yǐnqǐ mànxìng wěisuōxìng wèiyán de yuányīn hěn duō，rú dòngmài yìnghuà，bú hǎo de yān、 jiǔ、chá、yǐnshí xíguàn děng dōu róngyì sǔnhài wèi niánmó, yǐnqǐ mànxìng wěisuōxìng wèiyán。Mànxìng wěisuōxìng wèiyán de línchuáng biǎoxiàn wéi shàng fùbù bǎozhàng、àiqì、wèinà jiǎntuì děng zhèngzhuàng。Wèijìng jiǎnchá shì mùqián mànxìng wěisuōxìng wèiyán de zhǔyào zhěnduàn fāngfǎ,dànshì gèng shēnrù de jiǎnchá hái xūyào bìnglǐ zǔzhīxué jiǎnchá。

Mànxìng wěisuōxìng wèiyán kěyǐ yòng yàowù zhìliáo,xūyào jījí zhìliáo yōumén luógǎnjūn,háiyào dìngqī zuò wèijìng fùchá,zhèyàng cáinéng jǐnliàng jiǎnshǎo bìngbiàn,bìmiǎn áibiàn。

Chronic atrophic gastritis

Chronic atrophic gastritis is one of the common diseases in digestive system,accounting for 10% – 30% of chronic gastritis.

There are many causes of chronic atrophic gastritis,such as arteriosclerosis,alcohol consumption,smoking and excess consumption of tea and so on. This can easily damage gastric mucosa and cause the disease. The clinical manifestations of disease are upper abdominal distention,belching,decreased appetite and similar other symptoms. Gastroscopy is the main diagnostic method for chronic atrophic gastritis,but biopsy for histopathological examination is necessary to rule out the disease.

Chronic atrophic gastritis can be treated with drugs,and it needs to treat *Helicobacter pylori* actively. Routine gastroscopy is recommended. In this way the recurrence of disease can be minimized and the gastric cancer can be avoided.

【汉字知识】

部首"火"

部首"火"的意思为"燃烧",一般出现在汉字左侧。以"火"为部首的汉字大都跟燃烧有关。如"燃""烧""炮""烦""焰""烂""灶"等。此类汉字多为形声结构,左侧的部首为形旁,右侧的部件为声旁,代表字音。

例如:烦——心烦　烦躁　烦恼
　　　烂——溃烂　糜烂　腐烂

构词

——炎　表示"炎症"。

例如:胃炎、慢性胃炎、萎缩性胃炎、结膜炎、黏膜炎、关节炎。

——部　表示"身体部位"。

例如:头部、颈部、胸部、腿部、腹部、眼部。

【练习】

一、选择你听到的词语。

1.(　　　) A.呕吐　B.食欲　C.厌食　D.恶心

2.(　　　) A.病因　B.病源　C.病体　D.病症

3.(　　　) A.饱腹　B.腹痛　C.腹胀　D.腹部

4.(　　　) A.胃痛　B.反酸　C.胃炎　D.紊乱

5.(　　　) A.嗳气　B.胀气　C.疝气　D.酸气

二、根据听到的句子排列词语和短语。

1.感染　幽门螺杆菌　最主要　是　的　病因

2.胃炎　考虑　的　是　得　您　慢性　我

3. 痛　我　厉害　得　肚子

4. 胃镜检查　还需要　明确诊断　做　进一步　才能

三、仿照句子造句。

1. 您先去办住院手续,之后医生会对您进行系统治疗。

_____先去_____,之后_____。

_____先去_____,之后_____。

2. 我去药店买了吗丁啉吃,但是没有用。

_____,但是_____。

_____,但是_____。

3. 我肚子痛得厉害。

_____得厉害。

_____得厉害。

4. 根据您的症状,我考虑您得的是慢性胃炎。

根据_____,我考虑您得的是_____。

根据_____,我考虑您得的是_____。

四、选词填空。

呕吐物　诊断　复查　上腹部　胃炎

1. 查体可有_____轻压痛。

2. 定期做胃镜_____,可以减少病变,避免癌变。

3. 慢性胃炎的_____方法主要是什么?

4. 慢性_____主要有什么临床表现?

5. _____里面有血吗?

五、完成下面的对话和句子。

（一）

李　可:王医生,我肚子_____。

王　华:肚子痛了多久了?

李　可:大概有 1 个星期了,特别是吃完饭以后。

王　华:是吃了什么生、冷、硬、辣的东西吗?

李　可:没有。

王　华:肚子痛的时候有没有_____、_____?

李　可:有时候会有,吃的东西都吐出来了。

王　华:_____里面有血吗?

李　可:没有。

王　华:这段时间精神、_____、大小便怎么样?

李　可:食欲不太好,不太想吃东西。去药店_____,但还是很痛。

王　华:根据您的症状,我考虑您得的是_____。目前还需要给您做_____才能

进一步_____。

（二）

1. 不同病因引起的各种慢性_____病变。

2. 慢性胃炎最常见的_____是什么?

3. 大多数患者_____。

4. 辅助检查：＿＿＿＿＿＿＿＿、＿＿＿＿＿＿＿＿＿＿及＿＿＿＿＿＿＿检测。

六、根据对话和短文内容回答问题。

1. 慢性胃炎最常见的病因是什么？

2. 李可肚子痛了多久了？

3. 医生给李可安排了什么检查？

4. 慢性萎缩性胃炎在慢性胃炎中占多少比例？

5. 慢性萎缩性胃炎应该怎么治疗？

七、交际练习。

患者 A 因肚子痛来到医院消化内科就诊,医生 B 向患者 A 询问了症状。患者 A 说他肚子痛了 1 个星期了,伴随恶心、呕吐,自行从药店买了胃药来吃,但是没有效果,发病以来食欲差,体重变轻,所以就来医院就诊。医生给他安排了胃镜检查,并得出初步诊断。

两人一组,分别扮演角色 A、B,组织一段 3 分钟左右的对话展现上文场景。

【补充医学词汇】

序号	词语	拼音	词义
1	微生物	wēishēngwù	microorganism
2	毒素	dúsù	toxin
3	胆汁	dǎnzhī	bile
4	水肿	shuǐzhǒng	edema
5	糜烂	mílàn	erosion

（蒋　伟　马生元）

第二单元

消化内科（二）——消化性溃疡

除了肚子痛，还有什么不舒服吗

【学习目的】

1. 学会用汉语表述消化系统的主要器官。
2. 学会用汉语问诊典型消化性溃疡病例。
3. 了解消化性溃疡的相关医学常识。

【热身】

一、给下面的词语选择对应的字母。

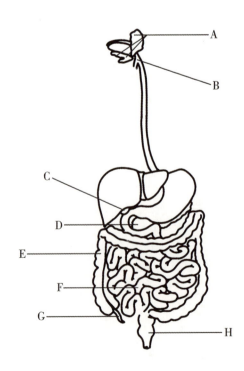

1. 唾液腺_____ 2. 大肠_____ 3. 胆囊_____ 4. 小肠_____ 5. 咽_____

6. 胰腺_____ 7. 阑尾_____ 8. 直肠_____

二、下面消化系统各器官排列顺序正确的是(　　　　)。

A. 咽、阑尾、胰腺、小肠、大肠

B. 唾液腺、阑尾、胰腺、咽、大肠、小肠

C. 唾液腺、咽、胆囊、胰腺、大肠、小肠

D. 咽、胆囊、胰腺、小肠、大肠、阑尾

【会话】

场景简介:

人物:患者——艾维(女,22 岁)

　　　医生——李玲(女,45 岁)

地点:消化内科门诊

对话一

生词

序号	词语	词性	拼音	词义
1	打嗝	动	dǎgé	hiccup
2	恶心	形	ěxin	nausea
3	反酸	动	fǎnsuān	sour regurgitation
4	黑便	名	hēibiàn	dark stools;melena
5	验血	动	yànxuè	blood test
6	血生化	名	xuè shēnghuà	blood biochemistry
7	心电图	名	xīndiàntú	electrocardiogram
8	消化性溃疡	名	xiāohuàxìng kuìyáng	peptic ulcer

艾　维:李医生好! 我肚子(指上腹部)很痛。

李　玲:这样大概多久了? 怎么痛的?

艾　维:4 年多了,偶尔隐隐的痛,特别是饭后和饮酒后。

李　玲:每次持续多久?

艾　维:每次约半个小时。

李　玲:除了肚子痛,还有什么不舒服吗?

艾　维:还打嗝、恶心、反酸。

李　玲:有呕吐、黑便吗?

艾　维:没有,但这周瘦了 2 斤。

李　玲:之前去医院检查过吗?

艾　维:做过验血,没什么问题。

李　玲:现在您需要做血生化、腹部 B 超、立位腹平片、心电图等检查。

(患者检查结果出来后)

李　玲:结合您的症状和检查结果,初步诊断您得的是消化性溃疡。您再做个胃镜检查才能进一步确定。这段时间请注意饮食和休息,不要吃刺激性食物。

艾　维：好，谢谢医生。

Ài Wéi：Lǐ yīsheng hǎo！Wǒ dùzi（zhǐ shàng fùbù）hěn tòng。

Lǐ Líng：Zhèyàng dàgài duō jiǔ le？zěnme tòng de？

Ài Wéi：4 nián duō le，óu'ěr yǐnyǐn de tòng，tèbié shì fàn hòu hé yǐnjiǔ hòu。

Lǐ Líng：Měi cì chíxù duōjiǔ？

Ài Wéi：Měi cì yuē bàn gè xiǎoshí。

Lǐ Líng：Chúle dùzi tòng，háiyǒu shénme bù shūfu ma？

Ài Wéi：Hái dǎgé、ěxin、fǎnsuān。

Lǐ Líng：Yǒu ǒutù、hēibiàn ma？

Ài Wéi：Méiyǒu，dàn zhè zhōu shòu le 2 jīn。

Lǐ Líng：Zhīqián qù yīyuàn jiǎnchá guò ma？

Ài Wéi：Zuò guò yànxuè，méi shénme wèntí。

Lǐ Líng：Xiànzài nín xūyào zuò xuè shēnghuà，fùbù B chāo，lì wèi fù píng piàn，xīndiàntú děng jiǎnchá。

（Huànzhě jiǎnchá jiéguǒ chūlái hòu）

Lǐ Líng：Jiéhé nín de zhèngzhuàng hé jiǎnchá jiéguǒ，chūbù zhěnduàn nín dé de shì xiāohuàxìng kuìyáng。Nín zài zuò gè wèijìng jiǎnchá cáinéng jìn yí bù quèdìng。Zhè duàn shíjiān qǐng zhùyì yǐnshí hé xiūxi，bú yào chī cìjīxìng shíwù。

Ài Wéi：Hǎo，xièxiè yīsheng。

Ai Wei：Hello Dr. Li，I have abdominal pain（pointing the upper abdomen）.

Li Ling：How long have you been like this？ How does it pain？

Ai Wei：It's more than four years，occasionally dull pain，especially after meal and after drinking wine.

Li Ling：Each time how long does it last？

Ai Wei：Each time about half an hour.

Li Ling：Do you have any other discomfort feeling beside abdominal pain？

Ai Wei：Hiccup，nausea and water brash.

Li Ling：Do you have vomiting，black stool？

Ai Wei：No，but this week I lose 1 kg weight.

Li Ling：Have you ever been to hospital for checking up before？

Ai Wei：I did blood test，there was no any problem.

Li Ling：Now you need to test blood biochemistry，ultrasound of abdomen，X-ray of abdomen，electro-cardiogram.

（After patient laboratory report is out）

Li Ling：With your symptoms and lab report，you are initially diagnosed as peptic ulcer. You need to do endoscopy before you can make further confirmation. Please pay attention to diet and rest，during this period and do not eat spicy food.

Ai Wei：OK，thanks doctor.

对话二

生词

序号	词语	词性	拼音	词义
1	胃窦	名	wèidòu	antrum of stomach
2	溃疡灶	名	kuìyáng zào	ulcer lesion
3	活检	动	huójiǎn	biopsies
4	胃溃疡	名	wèikuìyáng	gastric ulcer（GU）
5	麻醉	动	mázuì	anesthetic
6	戒	动	jiè	quit

李　玲：您的胃镜检查结果显示,在胃窦部发现溃疡灶,可以确诊您患的是胃溃疡。已为您取了活检,后续将做幽门螺杆菌检测和病理检查。

艾　维：谢谢医生。有什么需要注意的吗?

李　玲：现在麻醉作用还没有消失,不能喝水、吃东西,等检查完两个小时后才能吃流食。

李　玲：还要注意饮食和休息,戒烟戒酒,不要吃刺激性食物。

艾　维：好的,谢谢医生。

Lǐ Líng：Nín de wèijìng jiǎnchá jiéguǒ xiǎnshì,zài wèidòu bù fāxiàn kuìyáng zào,kěyǐ quèzhěn nín huàn de shì wèikuìyáng。Yǐ wéi nín qǔ le huójiǎn,hòuxù jiāng zuò yōumén luógǎnjūn jiǎncè hé bìnglǐ jiǎnchá。

Ài Wéi：Xièxiè yīsheng。Yǒu shénme xūyào zhùyì de ma?

Lǐ Líng：Xiànzài mázuì zuòyòng hái méiyǒu xiāoshī,bù néng hē shuǐ、chī dōngxi,děng jiǎnchá wán liǎnggè xiǎoshí hòu cái néng chī liúshí。

Lǐ Líng：Háiyào zhùyì yǐnshí hé xiūxi,jiè yān jiè jiǔ,bú yào chī cìjīxìng shíwù。

Ài Wéi：Hǎo de,xièxiè yīsheng。

Li Ling：Your gastro copy results show that the gastric ulcer is found in the solid part of the stomach. Biopsies have been taken for you, and *helicobacter pylori* detection and pathological examination will be done later.

Ai Wei：Thank you doctor. Is there anything for which I need to pay attention?

Li Ling：As for now the anesthetic effect has not disappeared, so you can't eat or drink anything, soon after two hours of inspection then you can eat only liquid food.

Li Ling：Also pay attention to diet and rest, quit smoking and drinking, do not eat spicy food.

Ai Wei：Okay, thank you doctor.

【短文】

生词

序号	词语	词性	拼音	词义
1	十二指肠	名	shí'èrzhǐcháng	duodenum
2	酸性	形	suānxìng	acidic

序号	词语	词性	拼音	词义
3	周期性	形	zhōuqīxìng	periodic
4	节律性	形	jiélǜxìng	rhythmic
5	唾液	名	tuòyè	saliva
6	胃灼热	形	wèi zhuórè	heartburn
7	反胃	形	fǎnwèi	regurgitation
8	钡餐	名	bèicān	barium meal
9	血清胃泌素	名	xuèqīng wèimìsù	serum gastric
10	根除	动	gēnchú	eradicate
11	抑制	动	yìzhì	inhibit

消化性溃疡

消化性溃疡主要是发生在胃和十二指肠的一种慢性溃疡。

引起消化性溃疡的原因主要是酸性胃液对胃黏膜的消化作用。男性更容易患这种病。消化性溃疡的临床表现为长期性、周期性、节律性的腹部疼痛,还有唾液分泌多、胃灼热、反胃、反酸、嗳气、恶心、呕吐等症状。一般采用的检查方式是十二指肠镜检查和黏膜活检、X 射线钡餐检查、幽门螺杆菌检测、血清胃泌素检测和胃液分析。

消化性溃疡患者需戒烟戒酒,服用药物根除幽门螺杆菌、抑制胃酸分泌、保护胃黏膜。严重的建议外科手术。

Xiāohuàxìng kuìyáng

Xiāohuàxìng kuìyáng zhǔyào shì fāshēng zài wèi hé shí'èrzhǐcháng de yì zhǒng mànxìng kuìyáng。

Yǐnqǐ xiāohuàxìng kuìyáng de yuányīn zhǔyào shì suānxìng wèiyè duì wèi niánmó de xiāohuà zuòyòng。Nánxìng gèng róngyì huàn zhè zhǒng bìng。Xiāohuàxìng kuìyáng de línchuáng biǎoxiàn wéi chángqīxìng、zhōuqīxìng、jiélǜxìng de fùbù téngtòng, háiyǒu tuòyè fēnmì duō、wèi zhuórè、fǎnwèi、fǎnsuān、àiqì、ěxin、ǒutù děng zhèngzhuàng。Yìbān cǎiyòng de jiǎnchá fāngshì shì shí'èrzhǐcháng jìng jiǎnchá hé niánmó huójiǎn、X shèxiàn bèicān jiǎnchá、yōumén luógǎnjūn jiǎncè、xuèqīng wèimìsù jiǎncè hé wèiyè fēnxī。

Xiāohuàxìng kuìyáng huànzhě xū jiè yān jiè jiǔ, fúyòng yàowù gēnchú yōumén luógǎnjūn、yìzhì wèisuān fēnmì、bǎohù wèi niánmó。Yánzhòng de jiànyì wàikē shǒushù。

Peptic ulcer

Peptic ulcer is mainly a chronic ulcer occurring in the stomach and duodenum.

The main cause of peptic ulcer is the digestion of gastric mucosa by acidic gastric juice. Men are more likely to suffer from this disease. The clinical manifestation of peptic ulcer are chronic, periodic rhythmic abdominal pain and many saliva secretion, heartburn, regurgitation, sour regurgitation, eructation, nausea, vomiting and other symptoms. Generally, duodenal examination and mucosal biopsy, X-ray barium meal examination Helicobacter pylori detection, serum gastric test and gastric juice analysis are commonly used.

Peptic ulcer patient need to quit smoking and drinking, take drugs to eradicate helicobacter pylori, inhibit gastric acid secretion, and protect gastric mucosa. Serious surgery is recommended.

【汉字知识】

部首"月"

部首"月"的意思为"肉体",一般出现在汉字的左侧。以"月"为部首的汉字大都跟身体有关。如"胖""肚""脸""腿""脑""肥""股""腹"等。此类汉字多为形声结构,左侧的部首为形旁,右侧的部件为声旁,代表字音。

　　例如:腹——腹部　小腹　腹痛

　　　　腿——大腿　腿部　抬腿

构词

——溃疡　表示"溃疡性病变"。

例如:口腔溃疡、胃溃疡、十二指肠溃疡。

——化　表示"性质或形态发生改变"。

例如:消化、钙化、绿化、美化、变化。

【练习】

一、选择听到的词语。

(　　　)1. A. 溃疡　B. 贵阳　C. 贵恙　D. 胃疡

(　　　)2. A. 恶性　B. 恶心　C. 二线　D. 恶习

(　　　)3. A. 呕吐　B. 呕血　C. 咯血　D. 欧雪

(　　　)4. A. 味精　B. 微晶　C. 卫星　D. 胃镜

(　　　)5. A. 吃惊　B. 刺激　C. 伺机　D. 次级

二、根据听到的句子排列词语和短语。

1. 是　诊断　消化性溃疡　您　初步　的　得

2. 确定　胃镜检查　您　进一步　才能　做　需要

3. 消失　麻醉作用　您　还　现在　没有

4. 病　男性　更容易　一般　这种　患

三、仿照句子造句。

1. 除了肚子痛,还有什么不舒服吗?

除了_____,还有_____。

除了_____,还有_____。

2. 结合您的症状和检查结果,初步诊断您得的是消化性溃疡。

结合_____,初步诊断_____。

结合_____,初步诊断_____。

3. 您现在麻醉作用还没有消失,还不能马上喝水吃东西。

您现在_____还没有_____,还不能_____。

您现在_____还没有_____,还不能_____。

四、选词填空。

　　　　　溃疡灶　胃镜　麻醉　消化性溃疡　血生化

1. 我之前去医院做过_____检查,没什么问题。

2. 结合您的症状和检查结果,初步诊断您得的是_____。

3. 现在您需要做_____、腹部 B 超、立位腹平片、心电图这些检查。

4. 您的检查结果显示,在胃窦部发现_____。

5. 现在_____作用还没有消失,不能喝水、吃东西。

五、完成下面的对话和句子。

(一)

艾　维:李医生好!

李　玲:_____?

艾　维:肚子痛得很厉害。

李　玲:_____?

艾　维:大约有 4 年多了,反反复复,时好时坏。

李　玲:_____、血生化、腹部 B 超、立位腹平片、心电图检查。

艾　维:好的,医生。

(二)

1. 消化性溃疡因其形成与酸性胃液对黏膜的_____有关而得名。

2. 伴有唾液分泌增多、胃灼热、反胃、反酸、_____、_____、_____等其他胃肠道症状。

3. 消化性溃疡一般需要_____。

4. _____主要指发生在胃部和十二指肠的一种_____。

5. 消化性溃疡临床表现为_____、_____、_____的腹痛。

六、根据对话和短文内容回答问题。

1. 消化性溃疡常见于哪个部位?

2. 消化性溃疡的临床表现是什么?

3. 消化性溃疡主要的实验室检查是什么?

4. 艾维有什么症状?

5. 胃镜活检后有什么注意事项?

七、交际练习。

患者 A 因晚饭后上腹痛来医院消化内科就诊,医生 B 向患者 A 询问症状。患者 A 说他前 1 天晚饭喝了酒,之后开始肚子痛,所以来医院就诊。医生 B 要求他先做血常规、大便常规检查。建议他以后戒酒。

两人一组,分别扮演角色 A、B,组织一段 3 分钟左右的对话展现上文场景。

【补充医学词汇】

序号	词语	拼音	词义
1	胃蛋白酶	wèi dànbái méi	pepsin
2	急性应激	jíxìng yìngjī	acute stress
3	穿孔	chuānkǒng	perforation
4	H_2 受体拮抗剂	H_2 shòutǐ jié kàng jì	H_2 receptor antagonist
5	质子泵抑制剂	zhìzǐ bèng yìzhì jì	proton pump inhibitor

(蒋　伟　马生元)

第三单元

呼吸内科（一）——肺炎

您的右下肺可以听到湿啰音

第三单元
生词、对话、短文

【学习目的】

1. 学会用汉语表述肺部结构。
2. 学会用汉语问诊典型肺炎病例。
3. 了解肺炎的相关医学常识。

【热身】

一、给下面的词语选择对应的字母。

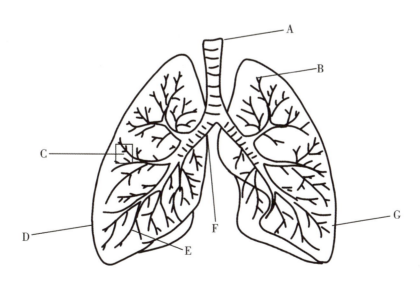

1. 支气管＿＿＿＿＿　2. 肺泡＿＿＿＿＿　3. 左肺＿＿＿＿＿　4. 右肺＿＿＿＿＿　5. 肺组织＿＿＿＿＿
6. 细支气管＿＿＿＿＿　7. 气管＿＿＿＿＿

二、根据拼音写汉字。

1. zuǒfèi _____

2. fèizǔzhī _____

3. fèipào _____

4. xìzhīqìguǎn _____

5. yòufèi _____

6. qìguǎn _____

7. zhīqìguǎn _____

【会话】

场景简介:
人物:患者——马明(男,40 岁)
　　　医生——秦兰(女,45 岁)
　　　实习医生——穆汗默德(男,20 岁,巴基斯坦人)
地点:呼吸内科门诊

对话一

生词

序号	词语	词性	拼音	词义
1	咳痰	动	kétán	cough with phlegm
2	阿莫西林	名	āmòxīlín	amoxicillin
3	过敏	动	guòmǐn	allergy
4	特殊	形	tèshū	special
5	疾病史	名	jíbìngshǐ	disease history
6	解开	动	jiěkāi	unclasp
7	听诊	动	tīngzhěn	auscultate
8	右下肺	名	yòuxiàfèi	lower right lung
9	湿啰音	名	shī luóyīn	moist rales
10	支气管炎	名	zhīqìguǎnyán	bronchitis
11	肺炎	名	fèiyán	pneumonia
12	血常规	名	xuèchángguī	blood routine
13	胸片	名	xiōngpiàn	chest X-ray
14	痰培养	动	tán péiyǎng	sputum culture

秦　兰:您好! 哪里不舒服?
马　明:我最近咳嗽、咳痰,痰是黄色的,特别是晚上咳得厉害。
秦　兰:多长时间了?
马　明:1 个星期了。
秦　兰:发热吗?
马　明:发热,39 ℃左右。
秦　兰:吃过什么药物没有?

马　明:吃了阿莫西林。

秦　兰:有什么药物过敏或者特殊疾病史吗?

马　明:没有。

秦　兰:您把外套解开,我给您做听诊检查。

马　明:好。

秦　兰:您的右下肺可以听到湿啰音,支气管炎或者肺炎的可能性大,需要做一下血常规、胸片和痰培养检查,查找咳嗽的病因。

马　明:好的。谢谢医生!

Qín Lán:Nín hǎo! Nǎlǐ bù shūfu?

Mǎ Míng:Wǒ zuìjìn késou、kétán,tán shì huángsè de,tèbié shì wǎnshang ké de lìhai。

Qín Lán:Duō cháng shíjiān le?

Mǎ Míng:Yí gè xīngqī le。

Qín Lán:Fārè ma?

Mǎ Míng:Fārè,39 shèshìdù zuǒyòu。

Qín Lán:Chī guò shénme yàowù méiyǒu?

Mǎ Míng:Chī le āòxīlín。

Qín Lán:Yǒu shénme yàowù guòmǐn huòzhě tèshū jíbìngshǐ ma?

Mǎ Míng:Méiyǒu。

Qín Lán:Nín bǎ wàitào jiěkāi,wǒ gěi nín zuò tīngzhěn jiǎnchá。

Mǎ Míng:Hǎo。

Qín Lán:Nín de yòuxiàfèi kéyǐ tīng dào shī luóyīn,zhīqìguǎnyán huòzhě fèiyán de kěnéngxìng dà,xūyào zuò yíxià xuèchángguī、xiōngpiàn hé tán péiyǎng jiǎnchá,cházhǎo késou de bìngyīn。

Mǎ Míng:Hǎo de。Xièxiè yīsheng!

Qin Lan:Hello,how can I help you?

Ma Ming:I had cough with yellow phlegm for last few days. It gets worse at night.

Qin Lan:How long has it been?

Ma Ming:It's just about a week.

Qin Lan:Do you have fever?

Ma Ming:Yes,it is around 39 degree centigrade.

Qin Lan:Did you take any medicine?

Ma Ming:Yes,I took Amoxicillin.

Qin Lan:Do you have history of any special disease and drugs allergy?

Ma Ming:No.

Qin Lan:Could you please take off your jacket so that I can auscultate your chest.

Ma Ming:OK.

Qin Lan:I can hear moist rales in lower right lung. Routine exam of blood,chest X-ray and sputum culture are required to rule out the cause of cough.

Ma Ming:OK,doctor. Thank you.

对话二

生词

序号	词语	词性	拼音	词义
1	肺炎链球菌	名	fèiyán liànqiújūn	streptococcus bacteria
2	斑片状浸润影	–	bānpiànzhuàng jìnrùnyǐng	patchy infiltrating shadow
3	白细胞	名	báixìbāo	leukocytosis
4	中性粒细胞	名	zhōngxìng lìxìbāo	neutrophil
5	比例	名	bǐlì	proportion
6	体征	名	tǐzhēng	sign
7	结合	动	jiéhé	combine
8	青霉素	名	qīngméisù	penicillin
9	抗菌	动	kàngjūn	antibiotic

马　　明：医生，这是我的检查结果。

秦　　兰：穆汗默德，你看一下。

穆汗默德：秦医生，他的痰培养结果显示痰里有大量的肺炎链球菌。

秦　　兰：胸片呢？

穆汗默德：他的胸片显示右下肺有一个斑片状浸润影。

秦　　兰：血常规有什么变化？

穆汗默德：白细胞增多，中性粒细胞比例增高。

秦　　兰：马明，根据您的临床表现和体征，结合胸部的 X 射线检查及痰培养和血常规检查，可以确诊您是得了肺炎。

马　　明：医生，要怎么治疗啊？

秦　　兰：可以用青霉素先进行抗菌药物治疗。

Mǎ Míng：Yīsheng，zhè shì wǒde jiǎnchá jiéguǒ。

Qín Lán：Mùhànmòdé，nǐ kàn yí xià。

Mùhànmòdé：Qín yīsheng，tā de tán péiyǎng jiéguǒ xiǎnshì tán lǐ yǒu dàliàng de fèiyán liànqiújūn。

Qín Lán：Xiōngpiàn ne？

Mùhànmòdé：Tā de xiōngpiàn xiǎnshì yòuxiàfèi yǒu yí gè bānpiànzhuàng jìnrùnyǐng。

Qín Lán：Xuèchángguī yǒu shénme biànhuà？

Mùhànmòdé：Báixìbāo zēngduō，zhōngxìnglì xìbāo bǐlì zēnggāo。

Qín Lán：Mǎ Míng，gēnjù nín de línchuáng biǎoxiàn hé tǐzhēng，jiéhé xiōngbù de X shè xiàn jiǎnchá jí tánpéiyǎng hé xuèchángguī jiǎnchá，kéyǐ quèzhěn nín shì dé le fèiyán。

Mǎ Míng：Yīsheng，yào zěnme zhìliáo a？

Qín Lán：Kěyǐ yòng qīngméisù xiān jìnxíng kàngjūn yàowù zhìliáo。

Ma Ming：Doctor，here are my test reports.

Qin Lan：Muhammad，have a look.

Muhammad：Doctor Qin，his sputum culture shows there are a lot of streptococcus pneumoniae in his sputum.

Qin Lan：What about the chest film?

Muhammad：Chest X-ray shows patchy infiltrating shadow in right lower lung.

Qin Lan：What are the changes in blood routine examination?

Muhammad：Leukocytosis，neutrophil count is higher.

Qin Lan：Ma Ming，according to clinical presentation combined with chest X-ray，sputum culture and blood routine examination，you are diagnosed to have pneumonia.

Ma Ming：Doctor，what about the treatment?

Qin Lan：You need to take penicillin antibiotic.

【短文】

生词

序号	词语	词性	拼音	词义
1	器官	名	qìguān	organ
2	呼吸	动	hūxī	breath
3	细菌	名	xìjūn	bacteria
4	鼻腔	名	bíqiāng	nasal cavity
5	咽腔	名	yānqiāng	trachea
6	致病	形	zhìbìng	pathogenic
7	病原体	名	bìngyuántǐ	causative agent
8	过滤	动	guòlǜ	filter
9	免疫力	名	miǎnyìlì	immune capacity
10	细菌性	形	xìjūnxìng	baterial
11	威胁	动	wēixié	threat
12	受凉	动	shòuliáng	catch cold
13	上呼吸道	名	shànghūxīdào	upper respiratory tract
14	忽视	动	hūshì	neglect
15	导致	动	dǎozhì	result in
16	抗生素	名	kàngshēngsù	antibiotics

肺　炎

肺是人体器官中最容易被感染的器官。人们呼吸的空气每时每刻都有细菌。空气通过鼻腔、咽腔进入气管，然后进入肺部。虽然大部分致病病原体被鼻腔、咽腔过滤了，但仍然有很多病原体随着空气进入肺部。当人体免疫力降低时，肺部就会被感染。

细菌性肺炎是最常见的肺炎，对儿童和老年人的健康威胁最大。细菌性肺炎多数是因为受凉引起的，患者一般会有咳嗽、高热、胸痛和上呼吸道感染的症状。很多细菌性肺炎患者，刚患病时症状不明显，因此忽视了治疗，导致病情加重。治疗多选用抗生素。

Fèiyán

Fèi shì réntǐ qìguān zhōng zuì róngyì bèi gǎnrǎn de qìguān。Rénmen hūxī de kōngqì měishíměikè dōu yǒu xìjūn。Kōngqì tōngguò bíqiāng、yānqiāng jìnrù qìguān,ránhòu jìnrù fèibù。Suīrán dà bùfen zhìbìng bìngyuántǐ bèi bíqiāng、yānqiāng guòlǜ le,dàn réngrán yǒu hěnduō bìngyuántǐ suízhe kōngqì jìnrù fèibù。Dāng réntǐ miǎnyìlì jiàngdī shí,fèibù jiù huì bèi gǎnrǎn。

Xìjūnxìng fèiyán shì zuì chángjiàn de fèiyán,duì értóng hé lǎoniánrén de jiànkāng wēixié zuì dà。Xìjūnxìng fèiyán duōshù shì yīnwèi shòuliáng yǐnqǐ de,huànzhě yìbān huì yǒu késou、gāorè、xiōngtòng hé shànghūxīdào gǎnrǎn de zhèngzhuàng。Hěn duō xìjūnxìng fèiyán huànzhě,gāng huànbìng shí zhèngzhuàng bù míngxiǎn,yīncǐ hūshì le zhìliáo,dǎozhì bìngqíng jiāzhòng。Zhìliáo duō xuǎnyòng kàngshēngsù。

Pneumonia

Lungs are the most susceptible organs to cause infection in human body. The air we breath contains various kinds of pathogens. These pathogens along with air enters through nasal cavity to pharynx, trachea and finally to the lungs. Although most pathogens are filtered in nasal cavity and pharynx, there are still many pathogens that enter lungs with air. When immune capacity of our body decreases, the lungs become infected.

Bacterial pneumonia is the most common among children and old population. Major cause of bacterial pneumonia is after catching cold. Patient usually has symptoms of cough, high fever, chest pain and upper respiratory tract infection. Most of time patient with minor symptoms neglect the required treatment, which in turn aggravate the disease condition. Multiple antibiotics therapy is the treatment.

【汉字知识】

部首"口"

部首"口"的意思是"嘴",一般出现在汉字的左侧。以"口"为部首的汉字多与嘴或相关动作有关。如:"吃""喝""呼吸""咬""吹""咳嗽""咽喉"等。此类汉字多为形声结构,左侧的部首为形旁,右侧的部件为声旁,代表字音。

例如:呼——呼吸　呼气　招呼

　　　吸——吸气　吐吸　吸入

构词

——诊　表示"医生为断定病症而察看患者身体的情况"。

例如:听诊、问诊、触诊、视诊。

——病　表示"生物体发生的不健康的现象"。

例如:致病、糖尿病、手足口病、妇科病、心脏病。

【练习】

一、选择听到的词语。

1.(　　) A.咳嗽　　B.瞌睡　　C.吐痰　　D.咳痰

2.(　　) A.过去　　B.过敏　　C.过来　　D.过分

3.(　　) A.抗菌　　B.抗炎　　C.抗体　　D.细菌

4.(　　) A.呼吸　　B.呼气　　C.呼入　　D.吸入

5.（　　　）A.过去　　　B.过滤　　　C.过来　　　D.过程

二、根据听到的句子排列词语和短语。

1.最近　咳嗽　我　咳得　厉害

2.是　应该　或者　支气管炎　肺炎　的　大　可能性

3.胸片　他的　右下肺　显示　一个　有　斑片状　浸润影

4.人体　是　肺　器官中　被　最容易　器官　感染的

三、仿照句子造句。

1.您把外套解开,我给您做听诊检查。

您＿＿＿＿＿＿＿＿＿＿,我给您＿＿＿＿＿＿＿＿＿＿。

您＿＿＿＿＿＿＿＿＿＿,我给您＿＿＿＿＿＿＿＿＿＿。

2.还是要做一下血常规和胸片检查,查找咳嗽的病因。

还是要做一下＿＿＿＿＿＿＿＿＿＿检查,查找＿＿＿＿＿＿＿＿＿＿的病因。

还是要做一下＿＿＿＿＿＿＿＿＿＿检查,查找＿＿＿＿＿＿＿＿＿＿的病因。

3.他的胸片显示右下肺有一个斑片状浸润影。

他的＿＿＿＿＿＿＿＿＿＿显示＿＿＿＿＿＿＿＿＿＿。

他的＿＿＿＿＿＿＿＿＿＿显示＿＿＿＿＿＿＿＿＿＿。

四、选词填空。

痰培养　抗生素　湿啰音　青霉素　免疫力

1.我昨天晚上吃了＿＿＿＿＿＿＿＿＿＿。

2.您的右下肺可以听到＿＿＿＿＿＿＿＿＿＿。

3.他的＿＿＿＿＿＿＿＿＿＿结果显示痰里有大量的肺炎链球菌。

4.细菌性肺炎可采用＿＿＿＿＿＿＿＿＿＿治疗。

5.当人体＿＿＿＿＿＿＿＿＿＿降低时,肺部就会被感染。

五、完成下面的对话和句子。

（一）

穆汗默德:秦医生,他的痰培养结果显示痰里有大量的＿＿＿＿＿＿＿＿＿＿。

秦　　兰:胸片呢?

马　　明:他的胸片显示右下肺有一个＿＿＿＿＿＿＿＿＿＿。

秦　　兰:血常规有什么变化?

穆汗默德:＿＿＿＿＿＿＿＿＿＿增多,中性粒细胞＿＿＿＿＿＿＿＿＿＿。

秦　　兰:根据患者的临床表现和＿＿＿＿＿＿＿＿＿＿,结合＿＿＿＿＿＿＿＿＿＿及痰培养和血常规检查,可以确诊是＿＿＿＿＿＿＿＿＿＿。

（二）

1.仍然有很多＿＿＿＿＿＿＿＿＿＿随着空气进入肺的深处。

2.细菌性肺炎是最常见的肺炎,对儿童和老年人的健康＿＿＿＿＿＿＿＿＿＿最大。

3.因此＿＿＿＿＿＿＿＿＿＿了细菌性肺炎的治疗,＿＿＿＿＿＿＿＿＿＿病情加重。

4.细菌性肺炎多数是因为＿＿＿＿＿＿＿＿＿＿引起的。

5.当人体＿＿＿＿＿＿＿＿＿＿降低时,肺部就会被＿＿＿＿＿＿＿＿＿＿。

六、根据对话和短文内容回答问题。

1. 马明咳嗽多长时间了?

2. 秦兰让马明做了什么检查?

3. 马明的痰培养结果是什么?

4. 秦兰觉得应该怎么治疗?

5. 为什么肺部会感染?

6. 细菌性肺炎有哪些症状?

七、交际练习。

患者 A 因咳嗽、发烧 3 天前来就诊,医生 B 接待了 A。医生 B 向患者 A 询问了症状。医生 B 给他先做体格检查,考虑是肺炎,并让患者 A 做血常规、胸片和痰培养进一步检查。

两人一组,分别扮演角色 A、B,组织一段 3 分钟左右的对话展现上文场景。

【补充医学词汇】

序号	词语	拼音	词义
1	血象	xuè xiàng	hemogram
2	索条影	suǒtiáo yǐng	linear opacities
3	密度影	mìdù yǐng	density
4	纵隔	zòng gé	mediastinum
5	钙化	gài huà	calcification

（张均智　代　晶）

第四单元

呼吸内科(二)——慢性阻塞性肺疾病

您要注意休息,不能受凉

【学习目的】

1.学会用汉语表述慢性阻塞性肺疾病的相关术语。

2.学会用汉语问诊典型慢性阻塞性肺疾病病例。

3.了解慢性阻塞性肺疾病的相关医学常识。

【热身】

一、给下面的词语选择对应的字母。

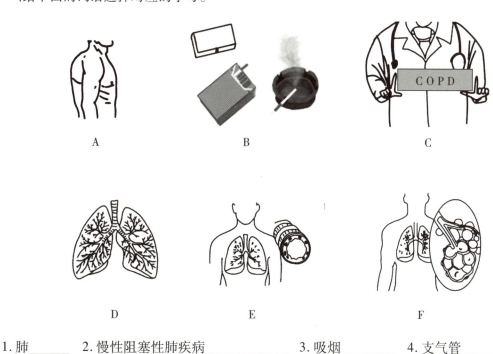

A   B   C

D   E   F

1.肺_____   2.慢性阻塞性肺疾病_____   3.吸烟_____   4.支气管_____

5.桶状胸_____   6.肺泡_____

二、根据英文写汉字。

1. barrel chest＿＿＿＿＿＿

2. chronic bronchitis＿＿＿＿＿＿

3. emphysema＿＿＿＿＿＿

4. alveolus＿＿＿＿＿＿

【会话】

> 人物:患者——赵光荣(男,80 岁)
>   患者家属——朱美艳(女,76 岁)
>   医生——陈林(男,38 岁)
>   实习医生——哈森（男,19 岁,印度人）
> 地点:呼吸内科住院部

对话一

生词

序号	词语	词性	拼音	词义
1	气喘	动	qìchuǎn	asthma
2	厉害	形	lìhai	powerful
3	痰	名	tán	sputum
4	垫	动	diàn	pad
5	枕头	名	zhěntou	pillow
6	抽烟	动	chōuyān	smoking
7	肺气肿	名	fèiqìzhǒng	emphysema
8	慢性支气管炎	名	mànxìng zhīqìguǎnyán	chronic bronchitis

陈　林:大爷,您哪儿不舒服?

朱美艳:他前天晚上受凉,这几天都咳嗽、气喘很厉害。咳嗽时有黄色的痰。走几步就气喘。

陈　林:还有哪儿不舒服?

赵光荣:晚上睡觉不能平躺,垫高枕头才感觉舒服点。

陈　林:抽烟吗?

朱美艳:抽,平均每天抽20 支,都30 年了。

陈　林:大妈,让大爷自己说吧。以前咳嗽、咳痰吗?

赵光荣:咳嗽、咳痰10 年了。冬天或天气冷的时候咳嗽、咳痰更厉害。

陈　林:住过院吗?

赵光荣:住过,医生诊断是肺气肿、慢性支气管炎,但不知道用的什么药。我以前上楼或快速走三四百米会气喘,这两年慢走100 米就气喘了,上坡也气喘。有时一年发病 3～4 次。

陈　林:大爷,您要戒烟,注意保暖。

　　Chén Lín:Dàyé,nín năr bù shūfu?

　　Zhū Měiyàn:Tā qiántiān wǎnshang shòu liáng,zhè jǐtiān dōu késou、qìchuǎn hěn lìhai。Késou shí yǒu huángsè de tán。Zǒu jǐ bù jiù qìchuǎn。

Chén Lín：Hái yǒu nǎr bù shūfu？

Zhào Guāngróng：Wǎnshang shuìjiào bù néng píngtǎng，diàngāo zhěntou cái gǎnjué shūfu diǎn。

Chén Lín：Chōuyān ma？

Zhū Měiyàn：Chōu，píngjūn měitiān chōu 20 zhī，dōu 30 nián le。

Chén Lín：Dàmā，ràng dàyé zìjǐ shuō ba。Yǐqián késou、kétán ma？

Zhào Guāngróng：Késou、kétán 10 nián le。Dōngtiān huò tiānqì lěng de shíhou késou、kétán gèng lìhai。

Chén lín：Zhù guò yuàn ma？

Zhào Guāngróng：Zhù guò，yīshēng zhěnduàn shì fèiqìzhǒng、mànxìng zhīqìguǎnyán。Dàn bù zhīdào yòng de shénme yào。Wǒ yǐqián shànglóu huò kuàisù zǒu sān-sì bǎi mǐ huì qìchuǎn，zhè liǎng nián mànzǒu 100 mǐ jiù qìchuǎn le，shàngpō yě qìchuǎn。Yǒushí yì nián fābìng 3～4 cì。

Chén Lín：Dàyé，nín yào jièyān，zhùyì bǎonuǎn。

Chen Lin：Grandpa，where are you feeling uncomfortable？

Zhu Meiyan：He caught cold at the night before last night. He has coughed and asthma in these days. He has yellow sputum when coughs and has an asthmatic attack after walking few steps.

Chen Lin：What else uncomfortable？

Zhao Guangrong：I can't lie down at night and feel comfortable when after raising the pillow.

Chen Lin：Do you smoke？

Zhu Meiyan：Yes，He has smoked for 30 years with an average of 20 sticks per day.

Chen Lin：Grandma，let grandpa himself speak. Did you cough and spectorate before？

Zhao Guangrong：I have been coughed and spectorated for 10 years. It is worse during winter or when it is cold.

Chen Lin：Have you ever been admitted in the hospital？

Zhao Guangrong：Yes，the doctor diagnosed it as emphysema and chronic bronchitis. But I do not know what medicine was used. I used to go upstairs or walk three or four hundred meters quickly before asthmatic attack. In the past two years，I have got asthmatic attack after walking 100 meters. When I go uphill，I also have wheezing. This occurrs 3–4 times a year.

Chen Lin：Grandpa，you have to quit smoking and keep warm.

对话二

生词

序号	词语	词性	拼音	词义
1	胸廓	名	xiōngkuò	thorax
2	异常	形	yìcháng	abnormal
3	减弱	动	jiǎnruò	weaken
4	干湿啰音	名	gānshī luóyīn	dry and moist rale
5	径	名	jìng	path
6	木桶	名	mùtǒng	barrel
7	桶状胸	名	tǒngzhuàng xiōng	barrel chest
8	慢性阻塞性肺疾病	名	mànxìng zǔsèxìng fèijíbìng	chronic obstructive pulmonary disease
9	加重期	名	jiāzhòng qī	aggravating period
10	增大	动	zēngdà	enlarge

陈　林:哈森,你去给7床患者做个检查。

哈　森:好。

陈　林:你先给他听听肺,再看看他的胸廓大小有什么异常。

哈　森:好的。

……

哈　森:他的双肺呼吸音减弱,有干湿啰音。胸廓前后径几乎与左右径相等,像个木桶。

陈　林:这种胸叫桶状胸,常见于严重的肺气肿患者。这个患者是慢性阻塞性肺疾病加重期。

哈　森:他的胸部CT检查结果上写着"双侧胸廓对称,前后径增大",指的是桶状胸吗?

陈　林:对的。

Chén Lín:Hā Sēn,nǐ qù gěi 7 chuáng huànzhě zuò ge jiǎnchá。

Hā Sēn:Hǎo。

Chén Lín:Nǐ xiān gěi tā tīngting fèi,zài kànkan tā de xiōngkuò dàxiǎo yǒu shénme yìcháng。

Hā Sēn:Hǎo de。

… …

Hā Sēn:Tā de shuāngfèi hūxīyīn jiǎnruò,yǒu gānshī luóyīn。Xiōngkuò qiánhòujìng jīhū yǔ zuǒyòujìng xiāngděng,xiàng gè mùtǒng。

Chén Lín:Zhèzhǒng xiōng jiào tǒngzhuàng xiōng,cháng jiànyú yánzhòng de fèiqìzhǒng huànzhě。Zhège huànzhé shì mànxìng zǔsèxìng fèijíbìng jiāzhòng qī。

Hā Sēn:Tā de xiōngbù CT jiǎnchá jiéguǒ shàng xiě zhe "shuāngcè xiōngkuò duìchèn,qiánhòu jìng zēngdà",zhǐ de shì tǒngzhuàngxiōng ma?

Chén Lín:Duì de。

Chen Lin:Hasson,please go to do a check for the patient of bed No.7.

Hasson:OK.

Chen Lin:First listen to the lungs,then the size of his chest.

Hasson:OK.

…

Hasson:He has breath sound weakened in both of his lungs,dry and moist rale. The anteroposterior diameter of the thorax is almost equal to that of the right and left,just like a wooden barrel.

Chen Lin:This kind of chest is called barrel chest,often happens when the patients has severe emphysema. This patient is an exacerbation of chronic obstructive pulmonary disease.

Hasson:His chest CT examination says,"bilateral thoracic symmetry,anteroposterior diameter increases". Does that refer to a barrel chest?

Chen Lin:Right.

【短文】

生词

序号	词语	词性	拼音	词义
1	细支气管	名	xì zhīqìguǎn	bronchiole
2	肺泡	名	fèipào	alveoli
3	毛细血管	名	máoxì xuèguǎn	capillaries

序号	词语	词性	拼音	词义
4	二氧化碳	名	èryǎnghuàtàn	carbon dioxide
5	损坏	动	sǔnhuài	damage
6	有效的	形	yǒuxiàode	effective
7	烟雾	名	yānwù	smoke
8	胸闷	形	xiōngmèn	chest tightness
9	根治	动	gēnzhì	radical cure
10	缓解	动	huǎnjiě	ease

慢性阻塞性肺疾病

慢性阻塞性肺疾病是一种慢性气道阻塞性疾病的统称。

人们吸气时,空气会通过气管、支气管、细支气管,进入肺泡,最后进入毛细血管。呼气时,肺会将身体中产生的二氧化碳排出体外。吸气时,肺泡会扩张,呼气时,肺泡会收缩。慢性阻塞性肺疾病会对肺产生损坏,使患者慢慢失去有效的呼吸能力。

抽烟是引起慢性阻塞性肺疾病的主要原因,长期受到化学烟雾、烟尘、空气污染等刺激也可能引起慢性阻塞性肺疾病。慢性阻塞性肺疾病患者会有喘气、气短、胸闷、持续性咳嗽等症状。慢性阻塞性肺疾病无法根治,但积极治疗可以缓解症状,减缓疾病恶化进程。

Mànxìng zǔsèxìng fèijíbìng

Mànxìng zǔsèxìng fèijíbìng shì yì zhǒng mànxìng qìdào zǔsèxìng jíbìng de tǒngchēng.

Rénmen xīqì shí, kōngqì huì tōngguò qìguǎn、zhīqìguǎn、xì zhīqìguǎn, jìnrù fèipào, zuìhòu jìnrù máoxì xuèguǎn. Hūqì shí, fèihuì jiāng shēntǐ zhōng chǎnshēng de èryǎnghuàtàn páichū tǐwài. Xīqì shí, fèipào huì kuòzhāng, hūqì shí, fèipào huì shōusuō. Mànxìng zǔsèxìng fèijíbìng huì duì fèi chǎnshēng sǔnhuài, shǐ huànzhě mànman shīqù yǒuxiàode hūxīn nénglì.

Chōuyān shì yǐnqǐ mànxìng zǔsèxìng fèijíbìng de zhǔyào yuányīn, chángqī shòudào huàxué yānwù、yānchén、kōngqì wūrǎn děng cìjī yě kěnéng yǐnqǐ mànxìng zǔsèxìng fèijíbìng. Mànxìng zǔsèxìng fèijíbìng huànzhě huì yǒu chuǎnqì、qìduǎn、xiōngmèn、chíxùxìng késou děng zhèngzhuàng. Mànxìng zǔsèxìng fèijíbìng wúfǎ gēnzhì, dàn jījí zhìliáo kěyǐ huǎnjiě zhèngzhuàng, jiǎnhuǎn jíbìng èhuà jìnchéng.

Chronic obstructive pulmonary disease

Chronic obstructive pulmonary disease is a general term for chronic obstructive airway diseases.

When people inhale, air passes through the trachea, bronchi, bronchioles, into the alveoli, and finally into the capillaries. When exhale, the lungs excrete carbon dioxide from your body. The alveoli expands when you inhale and shrink when you exhale. Chronic obstructive pulmonary disease can damage the lungs, causing patients to slowly lose their effective breathing capacity.

Smoking is the main cause of chronic obstructive pulmonary disease. Long-term exposure to chemical smoke, smoke, air pollution, etc. may also cause chronic obstructive pulmonary disease. Patients with chronic obstructive pulmonary disease will have gasp, shortness of breath, chest tightness, persistent cough and other symptoms. Chronic obstructive pulmonary disease can not be cured, but aggressive treatment can relieve symptoms and slow the progression of the deterioration.

【汉字知识】

部首"讠"

部首"讠"表示"语言",一般出现在汉字的左侧。以"讠"为部首的汉字大都跟语言有关。如"询""诊""谈""详"等。此类汉字多为形声结构,左侧的部首为形旁,右侧的部件为声旁,代表字音。

例如:询——询问　询价　咨询
　　　诊——诊断　问诊　听诊

构词

——细胞　表示"细胞的分类"。

细胞——　表示"细胞的组织部分"。

例如:白细胞、红细胞、肝细胞、细胞核、细胞质。

——状　表示"呈现出不同形状"。

例如:桶状、杆状、带状、块状、点状。

【练习】

一、选择听到的词语。

1. (　　　) A. 气泡　　B. 肺叶　　C. 肺泡　　D. 费用

2. (　　　) A. 胸痛　　B. 胸廓　　C. 桶状　　D. 胸闷

3. (　　　) A. 损坏　　B. 胸怀　　C. 孙坏　　D. 弄坏

4. (　　　) A. 一张　　B. 异常　　C. 异样　　D. 衣裳

5. (　　　) A. 增大　　B. 枕头　　C. 针大　　D. 针头

二、根据听到的句子排列词语和短语。

1. 厉害　得　冬天　或者　天气冷　的　时候　咳嗽　气喘　更

2. 不可逆转　损坏　对　慢性阻塞性肺疾病　肺　的　是　的

3. 木桶　像个　左右径　几乎　前后径　胸廓　他的　与　相等

4. 肺泡　毛细血管　产生的　经过　二氧化碳　身体中　进入

三、仿照句子造句。

1. 通常是天气冷的时候,咳嗽、气喘得比较厉害。

通常是_____时候,_____得比较厉害。

通常是_____时候,_____得比较厉害。

2. 医生的诊断是肺气肿、慢性支气管炎。

医生的_____是_____。

医生的_____是_____。

3. 像这种情况,您需要戒烟,注意保暖。

像这种情况,您需要_____。

像这种情况,您需要_____。

四、选词填空。

桶状胸　胸廓　胸闷　有效的

1. 慢性阻塞性肺疾病患者会慢慢失去_____呼吸能力。

2. 这个患者的_____前后径几乎与左右径相等。

3. 他昨天上楼时感觉有些_____。

4. _____常见于严重的肺气肿患者。

五、完成下面的对话和句子。

（一）

陈林:哈森,今天那个大爷_____?

哈森:他走路_____,晚上睡觉_____,要_____才舒服点。

陈林:他以前住过院吗？诊断是什么病？

哈森:_____,医生诊断是_____。

陈林:他的_____大小有没有什么异常？

哈森:他的胸廓_____几乎跟_____相等,像个_____。

陈林:这种胸叫做_____,常见于严重的_____患者。

（二）

1. 我们吸气时,空气会进入_____、_____、_____,最后进入_____。

2. 吸气时,肺泡会_____,呼气时,肺泡会_____。

3. 呼气时,肺会将_____排出体外。

4. 慢性阻塞性肺疾病会使患者失去_____的呼吸功能。

六、根据对话和短文内容回答问题。

1. 赵光荣在什么天气咳嗽、气喘得比较厉害？

2. 医生诊断赵光荣得了什么病？

3. 赵光荣的胸廓有什么异常？

4. 桶状胸常见于什么疾病？

5. 什么是引起慢性阻塞性肺疾病的主要原因？

6. 慢性阻塞性肺疾病可以根治吗？

七、交际练习。

患者A反复咳嗽、咳痰、气促10年,有时伴下肢水肿。住院诊断为"慢性支气管炎、肺气肿"。今病情加重,前来就诊。医生B询问患者A的病情后,为患者A做胸部视诊和听诊,并要求患者A做胸部CT。结果诊断为慢性阻塞性肺疾病加重期。

两人一组,分别扮演角色A、B,组织一段3分钟左右的对话展现上文场景。

【补充医学词汇】

序号	词语	拼音	词义
1	呼吸衰竭	hūxī shuāijié	respiratory failure
2	气流受限	qìliú shòu xiàn	obstructive airflow
3	不可逆	bù kě nì	irreversible
4	血气分析	xuè qì fēnxī	blood gas analysis
5	肺功能	fèi gōngnéng	pulmonary function

（姜冬梅　王华民）

第五单元

神经内科——癫痫

发作时有没有抽搐

【学习目的】

1. 学会用汉语表述人脑各部位的名称和主要功能。

2. 学会用汉语问诊典型癫痫病例。

3. 了解癫痫的相关医学常识。

【热身】

一、给下面的词语选择对应的字母。

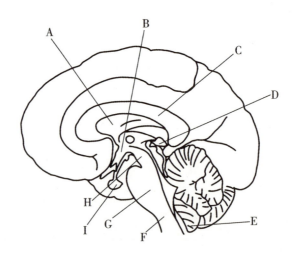

1. 丘脑_____   2. 下丘脑_____   3. 胼胝体_____   4. 松果体_____   5. 小脑_____

6. 延脑_____   7. 脑桥_____   8. 中脑_____   9. 垂体_____

二、请把下面脑区的划分及其相对应的功能连线。

1. 视觉功能   A. 额叶区

2. 听觉功能   B. 顶叶区

3. 体觉功能   C. 枕叶区

4. 思维功能   D. 颞叶区

【会话】

人物:患者——李中刚(男,65 岁)
   医生——赵光明(男,46 岁)
   实习医生——马克(男,21 岁,黎巴嫩人)
地点:神经内科门诊

对话一

生词

序号	词语	词性	拼音	词义
1	口吐白沫	–	kǒu tǔ báimò	foam started coming out of mouth
2	抽搐	动	chōuchù	convulsion
3	犯病	动	fànbìng	fall ill
4	持续	动	chíxù	continue
5	清醒	形	qīngxǐng	sober
6	癫痫	名	diānxián	epilepsy

马　克:您哪儿不舒服?

李中刚:昨天正吃着饭呢,我突然倒在地上什么都不知道了。

马　克:昨天发作时有没有抽搐?

李中刚:听家里人说有抽搐,而且两眼上翻,口吐白沫。

马　克:以前有过这种情况吗?

李中刚:有过一次,大概有 3 个月了。

马　克:犯病时大概持续了多长时间?

李中刚:有 10 分钟左右才完全清醒过来。

马　克:醒来后您知道刚才发生的事情吗?

李中刚:不知道,什么都想不起来了。

马　克:这些可能是癫痫的症状,让赵医生再给您诊断一下。

李中刚:好的,谢谢!

Mǎ　Kè:Nín nǎr bù shūfu?

Lǐ Zhōnggāng:Zuótiān zhèng chī zhe fàn ne,wǒ tūrán dǎo zài dì shàng shénme dōu bù zhīdào le。

Mǎ　Kè:Zuótiān fāzuò shí yǒu méi yǒu chōuchù?

Lǐ Zhōnggāng:Tīng jiālǐ rén shuō yǒu chōuchù,érqiě liǎng yǎn shàngfān,kǒu tǔ báimò。

Mǎ　Kè：Yǐqián yǒu guò zhè zhǒng qíngkuàng ma?

Lǐ Zhōnggāng：Yǒu guò yí cì, dàgài yǒu sān gè yuè le。

Mǎ　Kè：Fànbìng shí dàgài chíxù le duō cháng shíjiān?

Lǐ Zhōnggāng：Yǒu shí fēnzhōng zuǒyòu cái wánquán qīngxǐng guò lái。

Mǎ　Kè：Xǐng lái hòu nín zhīdào gāngcái fāshēng de shìqíng ma?

Lǐ Zhōnggāng：Bù zhīdào, shénme dōu xiǎng bù qǐlái le。

Mǎ　Kè：Zhè xiē kěnéng shì diānxián de zhèngzhuàng, ràng Zhào Guāngmíng zài gěi nín zhěnduàn yí xià。

Lǐ Zhōnggāng：Hǎo de, xièxie!

Mark：What seems to be the trouble?

Li Zhonggang：Yesterday, when I was having dinner, and I suddenly fell to the ground and didn't know anything.

Mark：When it happened, did you have any convulsions?

Li Zhonggang：Yes, my family said that I have got a convulsions, and my eyes started staring and foam started coming out of my mouth.

Mark：Have you ever experienced this before?

Li Zhonggang：Yes, I had it once before three months.

Mark：How long did it last?

Li Zhonggang：It took about ten minutes for me to completely regain my consciousness.

Mark：When you regained your consciousness, did you know what happened?

Li Zhonggang：No, I couldn't remember anything.

Mark：These are the symptoms of epilepsy, let Dr. Zhao give you another diagnosis.

Li Zhonggang：OK, thank you!

对话二

生词

序号	词语	词性	拼音	词义
1	输液	动	shūyè	infusion
2	确诊	动	quèzhěn	make definite diagnosis
3	病灶	名	bìngzào	focus of primary lesion
4	神经系统	名	shénjīng xìtǒng	nervous system
5	影像学	名	yǐngxiàng xué	imaging
6	脑脊液	名	nǎojǐyè	cerebrospinal fluid
7	头颅 CT	名	tóulú CT	head CT scan
8	动态脑电图	名	dòngtài nǎodiàntú	electroencephalogram（EEG）

（实习医生马克进行了简单的问诊后,由医生赵光明问诊）

赵光明：以前做过什么检查吗?

李中刚：没有,第一次犯病时就输了输液。

赵光明：您走几步让我看看。平时吃饭、睡觉怎么样?

李中刚：我不犯病时跟正常人一样,吃饭没问题,就是有时候休息不太好。

赵光明：家里父母有没有这样的情况？

李中刚：没有。

马　　克：他这是癫痫的症状吧？

赵光明：对。但是还需进一步检查才能确诊并找到病灶。

马　　克：嗯，找到病因病灶，才能对症治疗。

赵光明：除了神经系统、影像学，还要做血液和脑脊液的生化检查。

李中刚：我早上吃饭了，今天还能查血吗？

赵光明：明天早上空腹过来抽血。今天先做头颅 CT 和动态脑电图吧。

（shíxí yīsheng Mǎ Kè jìnxíng le jiǎndān de wènzhěn hòu, yóu yīsheng Zhào Guāngmíng wènzhěn）

Zhào Guāngmíng：Yǐqián zuò guò shénme jiǎnchá ma?

Lǐ Zhōnggāng：Méiyǒu, dì-yī cì fànbìng shí jiù shū le shū yè。

Zhào Guāngmíng：Nín zǒu jǐ bù ràng wǒ kànkan。 Píngshí chīfàn、shuìjiào zěnmeyàng?

Lǐ Zhōnggāng：Wǒ bú fànbìng shí gēn zhèngcháng rén yíyàng, chīfàn méiwèntí, jiùshì yǒushíhou xiūxi bú tài hǎo。

Zhào Guāngmíng：Jiālǐ fùmǔ yǒu méiyǒu zhèyàng de qíngkuàng?

Lǐ Zhōnggāng：Méiyǒu。

Mǎ Kè：Tā zhè shì diānxián de zhèngzhuàng ba?

Zhào Guāngmíng：Duì。 Dànshì hái xū jìn yí bù jiǎnchá cái néng quèzhěn bìng zhǎodào bìngzào。

Mǎ Kè：Èn, zhǎodào bìngyīn bìngzào, cái néng duìzhèng zhìliáo。

Zhào Guāngmíng：Chúle shénjīng xìtǒng、yǐngxiàng xué, háiyào zuò xuèyè hé nǎojǐyè de shēnghuà jiǎnchá。

Lǐ Zhōnggāng：Wǒ zǎoshang chīfàn le, jīntiān hái néng chá xuè ma?

Zhào Guāngmíng：Míngtiān zǎoshang kōngfù guòlái chōuxuè。 Jīntiān xiān zuò tóulú CT hé dòngtài nǎodiàntú ba。

（After a simple consultation with Mark, Dr. Zhao Guangming began to consult）

Zhao Guangming：Did you undergo any examination before?

Li Zhonggang：No, but I had an infusion when I had the episode for the first time.

Zhao Guangming：Let me see you walk few steps. How is your normal eating and sleeping habit?

Li Zhonggang：I am like a normal person when I don't have any problems, my eating habits are good, but I have problem with my sleeping.

Zhao Guangming：Do your parents or anyone in your family have this kind of problem?

Li Zhonggang：No.

Mark：Aren't these symptoms of epilepsy?

Zhao Guangming：Yes. But we should do the other examination to find the focus of primary lesion.

Mark：Mmm, but only if we confirm the cause and focus of the disease we can treat the patient.

Zhao Guangming：Other than the examination of central nervous system, Imaging, and biochemical examination of blood and cerebrospinal fluid should be done.

Li Zhonggang：I had my breakfast this morning. Can I still go for the blood test today?

Zhao Guangming：Then do the blood test tomorrow with an empty stomach. Today take head CT scan and EEG.

【短文】

生词

序号	词语	词性	拼音	词义
1	脑卒中	名	nǎocùzhòng	stroke
2	意识	名	yìshí	consciousness
3	丧失	动	sàngshī	loss
4	痉挛	动	jìngluán	spasm
5	原发性	形	yuánfāxìng	primary
6	继发性	形	jìfāxìng	secondary
7	代谢	动	dàixiè	metabolic
8	诱发	动	yòufā	induce
9	脑膜炎	名	nǎomóyán	meningitis
10	铅	名	qiān	plumbum
11	汞	名	gǒng	mercury

癫 痫

癫痫,俗称"羊角风",是神经系统常见疾病之一,患病率仅次于脑卒中。临床表现以反复发作的短暂意识丧失、肢体痉挛及抽搐为特点。癫痫根据病因可分为原发性、继发性两种。原发性癫痫原因不明,脑部无明显病理或代谢改变,体内外环境在生理范围内的各种改变可诱发其发病。原发性癫痫多在 5 岁左右或青春期发病。继发性癫痫是由脑内外各种疾病所引起,例如脑炎、脑膜炎、脑寄生虫病、脑瘤、脑外伤、脑缺氧、铅汞引起的脑中毒等。癫痫有一定遗传性。

Diānxián

Diānxián,súchēng "yángjiǎofēng",shì shénjīng xìtǒng chángjiàn jíbìng zhīyī,huànbìnglǜ jǐn cì yú nǎocùzhòng。Línchuáng biǎoxiàn yǐ fǎnfù fāzuò de duǎnzàn yìshí sàngshī,zhītǐ jìngluán jí chōuchù wéi tèdiǎn。Diānxián gēnjù bìngyīn kě fēnwéi yuánfāxìng、jìfāxìng liǎng zhǒng。Yuánfāxìng diānxián yuányīn bùmíng,nǎobù wú míngxiǎn bìnglǐ huò dàixiè gǎibiàn,tǐ nèiwài huánjìng zài shēnglǐ fànwéi nèi de gè zhǒng gǎibiàn kě yòufā qí fābìng。Yuánfāxìng diānxián duō zài 5 suì zuǒyòu huò qīngchūnqī fābìng。Jìfāxìng diānxián shì yóu nǎo nèiwài gè zhǒng jíbìng suǒ yǐnqǐ,lìrú nǎoyán、nǎomóyán、nǎo jìshēngchóngbìng、nǎoliú、nǎo wàishāng、nǎo quēyǎng、qiān gǒng yǐnqǐ de nǎo zhòngdú děng。Diānxián yǒu yídìng yíchuánxìng。

Epilepsy

Epilepsy,also known as Yangjiaofeng,is the second most common disease of nervous system,stroke being the first. Clinical manifestation is characterized by recurrent episodes of transient loss of consciousness, limb spasm and convulsion. Epilepsy can be divided into two types:primary and secondary epilepsy. The cause of primary epilepsy is unknown and there is no obvious pathological or metabolic changes in the brain. Various changes in the external environment can induce the pathogenesis within the body. Primary epilepsy occurs in about 5 years of age or in adolescence. Secondary epilepsy is caused by various diseases in and out of the brain,such as encephalitis,meningitis,brain parasitic disease,brain tumor,brain injury, cerebral hypoxia, lead mercury caused brain poisoning. Epilepsy has a certain heritability.

【汉字知识】

部首"疒"

部首"疒"的意思是人有疾病。以"疒"为部首的汉字多与疾病有关。如"病""痛""疼""瘤""癌"等。此类汉字多为形声结构,部首"疒"为形旁,"疒"内的部件为声旁,代表字音。

例如:

病—— 癫痫病　心脏病　妇科病

瘤—— 肿瘤　胰腺瘤　脑瘤　甲状腺瘤

构词

——性:表示"具有某种性质"。

例如:急性、慢性、萎缩性、生理性、病理性、溃疡性、原发性、继发性。

——脑:表示"人和动物神经系统的主要部分"。

例如:大脑、小脑、中脑、丘脑。

【练习】

一、选择听到的词语。

1. (　　　)A. 大脑　　　B. 间脑　　　C. 延脑　　　D. 小脑

2. (　　　)A. 额叶　　　B. 枕叶　　　C. 顶叶　　　D. 颞叶

3. (　　　)A. 清醒　　　B. 清楚　　　C. 清静　　　D. 情形

4. (　　　)A. 癌症　　　B. 癫痫　　　C. 疾病　　　D. 脑瘤

5. (　　　)A. 代谢　　　B. 代替　　　C. 代表　　　D. 代理

二、根据听到的句子排列词语和短语。

1. 症状　这些　应该　是　癫痫的　一些

2. 让　赵医生　诊断一下　最好　再　给　您

3. 第一次　犯病时　在　县医院　做了　我　头颅 CT

4. 癫痫　的　仅次于　脑卒中　患病率

5. 是　继发性　癫痫　由　所引起　脑内外　各种疾病

三、仿照句子造句。

1. 昨天我正吃着饭呢,突然倒在了地上。

我正＿＿＿＿＿＿＿＿＿＿呢,突然＿＿＿＿＿＿＿＿＿＿。

我正＿＿＿＿＿＿＿＿＿＿呢,突然＿＿＿＿＿＿＿＿＿＿。

2. 我吃饭没问题,就是有时候休息不太好。

我＿＿＿＿＿＿＿＿＿＿没问题,就是＿＿＿＿＿＿＿＿＿＿。

我＿＿＿＿＿＿＿＿＿＿没问题,就是＿＿＿＿＿＿＿＿＿＿。

3. 癫痫是神经系统常见疾病之一。

＿＿＿＿＿＿＿＿＿＿是＿＿＿＿＿＿＿＿＿＿之一。

＿＿＿＿＿＿＿＿＿＿是＿＿＿＿＿＿＿＿＿＿之一。

4. 还需要进一步检查才能确诊并找到病灶。

还需要＿＿＿＿＿＿才能＿＿＿＿＿＿。
还需要＿＿＿＿＿＿才能＿＿＿＿＿＿。

四、选词填空。

抽搐　持续　痉挛　确诊　诱发

1. 癫痫发作时,一般会＿＿＿＿＿2~5分钟。
2. 癫痫患者犯病时,眼睛上翻,口吐白沫,全身＿＿＿＿＿,意识丧失。
3. 如果要＿＿＿＿＿＿一种病,不能只看症状,还要做一系列的检查。
4. 肌肉突然紧张,不自主地抽搐的症状,就是＿＿＿＿＿,俗称抽筋。
5. 医学实验表明,脑内外的各种疾病易＿＿＿＿＿癫痫。

五、完成下面的对话和句子。

（一）

患　者:大夫,我头痛得厉害。
医　生:＿＿＿＿＿＿?
患　者:感觉头部胀痛,有压迫感。
医　生:＿＿＿＿＿?
患　者:除了头痛,我还感觉眩晕、胸闷、耳鸣。
医　生:＿＿＿＿＿。

（二）

1. 癫痫,俗称"＿＿＿＿＿",是神经系统常见疾病之一
2. 癫痫根据病因可分为＿＿＿＿＿、＿＿＿＿＿两种。
3. 继发性癫痫是由＿＿＿＿＿、＿＿＿＿＿、＿＿＿＿＿、＿＿＿＿＿、＿＿＿＿＿、＿＿＿＿＿、＿＿＿＿＿等
脑内外各种疾病所引起。

六、根据对话和短文内容回答问题。

1. 李中刚来就诊时,一共犯了几次病?
2. 李中刚犯病时都有哪些症状? 他知道犯病时发生的事情吗?
3. 李中刚以前做过检查吗?
4. 赵医生说要确诊癫痫病,还要做什么检查?
5. 癫痫病的症状和临床表现是什么?
6. 哪些病常常会诱发癫痫?

七、交际练习。

患者 A,男,65 岁,和朋友聊天时,突然眼睛上翻、口吐白沫,倒在地上失去意识。朋友急忙送其去
医院,在去医院的路上他清醒过来了,并不知道刚才所发生的事情。于是前来就诊。实习医生 B 为其
做了病情询问和初步检查,并与神经内科主任赵大夫讨论其病情。商量后决定让 A 先住院观察。

四人一组,分别扮演上述情景中的角色,组织一段 5 分钟左右的对话展现上文场景。

【补充医学词汇】

序号	词语	拼音	词义
1	脑出血	nǎochūxuè	cerebral hemorrhage
2	脱髓鞘	tuō suǐqiào	demyelination
3	颅高压	lú gāoyā	intracranial hypertention
4	失语	shī yǔ	aphasia
5	肌萎缩	jī wěisuō	amyotrophia

（吕兆格）

第六单元

心血管内科——心绞痛

您的检查结果出来了

【学习目的】

1. 学会用汉语表述心脏的主要解剖结构和主要功能。
2. 学会用汉语问诊心绞痛的典型病例。
3. 用汉语了解心血管系统疾病的相关医学常识。

【热身】

一、给下面的词语选择对应的字母。

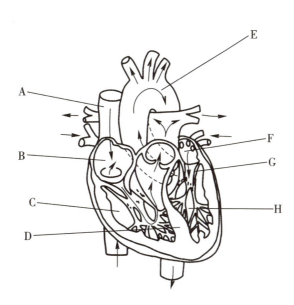

1. 静脉_____   2. 动脉_____   3. 左心房_____   4. 左心室_____
5. 右心房_____   6. 右心室_____   7. 室间隔_____   8. 二尖瓣_____

二、根据英文写汉字。

1. hypertension＿＿＿＿＿＿

2. hypotension＿＿＿＿＿＿

3. coronary artery heart disease＿＿＿＿＿＿

4. cardiac rhythm＿＿＿＿＿＿

5. cardiac muscle＿＿＿＿＿＿

【会话】

> 场景简介:
> 人物:患者——李爱国(男,54 岁)
> 　　　医生——张红华(女,40 岁)
> 　　　实习医生——哈桑(男,20 岁,印度人)
> 地点:心血管内科门诊

对话一

生词

序号	词语	词性	拼音	词义
1	硝酸甘油	名	xiāosuān gānyóu	nitroglycerin
2	频繁	副	pínfán	often;frequently
3	高血压	名	gāoxuèyā	hypertension
4	服(药)	动	fú(yào)	to take(medicine)

李爱国:张医生好!

张红华:您好! 您的胸口还痛吗?

李爱国:刚才含了硝酸甘油片,现在舒服一点儿了,但还是有点儿痛。

张红华:您以前有过这样的疼痛吗?

李爱国:两年前第一次发作,那时候没有这么痛,而且时间持续也不长,我以为是我没休息好。但是最近疼得越来越频繁,持续时间也越来越长了。

张红华:您有高血压病史吗?

李爱国:我患高血压已经五六年了。

张红华:那您坚持按时服药,定期复查了吗?

李爱国:真不好意思。有时候我觉得我的血压很好我就没吃药。

张红华:您呀! 高血压一定要坚持按时服药,定期复查。

李爱国:好的。以后我一定注意。

Lǐ Àiguó:Zhāng yīsheng hǎo!

Zhāng Hónghuá:Nínhǎo! Nín de xiōngkǒu hái tòng ma?

Lǐ Àiguó:Gāngcái hán le xiāosuān gānyóu piàn,xiànzài shūfu yìdiǎnr le,dàn háishì yǒu diǎnr tòng.

Zhāng Hónghuá:Nín yǐqián yǒu guò zhèyàng de téngtòng ma?

Lǐ Àiguó:Liǎng nián qián dì-yī cì fāzuò,nà shíhou méiyǒu zhè me tòng,érqiě shíjiān chíxù yě bù cháng,wǒ yǐwéi shì wǒ méi xiūxi hǎo。Dànshì zuìjìn téng de yuè lái yuè pínfán,chíxù shíjiān yě yuè lái yuè cháng le.

Zhāng Hónghuá：Nín yǒu gāoxuèyā bìngshǐ ma?

Lǐ Àiguó：Wǒ huàn gāoxuèyā yǐjīng wǔ–liù nián le.

Zhāng Hónghuá：Nà nín jiānchí ànshí fú yào, dìngqī fùchá le ma?

Lǐ Àiguó：Zhēn bùhǎoyìsi. Yǒu shíhou wǒ juéde wǒ de xuèyā hěn hǎo wǒ jiù méi chī yào.

Zhāng Hónghuá：Nín ya! gāoxuèyā yídìng yào jiānchí ànshí fú yào, dìngqī fùchá.

Lǐ Àiguó：Hǎo de. Yǐhòu wǒ yídìng zhùyì.

Li Aiguo：Hello, Doctor Zhang!

Zhang Honghua：Hello! Do you still have chest pain?

Li Aiguo：I just had Nitroglycerol. Now I am feeling better, but it still hurts a little.

Zhang Honghua：Have you ever had this kind of pain before?

Li Aiguo：The first time happened two years ago, it wasn't as painful, and it didn't last for such a long time. I thought it happened cause I didn't have a good rest. But recently the pain has become more frequent and longer.

Zhang Honghua：Do you have a history of Hypertension?

Li Aiguo：I have had Hypertension for five or six years.

Zhang Honghua：Do you insist on taking the medicine on time and recheck regularly?

Li Aiguo：I'm sorry. Sometimes I feel like my blood pressure is good and I'm not taking my medication.

Zhang Honghua：You ah! The patient who got Hypertension must insist on taking medicine regularly, and recheck regularly.

Li Aiguo：OK. I will pay attention later.

对话二

生词

序号	词语	词性	拼音	词义
1	毫米汞柱	量	háomǐgǒngzhù	mmHg
2	心前区	名	xīnqiánqū	pericardial region
3	心肌缺血	动	xīnjī quēxuè	myocardial ischemia
4	窦性心律	名	dòuxìng xīnlǜ	sinus rhythm
5	心肌坏死	动	xīnjī huàisǐ	myocardial necrosis
6	血清生物标志物	名	xuèqīng shēngwù biāozhìwù	serum biomarker
7	急性	形	jíxìng	acute
8	心肌梗死	动	xīnjī gěngsǐ	myocardial infarction（MI）
9	心绞痛	名	xīnjiǎotòng	angina

哈　桑：李先生，您的检查结果出来了。

李爱国：医生，结果怎么样？

哈　桑：您的情况需要住院治疗。血压很高，160/120 毫米汞柱，听诊情况心音有力，无杂音。心前区疼痛时，心电图结果是窦性心律、心肌缺血。心肌坏死血清生物标志物检查正常，可以基本排除急性心肌梗死。根据您的病史、体征及各项检查结果，王老师诊断您得的是冠心病、心绞痛。

李爱国：医生，这个病严重吗？

哈　桑：现在情况还好，但您一定要多注意情绪，不能太激动。还要积极配合医生的治疗。控制饮食，少吃油腻的食物。按时吃药，定期复查。

Hā Sāng：Lǐ xiānsheng，nín de jiǎnchá jiéguǒ chūlái le.

Lǐ Àiguó：Yīsheng，jiéguǒ zěnmeyàng?

Hā Sāng：Nín de qíngkuàng xūyào zhùyuàn zhìliáo. Xuèyā hěn gāo，160/120 háomǐgǒngzhù，tīngzhěn qíngkuàng xīnyīn yǒulì，wú záyīn. Xīnqiánqū téngtòng shí，xīndiàntú jiéguǒ shì dòuxìng xīnlǜ，xīnjī quēxuè. Xīnjī huàisǐ xuèqīng shēngwù biāozhìwù jiǎnchá zhèngcháng，kéyǐ jīběn páichú jíxìng xīnjī gěngsǐ. Gēnjù nín de bìngshǐ，tǐzhēng jí gèxiàng jiǎnchá jiéguǒ，Wáng lǎoshī zhěnduàn nín dé de shì guānxīnbìng，xīnjiǎotòng.

Lǐ Àiguó：Yīsheng，zhè ge bìng yánzhòng ma?

Hā Sāng：Xiànzài qíngkuàng hái hǎo，dàn nín yídìng yào duō zhùyì qíngxù，bù néng tài jīdòng. Háiyào jījí pèihé yīsheng de zhìliáo. Kòngzhì yǐnshí，shǎo chī yóunì de shíwù. Ànshí chīyào，dìngqī fùchá.

Hassan：Mr. Li，your examination results come out.

Li Aiguo：What's the result，doctor?

Hassan：Your condition requires hospitalization. High blood pressure，160/120 mmHg，During auscultation，the heart sounds powerful，with no murmur. The electrocardiograph indicates sinus rhythm and myocardial ischemia. Serum biomarkers of myocardial necrosis were normal，Acute myocardial infarction can be largely excluded. According to your medical history，physical signs and the results of different examinations，teacher Wang diagnosis you are coronary artery disease with angina.

Li Aiguo：Doctor，Is this serious?

Hassan：It's all right now，but you must pay more attention to your emotions and do not get too excited. And also you need actively cooperate with the doctor's treatment. Control your diet，eat less greasy food. Take your medicine on time，and come to recheck regularly.

【短文】

生词

序号	词语	词性	拼音	词义
1	由……组成	–	yóu……zǔchéng	be made up of；consist of
2	动力	名	dònglì	power
3	管道	名	guǎndào	pipeline
4	房间隔	名	fáng jiàngé	interatrial septum
5	室间隔	名	shì jiàngé	interventricular septum
6	互不	–	hù bù	be not…each other
7	静脉	名	jìngmài	vein
8	动脉	名	dòngmài	artery
9	腔	名	qiāng	cavity；antrum
10	冠状窦	名	guānzhuàngdòu	coronary sinus

序号	词语	词性	拼音	词义
11	血液循环	名	xuèyè xúnhuán	blood circulation
12	功能	名	gōngnéng	function
13	风湿性心脏病	名	fēngshī xìng xīnzàngbìng	rheumatic heart disease（RHD）
14	心肌炎	名	xīnjīyán	myocarditis

心血管系统

心血管系统由心脏和血管组成。心脏是动力器官,血管是运输血液的管道。

心脏由左心房、左心室、右心房和右心室组成,分别通过房间隔和室间隔分开,互不相通。心房接受静脉,心室发出动脉。右心房连接上、下腔静脉和冠状窦,左心房连接肺静脉。右心室发出肺动脉,左心室发出主动脉。血管由动脉、静脉和毛细血管组成。

心血管系统的基本功能是完成血液循环,保证身体功能。

心血管系统的常见疾病主要有高血压、动脉硬化、心肌梗死、冠心病、风湿性心脏病、心肌炎等。

Xīn xuèguǎn xìtǒng

Xīn xuèguǎn xìtǒng yóu xīnzàng hé xuèguǎn zǔchéng. Xīnzàng shì dònglì qìguān, xuèguǎn shì yùnshū xuèyè de guǎndào.

Xīnzàng yóu zuǒ xīnfáng, zuǒ xīnshì, yòu xīnfáng hé yòu xīnshì zǔchéng, fēnbié tōngguò fángjiāngé hé shìjiàngé fēnkāi, hù bù xiāngtōng. Xīnfáng jiēshòu jìngmài, Xīnshì fāchū dòngmài. Yòu xīnfáng liánjiē shàng、xià qiāng jìngmài hé guānzhuàngdòu, zuǒ xīnfáng liánjiē fèi jìngmài. Yòu xīnshì fāchū fèi dòngmài, zuǒ xīnshì fāchū zhǔ dòngmài. Xuèguǎn yóu dòngmài、jìngmài hé máoxì xuèguǎn zǔchéng.

Xīn xuèguǎn xìtǒng de jīběn gōngnéng shì wánchéng xuèyè xúnhuán, bǎozhèng shēntǐ gōngnéng.

Xīn xuèguǎn xìtǒng de chángjiàn jíbìng zhǔyào yǒu gāo xuèyā, dòngmài yìnghuà, xīnjī gěngsǐ, guānxīnbìng, fēngshī xìng xīnzàng bìng, xīnjīyán děng.

The cardiovascular system

The cardiovascular system consists of the heart and blood vessels. The heart is the power organ, the blood vessel is the conduit that carries blood.

The heart is composed of the left atrium, the left ventricle, the right atrium and the right ventricle, separated by room septum and ventricular septum respectively. The atrium receives the vein, the ventricle sends out the artery. The right atrium connects Upper and inferior vena cava and the coronary sinus, and the left atrium connects the pulmonary veins. The right ventricle gives out the pulmonary artery and the left ventricle gives out the aorta. Blood vessels are composed of arteries, veins and capillaries.

The basic function of the cardiovascular system is to complete the blood circulation and ensure the body function.

Common diseases of the cardiovascular system include hypertension, arteriosclerosis, myocardial infarction，coronary heart disease，rheumatic heart disease，myocarditis，etc.

【汉字知识】

部首"心"

部首"心"的意思为"心脏、内心"，一般出现在汉字底部。以"心"为部首的汉字多与心脏或者心理活动有关。如"想""您""急""怼"等。此类汉字多为形声结构，底部的部首为形旁，顶部的部件为声旁，代表字音。

例如：

想——想法　想念　思想

愿——愿望　祝愿　心愿

构词

——痛　表示"疼痛"。

例如：胸痛、头痛、腹痛、牙痛、脚痛、隐痛、阵痛、绞痛、放射痛、压榨痛。

——音　表示"声音"。

例如：呼吸音、心音、湿啰音、哮鸣音、肠鸣音、骨擦音。

【练习】

一、选择听到的词语。

1.（　　）A. 血压　　　　B. 血管　　　　C. 流血　　　　D. 血检

2.（　　）A. 头痛　　　　B. 胸痛　　　　C. 绞痛　　　　D. 不痛

3.（　　）A. 持续　　　　B. 频繁　　　　C. 复查　　　　D. 心音

4.（　　）A. 心前区　　　B. 心电图　　　C. 心脏病　　　D. 心绞痛

5.（　　）A. 毫米汞柱　　B. 甘油三酯　　C. 硝酸甘油　　D. 心肌缺血

二、根据拼音写汉字。

chíxù（　　　　）　　　bìngshǐ（　　　　）　　　dòuxìng xīnlǜ（　　　　　）

pínfán（　　　　）　　　gāoxuèyā（　　　　）

三、仿照句子造句。

1. 最近痛得越来越频繁。

越来越＿＿＿＿＿＿＿＿＿。

越来越＿＿＿＿＿＿＿＿＿。

2. 您一定要多注意情绪，不能太激动。

一定要＿＿＿＿＿＿＿＿＿。

一定要＿＿＿＿＿＿＿＿＿。

3. 心血管系统由心脏和血管组成。

由＿＿＿＿＿＿＿和＿＿＿＿＿＿＿组成。

由＿＿＿＿＿＿＿和＿＿＿＿＿＿＿组成。

四、选词填空。

频繁　坚持　急性　硝酸甘油　血液循环　毫米汞柱

1. 王老师诊断23床的患者得的是＿＿＿＿＿＿心肌梗死。

2. 最近我胸口痛得越来越＿＿＿＿＿＿了。

3. 20床的患者胸痛又发作了，快给他含＿＿＿＿＿＿＿。

4. 心血管系统的基本功能是完成＿＿＿＿＿＿＿，保证身体功能。

5. 张奶奶，出院以后您一定要＿＿＿＿＿＿＿按时吃药，定期复查。

6. 您的血压很高，160/120＿＿＿＿＿＿＿。

五、完成下面的对话和句子。

（一）

患　者：医生，_____？

医　生：结果出来了。您的_____很高，160/120毫米汞柱，听诊情况_____。血常规检查发现_____和_____都比较高。心电图结果是_____。心肌坏死血清生物标志物检查_____，可以基本_____急性心肌梗死。根据_____，我们诊断您得的是_____。

患　者：医生，_____？

医　生：不太严重，但您_____多注意情绪，不能_____。坚持_____吃药，_____复查。

（二）

1. 心血管系统由_____和_____组成。

2. 心血管系统的主要功能是_____、_____。

3. 心脏由_____、_____、_____和_____4个部分组成。

4. 血管由_____、_____和_____组成。心房接受_____，心室发出_____。

六、根据对话和短文内容回答问题。

1. 李可现在感觉怎么样？还胸痛吗？

2. 李可患高血压多长时间了？

3. 李可的检查结果是什么？

4. 李可得了什么病？

5. 心血管系统由什么组成？

6. 心血管系统的基本功能是什么？

七、交际练习。

患者A，男，42岁，昨天上午突发性胸痛到医院就诊。心血管内科医生B和实习医生C为其做了病情询问和初步检查，并告知患者病情。

三人一组，分别扮演角色A、B、C，组织一段5分钟左右的对话展现上文场景。

【补充医学词汇】

序号	词语	拼音	词义
1	二尖瓣	èr jiān bàn	mitral valve
2	三尖瓣	sān jiān bàn	tricuspid valve
3	主动脉瓣	zhǔ dòngmài bàn	aortic valve
4	肺动脉瓣	fèi dòngmài bàn	pulmonary valve

（张　勇）

第七单元

血液内科——缺铁性贫血

我们考虑您得的是缺铁性贫血

【学习目的】

1. 学会用汉语表述血液系统专有名词。
2. 学会用汉语问诊典型缺铁性贫血病例。
3. 了解缺铁性贫血的相关医学常识。

【热身】

一、给下面的词语选择对应的字母。

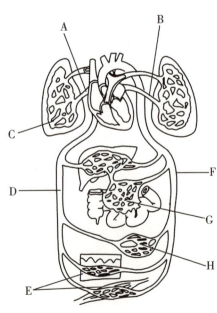

1. 主动脉_____ 2. 系统性毛细血管床_____ 3. 右肺毛细血管_____ 4. 下腔静脉_____
5. 左肺静脉_____ 6. 右肺静脉_____ 7. 肠毛细血管_____ 8. 肾毛细血管_____

二、根据英文写汉字。

1. pulmonary artery _____

2. capillary _____

3. aorta _____

4. vein _____

5. inferior vena cava _____

【会话】

场景简介：

人物：患者——李风（男，64 岁）

　　　医生——赵华（男，48 岁）

　　　实习医生——比诺德（男，23 岁，尼泊尔人）

地点：血液内科门诊

会话一

生词

序号	词语	词性	拼音	词义
1	风湿病	名	fēngshībìng	rheumatism
2	缺铁性贫血	名	quētiěxìng pínxuè	iron deficiency anemia

李　风：赵医生好！我 1 周前开始头晕、眼花、浑身没力气。

赵　华：有没有别的不舒服，例如恶心、呕吐？

李　风：都没有，但有时候肚子痛，有黑便。

赵　华：以前得过别的病吗？

李　风：我有风湿病，10 多年了，一直在吃止痛药。

赵　华：之前有做过手术吗？有没有什么病史？

李　风：都没有。

赵　华：我考虑您得的是贫血，还需要给您做血常规检查才能进一步确认。

（患者血常规结果显示：WBC 9.0×10^9/L, Hb 46 g/L, PLT 285×10^9/L, MCV 81. 66 fl, MCH 18. 29 pg, MCHC 223. 92 g/L）

赵　华：您的血常规结果已经拿到了。结合您的临床表现和血常规结果，我初步诊断您得的是缺铁性贫血。需要住院后做更详细的检查，并制定系统的治疗方案。

李　风：好的，谢谢医生。

Lǐ Fēng：Zhào Guāngmíng hǎo！Wǒ yìzhōu qián kāishǐ tóuyūn、yǎnhuā、húnshēn méi lìqi。

Zhào Huá：Yǒu méiyǒu biéde bù shūfu，lìrú ěxin、ǒutù？

Lǐ Fēng：Dōu méiyǒu，dàn yǒushíhou dùzi tòng，yǒu hēibiàn。

Zhào Huá：Yǐqián dé guò biéde bìng ma？

Lǐ Fēng：Wǒ yǒu fēngshībìng，shí duō nián le，yìzhí zài chī zhǐtòngyào。

Zhào Huá：Zhīqián yǒu zuò guò shǒushù ma？Yǒu méiyǒu shénme bìngshǐ？

Lǐ Fēng：Dōu méiyǒu。

Zhào Huá：Wǒ kǎolǜ nín dé de shì pínxuè，hái xūyào gěi nín zuò xuèchángguī jiǎnchá cái néng jìnyíbù quèrèn。

　　（Huànzhě xuèchángguī jiéguǒ xiǎnshì：WBC 9.0×10^9/L，Hb 46 g/L，PLT 285×10^9/L，MCV 81.66 fl，MCH 18.29 pg，MCHC 223.92 g/L）

　　Zhào Huá：Nín de xuèchángguī jiéguǒ yǐjīng ná dào le。Jiéhé nín de línchuáng biǎoxiàn hé xuèchángguī jiéguǒ，wǒ chūbù zhěnduàn nín dé de shì quētiěxìng pínxuè。Xūyào zhùyuàn hòu zuò gèng xiángxì de jiǎnchá，bìng zhìdìng xìtǒng de zhìliáo fāng'àn。

　　Lǐ Fēng：Hǎo de，xièxie yīsheng。

　　Li Feng：Doctor Wang！I started dizziness，eyesight and no strength all a week ago.

　　Zhao Hua：Is there anything else that is uncomfortable，such as nausea and vomiting?

　　Li Feng：No，but sometimes there is stomach ache and melena.

　　Zhao Hua：Have you had any other disease before?

　　Li Feng：I have rheumatism for more than 10 years and I have been taking painkillers.

　　Zhao Hua：Have you been any operation before? What is the history of the disease?

　　Li Feng：None.

　　Zhao Hua：I consider that you have anemia and you need routine blood test to confirm it.

　　（Patient blood routine results：WBC 9.0×10^9/L，Hb 46 g/L，PLT 285×10^9/L，MCV 81.66 fl，MCH 18.29 pg，MCHC 223.92 g/L）

　　Zhao Hua：Your blood routine results have been obtained. Combined with your clinical presentation and blood routine result，we initially diagnosed you as iron deficiency anemia. More details examination is needed after admit in hospital（hospitalization）and systematic treatment.

　　Li Feng：OK. Thank you.

对话二

生词

序号	词语	词性	拼音	词义
1	红细胞	名	hóngxìbāo	red blood cell
2	低色素	名	dī sèsù	hypochromic
3	铁蛋白	名	tiě dànbái	ferritin

　　赵　华：我初步考虑这位患者得的是缺铁性贫血。贫血的诊断步骤有哪几步？

　　比诺德：确立诊断、明确贫血类型、病因诊断。

　　赵　华：贫血按红细胞形态可分为哪几类？

　　比诺德：贫血按红细胞形态可分为大细胞性贫血、正常细胞性贫血、小细胞低色素性贫血。

　　赵　华：临床上最常见的贫血是什么？其患者的改变是什么？

　　比诺德：是缺铁性贫血。患者改变为血清铁降低，铁蛋白降低，总铁结合力升高。

　　赵　华：很好。请尽快与患者谈住院事宜。

　　Zhào Huá：Wǒ chūbù kǎolǜ zhè wèi huànzhě dé de shì quētiěxìng pínxuè。Pínxuè de zhěnduàn bùzhòu yǒu nǎ jǐ bù?

　　Bǐnuòdé：Quèlì zhěnduàn、míngquè pínxuè lèixíng、bìngyīn zhěnduàn。

　　Zhào Huá：Pínxuè àn hóngxìbāo xíngtài kě fēnwéi nǎ jǐ lèi?

Bǐnuòdé：Pínxuè àn hóngxìbāo xíngtài kě fēnwéi dà xìbāo xìng pínxuè、zhèngcháng xìbāo xìng pínxuè、xiǎoxìbāo dī sèsùxìng pínxuè。

Zhào Huá：Línchuáng shàng zuì chángjiàn de pínxuè shì shénme？Qí huànzhě de gǎibiàn shì shénme？

Bǐnuòdé：Shì quētiěxìng pínxuè。Huànzhě gǎibiàn wéi xuèqīng tiě jiàngdī，tiě dànbái jiàngdī，zǒng tiě jiéhélì shēnggāo。

Zhào Huá：Hěn hǎo。Qǐng jìnkuài yǔ huànzhě tán zhùyuàn shìyí。

Zhao Hua：We initially considered the patient suffering from iron deficiency anemia. What step should be taken to diagnose anemia?

Binod：Establish diagnosis，identify the type of anemia and diagnose the cause.

Zhao Hua：What kind of anemia can be divided according to red blood cells?

Binod：Anemia can be divided into large cell anemia and normal cell anemia，small cell hypo anemia according to the red blood cell.

Zhao Hua：What is the most common anemia in clinical practice？What's the change in patient？

Binod：Iron deficiency anemia. The patient serum iron level decreased. Ferritin decreased and total iron binding capacity increased.

Zhao Hua：Very good. Please talk to the patient about the hospitalization as soon as possible.

【短文】

生词

序号	词语	词性	拼音	词义
1	容量	名	róngliàng	capacity
2	心悸	动	xīnjì	palpitation
3	骨髓	名	gǔsuǐ	marrow
4	网织红细胞	名	wǎngzhī hóngxìbāo	reticulocyte
5	巨幼细胞贫血	名	jù yòu xìbāo pínxuè	megaloblastic anemia
6	叶酸	名	yèsuān	folic acid
7	溶血	名	róngxuè	hemolytic
8	脾	名	pí	spleen

贫 血

贫血是人体外周血红细胞容量减少，比正常范围低，不能运输足够的氧气到组织而产生的一种常见的临床症状。贫血患者常常会头晕、头痛、乏力、心悸、气促、皮肤黏膜苍白，轻度贫血患者活动后呼吸加深、加快，重度贫血患者坐着时呼吸急促。诊断贫血的辅助检查有血常规、外周血涂片、骨髓检查、网织红细胞计数。

对于贫血需要改善体内缺氧的状态，减轻重度血细胞减少的影响。根据病因进行治疗，如缺铁性贫血应补充铁剂，并治疗缺铁的原发病；巨幼细胞贫血应补充叶酸或维生素 B_{12}；溶血性贫血采用糖皮质激素或脾切除术治疗。

Pínxuè

Pínxuè shì réntǐ wàizhōu xuè hóngxìbāo róngliàng jiǎnshǎo, bǐ zhèngcháng fànwéi dī, bù néng yùnshū zúgòu de yǎngqì dào zǔzhī ér chǎnshēng de yìzhǒng chángjiàn de línchuáng zhèngzhuàng。Pínxuè huànzhě chángcháng huì tóuyūn、tóutòng、fálì、xīnjì、qìcù、pífū niánmó cāngbái, qīngdù pínxuè huànzhě huódòng hòu hūxī jiāshēn、jiākuài, zhòngdù pínxuè huànzhě zuòzhe shí hūxī jícù。Zhěnduàn pínxuè de fǔzhù jiǎnchá yǒu xuèchángguī、wàizhōu xuè túpiàn、gǔsuǐ jiǎnchá、wǎngzhī hóngxìbāo jìshù。

Duìyú pínxuè xūyào gǎishàn tǐnèi quēyǎng de zhuàngtài, jiǎnqīng zhòngdù xuèxìbāo jiǎnshǎo de yíngxiǎng。Gēnjù bìngyīn jìnxíng zhìliáo, rú quētiěxìng pínxuè yīng bǔchōng tiějì, bìng zhìliáo quētiě de yuánfābìng; jù yòu xìbāo pínxuè yīng bǔchōng yèsuān huò wéishēngsù B$_{12}$; róngxuèxìng pínxuè cǎiyòng tángpízhì jīsù huò píqiēchúshù zhìliáo。

Anemia

Anemia is a kind of common clinical symptoms because of red blood cell volume in human peripheral blood which is lower than the normal range and can not transport enough oxygen to the tissues. Anemia patient often have dizziness, headache, fatigue palpitation, skin and mucous membrane pale. Mild anemia patient after the activity of breathing accelerated, severe anemia in patient with rapid breathing. The auxiliary examinations for anemia include blood routine, peripheral blood smear, bone marrow examination and reticulocyte count.

Anemia needs to improve the state of anoxia in the body and reduce the effect of severe. Hemolytic reduction according to the cause of the disease such as iron deficiency anemia should be supplemented with iron, and the treatment of iron deficiency anemia should be with megaloblastic anemia supplemented with Folic acid or vitamin B$_{12}$; hemolytic anemia is treated with gloco corticoid or splenectomy.

【汉字知识】

部首"钅"

部首"钅"的意思为"金属",一般出现在汉字的左侧。以"钅"为部首的汉字大都跟金属有关。如"钉""铁""铜""锡"等。此类汉字多为形声结构,左侧的部首为形旁,右侧的部件为声旁,代表字音。

例如:铁——缺铁　铁质　铁路

　　　钉——钉子　钉鞋　图钉

构词:

血——　表示"与人或动物的血液相关的液体组织"。

例如:血液、血清、血浆、血常规、血压、血糖、血脂。

——药　表示"某种药物"。

例如:胃药、消炎药、降压药、感冒药、麻醉药。

【练习】

一、选择听到的词语。

1.（　　　）A.血细胞　　B.红细胞　　C.白细胞　　D.血小板

2.（　　　）A.血浆　　　B.血液　　　C.血清　　　D.血型

3.（　　　）A.铁剂　　　B.钙剂　　　C.贴剂　　　D.铁机

4.（　　　）A.诊断　　　B.诊疗　　　C.诊治　　　D.诊所

5.（　　　）A.头晕　　　B.头疼　　　C.头痛　　　D.头部

二、根据听到的句子排列词语和短语。

1.是　我们　贫血　您　的　考虑　得

2.治疗方案　给　您　的　会　系统　我们　制定

3.人体　血　红细胞　贫血　减少　指　外周　容量

4.脾切除术　采用　糖皮质激素　溶血性贫血　或　治疗

三、仿照句子造句。

1.您得的是贫血。

＿＿＿＿＿＿＿＿得的是＿＿＿＿＿＿＿。

＿＿＿＿＿＿＿＿得的是＿＿＿＿＿＿＿。

2.什么时候开始头晕的？

什么时候开始＿＿＿＿＿＿＿？

什么时候开始＿＿＿＿＿＿＿？

3.有没有别的不舒服,例如恶心、呕吐？

有没有别的不舒服,例如＿＿＿＿＿＿＿＿＿＿？

有没有别的不舒服,例如＿＿＿＿＿＿＿＿＿＿？

四、选词填空

心悸　叶酸　红细胞　风湿病

1.贫血患者常常会头晕、头痛、乏力、＿＿＿＿＿、气促。

2.巨幼细胞贫血补充＿＿＿＿＿＿＿或维生素 B_{12}。

3.我有 10 多年的＿＿＿＿＿＿＿。

4.贫血按＿＿＿＿＿＿＿形态可分为哪几类？

五、完成下面的对话和句子。

（一）

赵　华：＿＿＿＿＿＿＿＿？

李　风：头晕、眼花、浑身没力气。

赵　华：什么时候开始头晕的？

李　风：＿＿＿＿＿＿＿＿。

赵　华：＿＿＿＿＿＿＿＿？

李　风：我有风湿病,10 多年了。

赵　华：＿＿＿＿＿＿＿＿？

李　风：有的,一直在吃止痛药。

赵　华：＿＿＿＿＿＿＿,还需要给您做血常规检查才能进一步确认。

（二）

1. 什么时候开始＿＿＿＿＿＿的？

2. 您的＿＿＿＿＿＿结果已经回来了。

3. 我初步＿＿＿＿＿＿您是缺铁性贫血。

4. 我＿＿＿＿＿＿会有肚子痛。

5. 住院后医生会给您做更＿＿＿＿＿＿的检查。

六、根据对话和短文内容回答问题。

1. 李明的这些症状是从什么时候开始的？

2. 李明既往有什么病史？

3. 贫血的诊断步骤是什么？

4. 诊断贫血的辅助检查有哪些？

5. 巨幼细胞贫血需要补充什么？

6. 溶血性贫血需要做什么治疗？

七、交际练习。

患者 A 因头晕、乏力、面色苍白 1 周来到医院血液内科就诊，医生 B 向患者 A 询问了症状，并要求他先做血常规检查，建议他住院接受系统诊治。

两人一组，分别扮演角色 A、B，组织一段 3 分钟左右的对话展现上文场景。

【补充医学词汇】

序号	词语	拼音	词义
1	造血细胞增殖	zàoxuè xìbāo zēngzhí	hematopoietic cell proliferation
2	造血干祖细胞	zàoxuè gàn zǔ xìbāo	hematopoietic stem progenitor cell
3	衰竭	shuāijié	failure
4	肿瘤	zhǒngliú	tumor
5	耳鸣	ěrmíng	tinnitus

（蒋　伟　马生元）

第八单元

内分泌科——糖尿病

问诊糖尿病患者时都需要注意什么

第八单元
生词、对话、短文

【学习目的】

1. 学会用汉语表述内分泌系统的主要器官。
2. 学会用汉语问诊糖尿病的典型病例。
3. 了解糖尿病的相关医学常识。

【热身】

一、给下面的词语选择对应的字母。

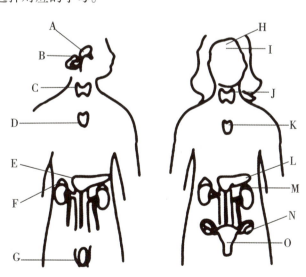

1. 胸腺_____   2. 甲状腺和甲状旁腺_____   3. 肾上腺_____   4. 脑垂体和下丘脑_____
5. 肝_____   6. 卵巢_____   7. 睾丸_____   8. 松果体_____   9. 子宫_____

二、连线题。

1. jiǎzhuàngxiàn		A. 松果体
2. gāowán		B. 脑垂体
3. yíxiàn		C. 下丘脑
4. xiàqiūnǎo		D. 甲状腺
5. luǎncháo		E. 甲状旁腺
6. sōngguǒtǐ		F. 胸腺
7. nǎochuítǐ		G. 胰腺
8. shènshàngxiàn		H. 肾上腺
9. jiǎzhuàngpángxiàn		I. 卵巢
10. xiōngxiàn		J. 睾丸

【会话】

场景简介：

人物：患者——孙天（男，62 岁）

　　　医生——李汉（男，45 岁）

　　　实习医生——珍妮弗（女，18 岁，摩洛哥人）

地点：内分泌科门诊

对话一

生词

序号	词语	词性	拼音	词义
1	重影	名	chóngyǐng	double image
2	空腹血糖	名	kōngfù xuètáng	fasting blood-glucose (FBG)
3	尿糖	名	niàotáng	urine glucose (UGLU)
4	型	名	xíng	type
5	冠心病	名	guānxīnbìng	coronary heart disease
6	脑梗死	名	nǎogěngsǐ	cerebral infarction
7	配合	名	pèihé	cooperation

孙　天：李医生好！我有糖尿病 15 年了，最近 1 个月看不清楚东西。

李　汉：除了看不清，还有没有其他问题，比如头痛、眼干、重影、黑影？

孙　天：都没有。

李　汉：以前是怎么发现糖尿病的？

孙　天：15 年前是因为口渴、多饮、多尿，到医院查空腹血糖 16 mmol/L、尿糖 4+，诊断为 2 型糖尿病。

李　汉：还有没有其他疾病，比如冠心病，有没有发生过脑梗死？

孙　天：这些都没有，就是有时候活动量大，感觉胸口有点痛。

李　汉：家人的身体状况都怎么样？有没有糖尿病、高血压？

孙　天：没有。

李　汉：好的。根据您的身体情况，接下来您需要住院接受进一步的治疗。谢谢您的配合。

孙　天:好的,谢谢李医生。

Sūn Tiān:Lǐ yīshēng hǎo! Wǒ yǒu tángniàobìng shíwǔ nián le, zuìjìn yí gè yuè kàn bù qīngchǔ dōngxi.

Lǐ Hàn:Chúle kàn bù qīng, hái yǒu méi yǒu qítā wèntí, bǐrú tóutòng, yǎngān, chóngyǐng, hēiyǐng?

Sūn Tiān:Dōu méi yǒu.

Lǐ Hàn:Yǐqián shì zěnme fāxiàn tángniàobìng de?

Sūn Tiān:Shíwǔ nián qián shì yīnwèi kǒu kě, duō yǐn, duō niào, dào yīyuàn chá kōngfù xuètáng 16 mmol/L, niàotáng 4+, zhěnduàn wéi èr xíng tángniàobìng.

Lǐ Hàn:Hái yǒu méi yǒu qítā jíbìng, bǐrú guānxīnbìng, yǒu méi yǒu fāshēngguo nǎogěngsǐ?

Sūn Tiān:Zhèxiē dōu méi yǒu, jiùshì yǒushíhòu huódòngliàng dà, gǎnjué xiōngkǒu yǒudiǎn tòng.

Lǐ Hàn:Jiārén de shēntǐ zhuàngkuàng dōu zěnmeyàng? Yǒu méi yǒu tángniàobìng, gāoxuèyā?

Sūn Tiān:Méi yǒu.

Lǐ Hàn:Hǎo de. Gēnjù nín de shēntǐ qíngkuàng, jiē xiàlái nín xūyào zhùyuàn jiēshòu jìnyībù de zhìliáo. Xièxie nín de pèihé.

Sūn Tiān:Hǎo de, xièxie Lǐ yīshēng.

Sun Tian:Hello, Dr. Li! I have been diabetic for 15 years and I can't see clearly in the last month.

Li Han:Besides being unable to see clearly, are there any other problems, such as headache, dry eyes, double vision and dark shadow?

Sun Tian:No.

Li Han:How did you find diabetes before?

Sun Tian:15 years ago, because of polydipsia, multiple drink and polyuria, I went to the hospital to check up. The fasting blood glucose was 16 mmol/L and urine sugar was 4+, so I was diagnosed with type 2 diabetes.

Li Han:Are there any other diseases, such as coronary heart disease or cerebral infarction?

Sun Tian:None of these things, but sometimes if there are amounts of activity, I feel a little pain in my chest.

Li Han:What about the health of your family? Do they have diabetes or hypertension?

Sun Tian:No.

Li Han:All right. According to your physical condition, next you need to be hospitalized for further treatment. Thank you for your cooperation.

Sun Tian:Yes. Thank you, Dr. Li.

对话二

生词

序号	词语	词性	拼音	词义
1	并发症	名	bìngfāzhèng	complication
2	糖化血红蛋白	名	tánghuà xuèhóng dànbái	glycosylated hemoglobin

序号	词语	词性	拼音	词义
3	代谢紊乱	名	dàixiè wěnluàn	metabolic disorder
4	葡萄糖耐量	名	pútaotáng nàiliàng	glucose tolerance
5	胰岛素释放试验	名	yídǎosù shìfàng shìyàn	insulin release test
6	分型	名	fēn xíng	type
7	针对性	名	zhēnduìxìng	pertinence
8	制定	动	zhìdìng	formulate
9	方案	名	fāng'àn	scheme
10	综合	动	zōnghé	synthesize
11	控制	动	kòngzhì	control
12	手段	名	shǒuduàn	means

珍妮弗：李医生，问诊糖尿病患者时都需要注意什么？

李　汉：首先要问一下患者是怎么发现的，还要了解患者的个人生活习惯和有无糖尿病的急、慢性并发症。

珍妮弗：都需要做哪些检查？

李　汉：通过查血脂、血糖、糖化血红蛋白及肝肾功能等，了解代谢紊乱情况；通过葡萄糖耐量及胰岛素释放试验来了解胰岛功能。

珍妮弗：那确诊以后，怎么治疗呢？

李　汉：先要确定糖尿病的分型，然后有针对性地制定治疗方案。无论是哪种糖尿病，都需要综合饮食控制、运动、降糖药物等治疗手段，通过定期检查血糖和糖化血红蛋白了解控制情况，还要每年查一次有无并发症。

Zhēnnífú：Lǐ yīshēng, wènzhěn tángniàobìng huànzhě shí dōu xūyào zhùyì shénme?

Lǐ　Hàn：Shǒuxiān yào wèn yīxià huànzhě shì zěnme fāxiàn de, hái yào liǎojiě huànzhě de gèrén shēnghuó xíguàn hé yǒu wú tángniàobìng de jí、màn xìng bìngfāzhèng.

Zhēnnífú：Dōu xūyào zuò nǎxiē jiǎnchá?

Lǐ　Hàn：Tōngguò chá xuèzhī, xuètáng, tánghuà xuèhóng dànbái jí gān shèn gōngnéng děng, liǎojiě dàixiè wěnluàn qíngkuàng; tōngguò pútaotáng nàiliàng jí yídǎosù shìfàng shìyàn lái liǎojiě yídǎo gōngnéng.

Zhēnnífú：Nà quèzhěn yǐhòu, zěnme zhìliáo ne?

Lǐ　Hàn：Xiān yào quèdìng tángniàobìng de fēn xíng, ránhòu yǒu zhēnduìxìng de zhìdìng zhìliáo fāng'àn. Wúlùn shì nǎ zhǒng tángniàobìng, dōu xūyào zōnghé yǐnshí kòngzhì, yùndòng, jiàngtáng yàowù děng zhìliáo shǒuduàn, tōngguò dìngqī jiǎnchá xuètáng hé tánghuà xuèhóngdànbái lái liǎojiě kòngzhì qíngkuàng, hái yào měi nián chá yī cì yǒu wú bìngfāzhèng.

Gennifer：Dr. Li, what do we need to pay attention to when we ask diabetes patients?

Li　Han：First, we should ask how the patient found the disease, know the patient's personal habits and if they have acute or chronic complications of diabetes.

Gennifer：What kind of tests do diabetes patients need?

Li　Han：We learned about metabolic disorders by checking blood fats, blood glucose, glycosylated hemoglobin, liver and kidney function. The pancreatic islet function was understood by glucose tolerance and insulin release test.

Gennifer: How to treat it after the diagnosis?

Li Han: The first step is to determine the type of diabetes, and then make a targeted treatment plan. No matter what type of diabetes, it requires combination treatments of diet control, exercise and glucose-lowering drugs. We need to understand the control situation through regular inspection of blood sugar and glycosylated hemoglobin, and check every year for any complications.

【短文】

生词

序号	词语	词性	拼音	词义
1	分泌	动	fēnmì	secrete
2	缺陷	名	quēxiàn	defect
3	佳	形	jiā	fine
4	伴发	动	bànfā	concomitant
5	损害	名	sǔnhài	damage
6	残疾	名	cánjí	disability
7	妊娠	名	rènshēn	pregnancy
8	典型	形	diǎnxíng	typical
9	分割点	名	fēngē diǎn	break point
10	人为	形	rénwéi	man-made; artificial
11	依据	动	yījù	according to
12	危害	动	wēihài	harm
13	程度	名	chéngdù	degree

糖尿病

糖尿病是一组由于胰岛素分泌及(或)作用缺陷引起的以血糖增高为特征的代谢病。长期血糖控制不佳的糖尿病患者,可伴发各种器官,尤其是眼、心、血管、肾、神经的损害,功能不全或衰竭,甚至导致残疾或者早亡。糖尿病可分为 1 型、2 型、其他特殊类型及妊娠糖尿病 4 种,典型症状是"三多一少"(多饮、多食、多尿、体重减轻)。糖尿病的诊断由血糖水平确定,其判断为正常或异常的分割点是人为制定的,主要是依据血糖水平对人类健康的危害程度。

Tángniàobìng

Tángniàobìng shì yī zǔ yóuyú yídǎosù fēnmì jí(huò) zuòyòng quēxiàn yǐnqǐ de yǐ xuètáng zēnggāo wéi tèzhēng de dàixièbìng. Chángqī xuètáng kòngzhì bù jiā de tángniàobìng huànzhě, kě bànfā gè zhǒng qìguān, yóuqí shì yǎn、xīn、xuèguǎn、shèn、shénjīng de sǔnhài, gōngnéng bù quán huò shuāijié, shènzhì dǎozhì cánjí huòzhě zǎo wáng. Tángniàobìng kě fēn wéi yī xíng、èr xíng、qítā tèshū lèixíng jí rènshēn tángniàobìng sì zhǒng, diǎnxíng zhèngzhuàng shì "sān duō yī shǎo"(duō yǐn, duō shí, duō niào, tǐzhòng jiǎnqīng). Tángniàobìng de zhěn duàn yóu xuètáng shuǐpíng quèdìng, qí pànduàn wéi zhèngcháng huò yìcháng de fēngē diǎn shì rénwéi zhìdìng de, zhǔyào shì yījù xuètáng shuǐpíng duì rénlèi jiànkāng de wēihài chéngdù.

Diabetes

Diabetes is a group of metabolic diseases characterized by increased blood sugar due to insulin secretion and/or dysfunction. Diabetic patients who have not been well controlled for long periods of time may develop various organs, especially eyes, heart, blood vessels, kidneys, nerve damage, dysfunction or failure, leading to disability or early death. Diabetes can be divided into four types: type 1, type 2, other special types and gestational diabetes, and the typical symptoms are "three more and one less"(more drinks, more food, more urine, less weight). The diagnosis of diabetes is determined by blood glucose level, and the dividing point which is judged as normal or abnormal is artificially formulated, mainly according to the harmful degree of blood glucose level to human health.

【汉字知识】

部首"氵"

部首"氵"的形状和意思为"水",一般出现在汉字的左侧。以"氵"为部首的汉字大都跟水有关。如"消""液""溶""混""油""浊""清""泡"等。此类汉字多为形声结构,左侧的部首为形旁,右侧的部件为声旁,代表字音。

例如:消——消毒　消化　消灭

　　　液——液体　液态　血液

构词

——腺　表示"生物体内由腺细胞组成的能分泌某些化学物质的组织"。

例如:胰腺、唾液腺、甲状腺。

——糖　表示"有机化合物的一类,又叫碳水化合物,是人体内产生热能的主要物质"。

例如:血糖、尿糖、降糖。

【练习】

一、选择听到的词语。

1.(　　) A.重要　　　B.体重　　　C.重复　　　D.重影

2.(　　) A.血糖　　　B.尿糖　　　C.降糖　　　D.低糖

3.(　　) A.人身　　　B.妊娠　　　C.人生　　　D.认识

4.(　　) A.导致　　　B.控制　　　C.制定　　　D.指定

5.(　　) A.移居　　　B.一句　　　C.依据　　　D.已经

二、根据听到的句子排列词语和短语。

1.都　身体状况　家人　怎么样　的

2.诊断　由　确定　的　血糖　水平　糖尿病

3.有无　查　每年　并发症　一次

4.接受　需要　住院　您　进一步　的　治疗

三、仿照句子造句。

1. 先要确定糖尿病的分型,然后有针对性地制定治疗方案。

先要_____,然后_____。

先要_____,然后_____。

2. 无论是哪种糖尿病,都需要综合饮食控制、运动、降糖药物等治疗手段。

无论_____都_____。

无论_____都_____。

3. 通过定期检查血糖和糖化血红蛋白来了解控制情况。

通过_____了解_____。

通过_____了解_____。

四、选词填空。

空腹血糖　　控制　　制定　　配合　　并发症

1. 李医生刚才为您_____了一个新的治疗方案。

2. 糖尿病需要_____饮食。

3. 糖尿病的诊断主要依据_____水平确定。

4. 严重的糖尿病_____可导致残疾。

5. 希望您好好_____医生的治疗,早日出院。

五、完成下面的对话和句子。

(一)

患者:医生,我最近 2 个月感觉口渴,喝水特别多。

医生:_____?

患者:还觉得虽然吃得比以前多了很多,但是体重却减轻了。

医生:_____?

患者:感觉身体挺好的,没有检查过。

医生:好的,那先做一下检查吧。

(二)

1. 糖尿病可分为_____、_____、_____及_____4 种。

2. 糖尿病的典型症状是多_____、多_____、多_____和_____。

六、根据对话和短文内容回答问题。

1. 孙天因为什么病来医院?

2. 孙天怎么知道自己得的是糖尿病?

3. 糖尿病患者都需要做哪些检查? 怎么确诊?

4. 长期血糖控制不好的糖尿病患者会出现什么问题?

5. 糖尿病分为哪几种类型?

6. 糖尿病的典型症状是什么?

七、交际练习。

患者 A,男,32 岁,近 2 个月时常感觉口渴,多饮、多尿,无尿痛及发热。食量及运动量未变,但体重下降 4 kg,无乏力及心前区疼痛,无手足麻木及视物模糊。偶尔午餐前出现心慌、出汗,但是吃点东西就好了。实习医生 B 为其做了病情询问,并与内分泌科副主任 C 讨论病情。C 和 A 商量后建议做进一步检查。

三人一组,分别扮演角色 A、B、C,组织一段 5 分钟左右的对话展现上文场景。

【补充医学词汇】

序号	词语	拼音	词义
1	激素	jīsù	hormone
2	甲状腺功能亢进症（甲亢）	jiǎzhuàngxiàn gōngnéng kàngjìn zhèng（jiǎ kàng）	hyperthyroidis
3	甲状腺功能减退症（甲减）	jiǎzhuàngxiàn gōngnéng jiǎntuì zhèng（jiǎ jiǎn）	hypothyroidism
4	甲状腺结节	jiǎzhuàngxiàn jiéjié	thyroid nodule
5	黏液性水肿	niányèxìng shuǐzhǒng	myxedema

（毛　雪）

第九单元

普外科（一）——肠梗阻

出院后要注意饮食，少食多餐

【学习目的】

1.学会用汉语表述消化系统的相关器官名称。

2.学会用汉语问诊肠梗阻典型病例。

3.了解肠梗阻的相关医学知识。

【热身】

一、给下面的词语选择对应的字母。

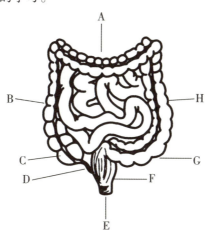

1.肛门_____ 2.直肠_____ 3.阑尾_____ 4.盲肠_____ 5.横结肠_____

6.升结肠_____ 7.降结肠_____ 8.乙状结肠_____

二、根据英文写汉字。

1. sigmoid colon_____

2. rectum_____

3. anus_____

4. vermiform appendix_____

5. cecum_____

6. ascending colon _____

7. transverse colon _____

8. descending colon _____

【会话】

场景简介:

人物:患者——王文(男,49 岁)

患者家属——陈姣娃(女,45 岁)

医生——刘合(男,25 岁)

实习医生——马克(男,21 岁,黎巴嫩人)

地点:消化内科住院部

对话一

生词

序号	词语	词性	拼音	词义
1	采集	动	cǎijí	collect
2	蔓延	动	mànyán	spread
3	触诊	名	chùzhěn	palpation
4	压痛感	名	yātònggǎn	tenderness
5	肠鸣音	名	chángmíngyīn	bowel sound
6	内容物	名	nèiróng wù	content
7	排气	动	páiqì	fart
8	禁食	动	jìnshí	fast
9	肠梗阻	名	chánggěngzǔ	intestinal obstruction

刘　合:马克,3 床的病史采集完了吗?

马　克:采集完了。患者说开始是下腹部阵发性疼痛,然后持续加重,现在蔓延至全腹了。我给他做了触诊和听诊,有压痛感,肠鸣音弱。

刘　合:呕吐吗?

马　克:吐了 5～6 次。

刘　合:有咖啡样呕吐物吗?

马　克:没有,都是胃内容物。

刘　合:大便正常吗?

马　克:有 1 天没有大便和肛门排气了。刘医生,这会是什么病?

刘　合:可能是肠梗阻,让患者暂禁食,先做立卧位腹平片检查。

马　克:好的。

Liú　Hé:Mǎ Kè,3 chuáng de bìngshǐ cǎijí wán le ma?

Mǎ　Kè:Cǎijí wán le。Huànzhě shuō kāishǐ shì xiàfùbù zhènfāxìng téngtòng,ránhòu chíxù jiāzhòng,xiànzài mànyán zhì quán fù le。Wǒ gěi tā zuò le chùzhěn hé tīngzhěn,yǒu yātònggǎn, chángmíngyīn ruò。

Liú　Hé：Outù ma?

Mǎ　Kè：Tù le 5~6 cì。

Liú　Hé：Yǒu kāfēiyàng ǒutùwù ma?

Mǎ　Kè：Méi yǒu，dōu shì wèi nèiróng wù。

Liú　Hé：Dàbiàn zhèngcháng ma?

Mǎ　Kè：Yǒu 1 tiān méiyǒu dàbiàn hé gāngmén páiqì le。Liú yīshēng，zhè huì shì shénme bìng?

Liú　Hé：Kěnéng shì chánggěngzǔ，ràng huànzhě zàn jìnshí，xiān zuò lì wò wèi fùpíngpiàn jiǎnchá。

Mǎ　Kè：Hǎo de。

Liu He：Mark，is the history of bed No. 3 taken?

Mark：It's done. The patient complained the paroxysmal pain in the lower abdomen. It increasingly became more serious，and it spread to the entire abdomen. I did palpation and auscultation for him. There was tenderness and weak bowel sounds.

Liu He：Did he vomit?

Mark：Spitted 5-6 times.

Liu He：Was the vomit things brown?

Mark：No，it was just stomach contents.

Liu He：Are the stool normal?

Mark：He has not defecatd for 1 day，nor fart. Dr. Liu，what can this disease be?

Liu He：Maybe intestinal obstruction，Ask him not to eat and let him do a plain abdominal examination.

Mark：OK.

对话二

生词

序号	词语	词性	拼音	词义
1	好转	动	hǎozhuǎn	be better
2	叮嘱	动	dīngzhǔ	advise；warn
3	清淡	形	qīngdàn	light
4	半流质	形	bàn liúzhì	semi-liquid
5	高蛋白	形	gāo dànbái	high protein

马　克：您好！今天感觉怎么样?

陈姣娃：很好。我丈夫可以出院了吗?

马　克：应该快了。您丈夫的腹部立卧位平片检查结果比第一次好多了，说明不完全肠梗阻已经好转。

陈姣娃：那太好了。

马　克：(对王文)您的肚子还痛吗?

王　文：不痛了。

马　克：我给您检查下。这儿痛不痛?

王　文：不痛。这几天没有恶心、呕吐了。大便也正常了。

马　克：那很好。

陈姣娃：出院后要注意些什么？

马　克：刘医生要我叮嘱他，出院后要注意饮食，少吃多餐，以清淡、易消化、高蛋白、半流质饮食为主。

陈姣娃：知道了，谢谢！

Mǎ　Kè：Nín hǎo！Jīntiān gǎnjué zěnmeyàng？

Chén Jiāowá：Hěn hǎo。Wǒ zhàngfu kěyǐ chūyuàn le ma？

Mǎ　Kè：Yīnggāi kuài le。Nín zhàngfu de fùbù lì wò wèi píngpiàn jiǎnchá jiéguǒ bǐ dì-yī cì hǎo duō le，shuōmíng bùwánquán chánggěngzǔ yǐjīng hǎozhuǎn。

Chén Jiāowá：Nà tài hǎo le。

Mǎ　Kè：（Duì wáng wén）Nín de dùzi hái tòng ma？

Wáng　Wén：Bú tòng le。

Mǎ　Kè：Wǒ gěi nín jiǎnchá xià。Zhèr tòng bu tòng？

Wáng　Wén：Bú tòng。Zhè jǐ tiān méiyǒu ěxin、ǒutù le。Dàbiàn yě zhèngcháng le。

Mǎ　Kè：Nà hěn hǎo。

Chén Jiāowá：Chūyuàn hòu yào zhùyì xiē shénme？

Mǎ　Kè：Liú yīshēng yào wǒ dīngzhǔ tā，chūyuàn hòu yào zhùyì yǐnshí，shǎo chī duō cān，yǐ qīngdàn、yì xiāohuà、gāo dànbái、bàn liúzhì yǐnshí wéi zhǔ。

Chén Jiāowá：Zhīdào le，xièxie！

Mark：Hello！how do you feel today？

Chen Jiaowa：Very good. Can my husband be discharged？

Mark：It should be fast. The result of your husband's abdominal plain film examination is much better than the first，indicating that your incomplete intestinal obstruction has improved.

Chen Jiaowa：That's great.

Mark：（To Wang Wen）Do you still have stomach pain？

Wang Wen：No.

Mark：OK. Let me checke for you. Isn't it painful here？

Wang Wen：No pain. These days I'm not feeling disgusted nor do I vomit. My stool is normal.

Mark：OK.

Chen Jiaowa：What shall we need to pay attention to after being discarded from the hospital？

Mark：Dr. Liu asked me to advisehim to pay attention to the diet after leaving the hospital. He should take semi-liquid diet and eat light，digestible，high protein foods.

Chen Jiaowa：Oh，I know. Thank you！

【短文】

生词

序号	词语	词性	拼音	词义
1	急腹症	名	jífùzhèng	acute abdomen diseases
2	障碍	名	zhàng'ài	obstruction
3	通过	动	tōngguò	pass

序号	词语	词性	拼音	词义
4	胀	形	zhàng	bloating
5	闭	动	bì	closure
6	脆弱	形	cuìruò	fragile
7	富含	动	fù hán	be rich in

肠梗阻

肠梗阻是一种常见的消化系统疾病,也是外科常见的急腹症之一,主要发生在小肠。急腹症是腹部急性疾病的总称,如急性阑尾炎、肠梗阻、急性胰腺炎等。医学上把各种原因引起的肠道内容物通过障碍疾病,也就是肠道不通,叫肠梗阻。

肠梗阻的典型症状是"痛、吐、胀、闭"。"痛"是指腹痛,"吐"是指呕吐,"胀"是指腹胀,"闭"是指停止排气、排便。无论是婴儿还是老人都有患病的可能。

一般经过手术的肠梗阻患者,肠道功能比较脆弱,应吃清淡、易消化、富含蛋白质及铁质的食物,如蛋汤、面、蔬菜、水果、瘦肉、鱼虾等。

Chánggěngzǔ

Chánggěngzǔ shì yìzhǒng chángjiàn de xiāohuà xìtǒng jíbìng, yě shì wàikē chángjiàn de jífùzhèng zhīyī, zhǔyào fāshēng zài xiǎocháng。Jífùzhèng shì fùbù jíxìng jíbìng de zǒngchēng, rú jíxìng lánwěiyán、chánggěngzǔ、jíxìng yíxiànyán děng。Yīxué shang bǎ gè zhǒng yuányīn yǐnqǐ de chángdào nèiróngwù tōngguò zhàng'ài jíbìng, yě jiùshì chángdào bù tōng, jiào chánggěngzǔ。

Chánggěngzǔ de diǎnxíng zhèngzhuàng shì "tòng、tǔ、zhàng、bì"。"Tòng" shì zhǐ fùtòng, "tǔ" shì zhǐ ǒutù, "zhàng" shì zhǐ fùzhàng, "bì" shì zhǐ tíngzhǐ páiqì、páibiàn。Wúlùn shì yīng'ér háishì lǎorén dōu yǒu huàn bìng de kěnéng。

Yìbān jīngguò shǒushù de chánggěngzǔ huànzhě, chángdào gōngnéng bǐjiào cuìruò, yīng chī qīngdàn、yì xiāohuà、fù hán dànbáizhì jí tiězhì de shíwù, rú dàntāng、miàn、shūcài、shuǐguǒ、shòuròu、yúxiā děng。

Intestinal obstruction

Intestinal obstruction is a common digestive system disease, and one of the most common acute abdomen diseases. It mainly occurs in the small intestine. Acute abdomen is referring to the diseases such as acute appendicitis, intestinal obstruction, acute pancreatitis. Intestinal obstruction is a mechanical or functional obstruction of the intestines which prevents the intestinal content smoothly pass through because of different causes.

Typical symptoms of intestinal obstruction are "pain, vomiting, bloating, and closure". "Pain" is abdominal pain, "spit" is vomiting, "bloating" is abdominal bloating, and "closure" is stopping passing gas and defecate. Both infants and the elderly are equally susceptible.

Patients with intestinal obstruction who had surgery have a relatively weak intestinal function and should eatfood which is light, easily digested, rich in proteins and iron such as egg soup, noodles, vegetables, fruits, lean meat, fish Shrimp and so on.

【汉字知识】

部首"木"

部首"木"的意思为"木头",一般出现在汉字的左侧。以"木"为部首的汉字大都跟树木有关。如"检""椎""案""栓""梗""根"等。此类汉字多为形声结构,左侧的部首为形旁,右侧的部件为声旁,代表字音。

例如:检——检查　检疫　检验
　　　梗——肠梗阻　脑梗死　心肌梗死

构词

高——　表示"在一般标准或平均程度之上"。

例如:高蛋白、高血压、高血糖、高血脂。

——肠　表示"肠道的不同部位"。

例如:直肠、盲肠、小肠、大肠、结肠、升结肠、横结肠、降结肠。

【练习】

一、选择听到的词语。

1. (　　　) A.再见　B.彩旗　　C.采集　　D.气息
2. (　　　) A.满眼　B.慢行　　C.浪漫　　D.蔓延
3. (　　　) A.叮嘱　B.挺住　　C.听清　　D.盯住
4. (　　　) A.内脏　B.障碍　　C.障眼　　D.丈夫
5. (　　　) A.系列　B.细致　　C.距离　　D.剧烈

二、根据听到的句子排列词语和短语。

1. 两天　已经　了　他　排气　没有　　排便

2. 清淡　叮嘱　他　食物　的　多吃　易消化　医生　有营养

3. 急腹症　是　肠梗阻　常见　之一　外科　　的

4. 胀　肠梗阻　吐　的　闭　典型　是　症状　痛

三、仿照句子造句。

1. 这名患者是因为2天前突然出现腹部疼痛来看病的。
　　_____是因为_____来看病的。
　　_____是因为_____来看病的。
2. 肠梗阻是一种常见的消化系统疾病。
　　_____是一种常见的_____疾病。
　　_____是一种常见的_____疾病。
3. 肠梗阻是外科常见的急腹症之一。
　　_____是_____常见的_____之一。
　　_____是_____常见的_____之一。

四、选词填空。

采集　内容物　叮嘱　蔓延　半流质

1. 他刚做完手术出院,应该以吃_____食物为主,如粥、面等。
2. 医生_____他出院后一定要注意休息。

3. 他已经吐了 3 次了,_____有咖啡样的东西。

4. 你记得_____完病史就马上跟陈医生汇报。

5. 他的疼痛已_____至全腹了。

五、完成下面的对话和句子。

(一)

医生:_____?

患者:我下腹部疼痛。

医生:多长时间了?

患者:_____。

医生:呕吐吗?

患者:_____。

医生:有没有拉大便?

患者:_____。

医生:您先去做个检查,我给您开化验单。

(二)

1. 肠梗阻是外科常见的_____之一。

2. "_____"是肠梗阻的典型症状。

3. 一般经过手术的肠梗阻患者,应吃_____、_____、_____及_____食物。

六、根据对话和短文内容回答问题。

1. 3 床患者为什么来看病?

2. 3 床患者呕吐的是什么内容物?

3. 刘医生叮嘱 3 床出院后要注意什么?

4. 肠梗阻的典型症状是什么?

5. 肠梗阻在发病年龄上有没有差异?

七、交际练习。

患者 A 腹胀、腹痛 13 小时来医院就诊,医生 B 询问其病情,发现其恶心、呕吐 3 次,停止排气排便 2 天,考虑肠梗阻,要求其做立位腹平片检查。

两人一组,分别扮演角色 A、B,组织一段 3 分钟左右的对话展现上文场景。

【补充医学词汇】

序号	词语	拼音	词义
1	机械性肠梗阻	jīxièxìng chánggěngzǔ	mechanicalintestinal obstruction
2	动力性肠梗阻	dònglìxìng chánggěngzǔ	dynamic intestinal obstruction
3	血管性肠梗阻	xuèguǎnxìng chánggěngzǔ	vascular intestinal obstruction
4	单纯性肠梗阻	dānchúnxìng chánggěngzǔ	simple intestinal obstruction
5	绞窄性肠梗阻	jiǎozhǎixìng chánggěngzǔ	strangulateintestinal obstruction
6	不完全性肠梗阻	bùwánquánxìng chánggěngzǔ	imcompleteintestinal obstruction
7	完全性肠梗阻	wánquánxìng chánggěngzǔ	complete intestinal obstruction

(姜冬梅 王华民)

第十单元

普外科（二）——急性阑尾炎

是胀痛还是绞痛

【学习目的】

1. 学会用汉语表述盲肠和阑尾的内部结构。
2. 学会用汉语问诊典型急性阑尾炎病例。
3. 了解阑尾炎的相关医学常识。

【热身】

一、给下面的词语选择对应的字母。

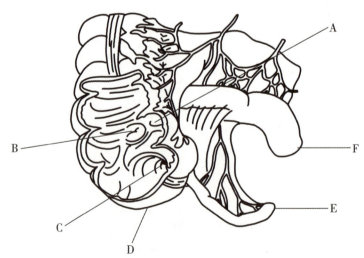

1. 阑尾_____ 2. 回肠口_____ 3. 回盲瓣_____ 4. 阑尾口_____ 5. 回肠_____

6. 盲肠_____

二、根据拼音写汉字。

1. mángcháng_____

2. huímángbàn_____

3. lánwěi _____

4. lánwěi kǒu _____

5. huícháng _____

6. huícháng kǒu _____

【会话】

场景简介:

人物:患者——夏天(女,27 岁)

　　　医生——赵雨(男,38 岁)

　　　实习医生——穆汗默德(男,21 岁,巴基斯坦人)

地点:急诊科

对话一

生词

序号	词语	词性	拼音	词义
1	阵痛	动	zhèntòng	labour pain
2	胀痛	动	zhàngtòng	swelling pain
3	绞痛	动	jiǎotòng	colic pain
4	拉肚子	动	lādùzi	diarrhea
5	体格	名	tǐgé	physigue
6	尿常规	名	niàochángguī	urine routine
7	腹部 X 射线	名	fùbù X shèxiàn	abdominal X-ray

穆汗默德:您好,哪里不舒服?

夏　天:我昨晚开始肚子痛得厉害,有 10 个小时了。

穆汗默德:哪个地方痛?

夏　天:开始痛的时候是肚子中间,后面就到右下面了。

穆汗默德:是一直痛还是阵痛?或者胀痛还是绞痛?

夏　天:一阵阵胀痛,有时会缓解。

穆汗默德:还有其他不舒服吗?

夏　天:可能发热了,有些怕冷。

穆汗默德:有没有拉肚子或者恶心、呕吐?

夏　天:呕吐了 1 次,没有拉肚子。

穆汗默德:请躺下做个体格检查。我摸到您感觉痛的地方时告诉我。

夏　天:这里好痛。

穆汗默德:我现在放手,痛不痛?

夏　天:痛。

穆汗默德:可以起来了。赵医生,他可能是急性阑尾炎。

赵　雨:我知道了。您跟他先去验血常规和尿常规,再拍腹部 X 射线片,等结果出来给我看。

穆汗默德:好的。夏天,跟我来。

夏　天:好,谢谢医生。

Mùhànmòdé：Nín hǎo，nǎlǐ bù shūfu？

Xià Tiān：Wǒ zuó wǎn kāishǐ dùzi tòng dé lìhai，yǒu 10 gè xiǎoshí le。

Mùhànmòdé：Nǎ gè dìfang tòng？

Xià Tiān：Kāishǐ tòng de shíhou shì dùzi zhōngjiān，hòumian jiù dào yòu xiàmian le。

Mùhànmòdé：Shì yìzhí tòng háishì zhèntòng？ Huòzhě zhàngtòng háishì jiǎotòng？

Xià Tiān：Yí zhènzhèn zhàngtòng，yǒushí huì huǎnjiě。

Mùhànmòdé：Hái yǒu qítā bù shūfu ma？

Xià Tiān：Kěnéng fārè le，yǒuxiē pàlěng。

Mùhànmòdé：Yǒu méiyǒu lādùzi huòzhě ěxin、ǒutù？

Xià Tiān：Ǒutù le yí cì，méiyǒu lādùzi。

Mùhànmòdé：Qǐng tǎngxià zuò gè tǐgé jiǎnchá。 Wǒ mō dào nín gǎnjué tòng de dìfang shí gàosù wǒ。

Xià Tiān：Zhèlǐ hǎo tòng。

Mùhànmòdé：Wǒ xiànzài fàng shǒu，tòng bu tòng？

Xià Tiān：Tòng。

Mùhànmòdé：Kéyǐ qǐlái le。 Zhào Guāngmíng，tā kěnéng shì jíxing lánwěiyán。

Zhào Yǔ：Wǒ zhīdào le。 Nín gēn tā xiān qù yàn xuèchángguī hé niàochángguī，zài pāi fùbù X shèxiànpiān，děng jiéguǒ chūlái gěi wǒ kàn。

Mùhànmòdé：Hǎo de。 Xià Tiān，gēn wǒ lái。

Xià Tiān：Hǎo，xièxie yīshēng。

Muhammed：Hello，where are you feeling uncomfortable？

Xia Tian：Last night I had a stomachache badly，for 10 hours.

Muhammaed：Where hurts？

Xia Tian：When it started to hurt，it was between the middle of the stomach and later it shifted to the lower right bottom.

Muhammed：Is it a pain or tenderness？ Or swollen pain or colic？

Xia Tian：A lot of pain，sometimes relieved.

Muhammead：Is there anything else uncomfortable？

Xia Tian：Maybe I have a fever，some times I'm afraid of cold.

Muhammed：Do you have diarrhea，nausea or vomiting？

Xia Tian：Vomit one time，no diarrhea.

Muhammed：Please lie down，I will do a physical examination. Tell me when you feel the pain.

Xia Tian：It hurts.

Muhammed：I release my hands now，is there pain or not？

Xia Tian：It's pain.

Muhammed：You can get up. Dr. Zhao，he may have acute appendicitis.

Zhao Yu：I see. You should go tocheck the blood routine and urine routine with him first，then take the abdominal X-ray，and let me see the result.

Muhammed：All right. Xia Tian，come with me.

Xia Tian：OK，thank you，doctor.

对话二

生词

序号	词语	词性	拼音	词义
1	提示	动	tíshì	indicate
2	炎症	名	yánzhèng	inflammation

（检查结果出来后）

赵　雨：您的检查结果除了血常规提示有炎症的表现，其他检查都没有问题。根据您的检查结果还有体格检查，目前考虑您是急性阑尾炎，需要手术治疗。

夏　天：这么严重？可以不做手术吗？

赵　雨：如果不做手术，可能有危险。手术治疗主要是切除病变的阑尾，达到彻底治疗的目的。

夏　天：那我还是手术吧。

赵　雨：我现在给您办理住院手续，帮您安排到普外科住院。

夏　天：好的，谢谢医生。

（Jiǎnchá jiéguǒ chēlái hòu）

Zhào Yǔ：Nín de jiǎnchá jiéguǒ chúle xuèchángguī tíshì yǒu yánzhèng de biǎoxiàn，qítā jiǎnchá dōu méiyǒu wèntí。Gēnjù nín de jiǎnchá jiéguǒ hái yǒu tǐgé jiǎnchá，mùqián kǎolǜ nín shì jíxìng lánwěiyán，xūyào shǒushù zhìliáo。

Xià Tiān：Zhème yánzhòng？Kéyǐ bú zuò shǒushù ma？

Zhào Yǔ：Rúguǒ bú zuò shǒushù，kěnéng yǒu wēixiǎn。Shǒushù zhìliáo zhǔyào shì qiēchú bìngbiàn de lánwěi，dádào chèdǐ zhìliáo de mùdì。

Xià Tiān：Nà wǒ háishì shǒushù ba。

Zhào Yǔ：Wǒ xiànzài gěi nín bànlǐ zhùyuàn shǒuxù，bāng nǐ ānpái dào pǔwàikē zhùyuàn。

Xià Tiān：Hǎo de，xièxie yīsheng。

（After the result of the examination）

Zhao Yu：Your examination results show that there are no other problems except for blood routine indicating inflammation. According to your examination results and physical examination，now we consider that you are acute appendicitis and need surgical treatment.

Xia Tian：So serious？Is it okay not to have surgery？

Zhao Yu：If surgery is not done，there may be danger. Surgical treatment is mainly to remove the appendix of the lesion and achieve the goal of thorough treatment.

Xia Tian：OK，I accept the operation.

Zhao Yu：Now I'll go through the hospitalization procedure and arrange for you to be hospitalized in the department of general surgery.

Xia Tian：OK，thank you，doctor.

【短文】

生词

序号	词语	词性	拼音	词义
1	就医	动	jiùyī	see the doctor
2	盲管	名	mángguǎn	blind tube
3	扭曲	动	niǔqū	twist
4	压迫	动	yāpò	oppress
5	肠道	名	chángdào	intestine
6	粪	名	fèn	feces
7	异物	名	yìwù	foreign bodies
8	寄生虫	名	jìshēngchóng	parasites
9	阻塞	动	zǔsè	block
10	阑尾腔	名	lánwěi qiāng	appendix
11	转移	动	zhuǎnyí	transfer
12	麦氏点	名	Màishì diǎn	McBurney point
13	反跳痛	名	fǎntiàotòng	rebound symptoms

急性阑尾炎

急性阑尾炎是普外科常见的疾病之一,大多数患者能及时就医,获得良好的治疗效果。但是,有时诊断相当困难,处理不当时会发生一些严重的并发症。到目前为止,急性阑尾炎仍有 0.1% ~ 0.5% 的死亡率。

阑尾是一条又细又长的盲管。因为长,所以容易扭曲或被周围的东西压迫;因为细,所以容易被肠道里的粪块、异物、寄生虫阻塞,这些都可以造成阑尾腔的梗阻。因为是盲管,所以阻塞就四面不通。阑尾炎的主要症状是腹痛。外科医生通过转移性右下腹痛的病史,麦氏点压痛、反跳痛的体征和辅助检查来诊断阑尾炎。

Jíxìng lánwěiyán

Jíxìng lánwěiyán shì pǔ wàikē chángjiàn de jíbìng zhī yī, dà duōshù huànzhě néng jíshí jiùyī, huòdé liánghǎo de zhìliáo xiàoguǒ。Dànshì, yǒushí zhěnduàn xiāngdāng kùnnán, chúlǐ bùdāng shí huì fāshēng yìxiē yánzhòng de bìngfāzhèng。Dào mùqián wéi zhǐ, jíxìng lánwěiyán réng yǒu bǎifēnzhī líng diǎn yī dào bǎifēnzhī líng diǎn wǔ de sǐwáng lǜ。

Lánwěi shì yìtiáo yòu xì yòu cháng de mángguǎn。Yīnwèi cháng, suóyǐ róngyì niǔqū huò bèi zhōuwéi de dōngxi yāpò; yīnwèi xì, suóyǐ róngyì bèi chángdào lǐ de fènkuài、yìwù、jìshēngchóng zǔsè, zhèxiē dōu kéyǐ zàochéng lánwěi qiāng de géngzǔ。Yīnwèi shì mángguǎn, suóyǐ zǔsè jiù sìmiàn bù tōng。Lánwěiyán de zhǔyào zhèngzhuàng shì fùtòng。Wàikē yīsheng tōngguò zhuǎnyí xìng yòu xià fù tòng de bìngshǐ, Màishì diǎn yātòng、fǎntiàotòng de tǐzhēng hé fǔzhù jiǎnchá lái zhěnduàn lánwěiyán。

Acute appendicitis

Acute appendicitis is one of the common diseases in abdominal surgery. Most patients can get timely medical treatment and achieve good therapeutic effect. However, sometimes the diagnosis is rather difficult. If there is no treatment, some serious complications will occur. So far, acute appendicitis still has a mortality rate of 0.1% –0.5%.

The appendix is a thin and long blind tube. Because it is long, it is easily twisted or oppressed by the surrounding things; because of the fine, it is easily blocked by the feces, foreign bodies and parasites in the intestines, which can cause the obstruction of the appendix. Because it is a blind tube, the infarct will not work on all sides. The main symptom of appendicitis is abdominal pain. Surgeons diagnosed appendicitis by transferring the history of right lower quadrant pain, McBurney point tenderness, rebound symptoms and auxiliary examinations.

【汉字知识】

部首"亻"

部首"亻"的意思为"人"，一般出现在汉字的左侧。以"亻"为部首的汉字多与人有关。如"他""体""健""伤""借""你"等。此类汉字多为形声结构，左侧的部首为形旁，右侧的部件为声旁，代表字音。

例如：体——身体　体育　体能

健——健康　健在　健身

构词

——道　表示"泛指各种通道"。

例如：阴道、尿道、肠道、上呼吸道、下呼吸道。

——症　表示"身体出现某种症状或现象"。

例如：炎症、癌症、病症、多动症、厌食症、并发症。

【练习】

一、选择听到的词语。

1. (　　)A. 绞痛　　B. 头痛　　C. 阵痛　　D. 胀痛
2. (　　)A. 血常规　B. 尿常规　C. 常规性　D. 回盲肠
3. (　　)A. 恶心　　B. 可恶　　C. 恶人　　D. 中心
4. (　　)A. 阻塞　　B. 阻止　　C. 梗死　　D. 闭塞
5. (　　)A. 阑尾炎　B. 阑尾腔　C. 阑尾管　D. 阑尾口

二、根据听到的句子排列词语和短语。

1. 开始　昨晚　我　痛　厉害　得　肚子

2. 检查结果　除了　提示　您的　有　炎症的　表现　血常规　检查　其他　没有　都　问题

3. 急性阑尾炎　初期　典型的　腹部的　有　中上部位置　肚脐周围　或　疼痛

4. 通常　外科医生　根据　患者　麦氏点　的　右下腹　固定压痛　实验室检查　和　来　确诊　阑尾炎

三、仿照句子造句。

1. 我昨晚开始肚子痛得厉害,有 10 个小时了。

我_____开始_____,有_____了。

我_____开始_____,有_____了。

2. 有没有拉肚子或者恶心、呕吐?

有没有_____或者_____?

有没有_____或者_____?

3. 目前考虑您是急性阑尾炎,需要手术治疗。

目前考虑你是_____,需要_____。

目前考虑你是_____,需要_____。

四、选词填空。

提示　体格　胀痛　扭曲　盲管

1. 请躺下做个_____检查。

2. 一阵阵_____,有时会缓解。

3. 您的检查结果除了血常规_____有炎症的表现,其他检查都没有问题。

4. 阑尾因为长,所以容易_____或被周围的东西压迫。

5. 由于阑尾是条_____,阻塞就四面不通。

五、完成下面的对话和句子。

(一)

赵　雨:您的检查结果除了血常规提示_____,其他检查都没有问题。根据您的检查结果还有_____,目前考虑您是_____,需要手术治疗。

夏　天:这么严重? 可以_____吗?

赵　雨:如果不做手术,可能_____。手术治疗主要是_____,达到_____的目的。

夏　天:那我还是手术吧。

赵　雨:我现在给您办理_____,帮您安排到_____。

夏　天:好的,谢谢医生。

(二)

1. 阑尾是一条又细又长的_____。

2. 阑尾因为长,容易_____或被周围的东西_____。

3. 阑尾炎的主要症状是_____。

4. 外科医生通过_____右下腹痛的病史,_____压痛、_____的体征和辅助检查来诊断阑尾炎。

5. 阑尾因为细,容易被肠道里的_____、异物、_____阻塞。

六、根据对话和短文内容回答问题。

1. 夏天哪里不舒服?

2. 夏天得了什么病?

3. 赵雨给出了什么治疗方案?

4. 夏天为什么要进行手术治疗?

5. 阑尾为什么会阻塞?

6. 如何确诊阑尾炎?

七、交际练习。

患者 A 因右下腹疼痛 8 小时,伴恶心、发热前来就诊,医生 B 接待了患者 A。医生 B 向患者 A 询问了症状。医生 B 给他先做体格检查,考虑是急性阑尾炎,并让患者 A 做血常规、尿常规和腹部 X 射线片检查。

两人一组,分别扮演角色 A、B,组织一段 3 分钟左右的对话展现上文场景。

【补充医学词汇】

序号	词语	拼音	词义
1	血淀粉酶	xuè diànfěn méi	blood amylase
2	阑尾穿孔	lánwěi chuānkǒng	appendiceal perforation
3	荷包线缝合	hébāo xiàn fénghé	string suture
4	腰大肌试验	yāo dà jī shìyàn	psoas stretch
5	腹腔镜检查	fùqiāng jìng jiǎnchá	laparoscopy

（张均智　代　晶）

第十一单元

心胸外科——胸部损伤

初步诊断是左侧肋骨骨折

【学习目的】

1. 学会用汉语表述胸部各部位名称。

2. 学会用汉语问诊胸部损伤典型病例。

3. 学会用汉语表述心胸外科的常见疾病、主要症状、体征、常规检查和防治措施等。

4. 能够用汉语描述术前、术后的变化。

【热身】

一、给下面的词语选择对应的字母。

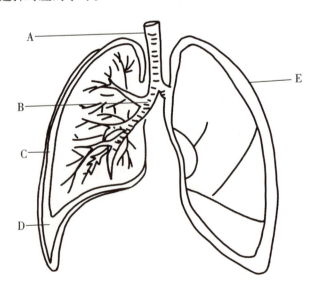

1. 胸膜腔_____   2. 支气管_____   3. 气管_____   4. 肋膈隐窝_____   5. 肺_____

二、给下面的词语选择对应的字母。

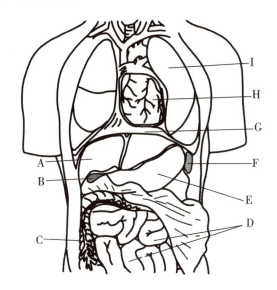

1.肝＿＿＿＿　2.胃＿＿＿＿　3.膈肌＿＿＿＿　4.小肠＿＿＿＿　5.胆囊＿＿＿＿

6.脾＿＿＿＿　7.大肠＿＿＿＿　8.肺＿＿＿＿　9.心脏＿＿＿＿

【会话】

对话一

场景简介：

人物:患者——王凯(男,25 岁)

　　　　医生——赵伟(男,43 岁)

地点:心胸外科 3 诊室

生词

序号	词语	词性	拼音	词义
1	车把	名	chēbǎ	handlebar
2	肋骨	名	lèigǔ	rib
3	胸带	名	xiōng dài	chest strap
4	胸壁	名	xiōngbì	chest wall
5	淤血	名	yūxuè	clotted blood
6	边缘	名	biānyuán	edge
7	避免	动	bìmiǎn	avoid
8	剧烈	形	jùliè	strenuous
9	随意	副	suíyì	arbitrarily

赵　伟:您哪里不舒服?

王　凯:昨天下雪路滑,我骑电动车时摔倒了,左边胸部撞到车把上,疼痛难忍,我就去当地医院拍了个胸部 CT,结果显示断了 3 根肋骨。大夫给我上了胸带,建议我来这里手术治疗。

赵　伟:CT 片子带来了吗?

王　凯：带着呢,片子在这儿。

赵　伟：(仔细看片子)确实是左侧肋骨骨折,左侧胸壁肿胀有淤血。(用手轻摸)这里还痛吗?

王　凯：哎哟! 痛死我了。

赵　伟：肿胀边缘压痛异常明显,您这种情况需要住院治疗。那您先办住院吧。

王　凯：大夫,我这需要做手术吗?

赵　伟：做完检查后,根据检查结果才能决定治疗方案。

王　凯：能不能先给我输点止痛药,我痛得受不了呀。

赵　伟：可以。您现在要避免剧烈活动,特别是胸部不能随意扭动。

王　凯：好的,谢谢医生!

Zhao Wei：What's wrong with you?

Wang Kai：Yesterday,when it was snowing,down the slippery road,I fell while riding the electric motorbike,left chest hit the handlebar's of bike. Pain was unbearable. I went to a local hospital and took a chest CT,and the result was I broke three ribs. The doctor gave me a chest strap and advised me to come here for surgery.

Zhao Wei：Did you bring the CT film?

Wang Kai：Yes,here it is.

Zhao Wei：(Carefully watching the CT film) It is indeed a fracture of the left rib and the left chest wall is swollen with clotted blood. (Touch lightly) Does it still hurt here?

Wang Kai：Ouch! It hurts.

Zhao Wei：The tenderness from the abnormally swollen edge is obvious. You need to be hospitalized in this situation. Hence,firstly get ready to hospitalize.

Wang Kai：Doctor,do I need surgery?

Zhao Wei：After completing the examination,based on the results,the treatment plan can be determined.

Wang Kai：Can I get pain medicine first? I can't withstand the pain.

Zhao Wei：Yes. Now,you must avoid strenuous activity,especially the chest can not be arbitrarily twisted.

Wang Kai：OK,thank you doctor!

对话二

场景简介:
人物:胸外科医生——王健(男,48岁)
　　　急诊科医生——李云龙(男,30岁)
　　　实习医生——马克(男,21岁,黎巴嫩人)
地点:急诊ICU

生词

序号	词语	词性	拼音	词义
1	车祸	名	chēhuò	accident
2	急促	形	jícù	tachypnea
3	稳定	形	wěndìng	stable
4	指标	名	zhǐbiāo	indicator

序号	词语	词性	拼音	词义
5	胸腔闭式引流	动	xiōngqiāng bìshì yǐnliú	closed thoracic drainage
6	液体	名	yètǐ	liquid
7	初步	形	chūbù	initial
8	挫伤	动	cuòshāng	contuse
9	血气胸	名	xuè qì xiōng	blood pneumothorax
10	进行性血胸	名	jìnxíngxìng xuèxiōng	progressive hemothorax
11	阴影	名	yīnyǐng	shadow
12	评估	动	pínggū	evaluate
13	耐受	动	nàishòu	tolerate
14	保守	形	bǎoshǒu	conservative
15	沟通	动	gōutong	communicate

马　克：老师您好！

王　健：先看患者吧，请把现有的片子拿来，我看一下。

马　克：好的，我先简单说一下他的情况：他是车祸中的小车司机，送来时意识丧失，呼吸急促，血压85/55 mmHg。

王　健：输血、补液后情况怎么样？

李云龙：血压还是不稳定，血常规各相关指标也下降明显，我们放了胸腔闭式引流，1个小时已经引出大概300 mL鲜红色液体了。

王　健：初步诊断是什么？

李云龙：我们考虑胸部这方面是肋骨骨折、肺挫伤、血气胸、进行性血胸。

王　健：其他情况怎么样？

马　克：X射线检查见肺部阴影逐渐增大，其他各系统据目前检查还未见异常。

王　健：进行性血胸的可能性极大，现在评估一下其他各部位情况，若能耐受手术就急诊手术治疗吧，保守治疗可行性小。

李云龙：好的，我先去跟家属沟通签字，马克你联系手术室准备手术。

马　克：好的。

Mark：Hello, Dr. Wang.

Wang Jian：Let's see the patient first. Please bring the existing film. Let me see.

Mark：Yes, let me talk briefly about his situation：He was the driver of the car in a car accident. He lost consciousness and breathlessness when admitted, and his blood pressure was 85/55 mmHg.

Wang Jian：What about the situation after blood transfusion?

Li Yunlong：Blood pressure was still unstable, and blood related indicators also decreased significantly. We put a closed thoracic drainage, and about 300 mL of bright red liquid had been drawn in one hour.

Wang Jian：What is the initial diagnosis?

Li Yunlong：We think that, aspect of the chest has rib fracture, pulmonary contusion, blood pneumothorax, and progressive hemothorax.

Wang Jian：What about other situations?

Mark：X-ray examination showed that the shadow of the lungs gradually increased, and other systems according to the current examination no abnormalities.

Wang Jian: The possibility of progressive hemothorax is extremely high. At present, let's evaluate the situation in other parts. If he can tolerate surgery, then emergency surgery is a good option. Conservative treatment is less feasible.

Li Yunlong: OK, I'll first communicate with the patient's relations. Mark, you contact the operating room for surgery.

Mark: OK.

【短文】

生词

序号	词语	词性	拼音	词义
1	损伤	动	sǔnshāng	injury
2	锐器	名	ruìqì	sharp
3	窒息	动	zhìxī	apnea
4	钝性伤	名	dùn xìng shāng	blunt trauma
5	穿透伤	名	chuāntòu shāng	penetrating injury
6	胸膜腔	名	xiōngmóqiāng	pleural cavity
7	支撑	动	zhīchēng	support
8	破裂	动	pòliè	rupture

胸部损伤

胸部损伤是由车祸、挤压伤、摔伤和锐器伤等所致,包括胸壁挫伤、裂伤、肋骨及胸骨骨折、气胸、血胸、肺挫伤、气管及主支气管损伤、心脏损伤、膈肌损伤、创伤性窒息等,有时可合并腹部损伤。根据损伤性质不同,胸部损伤可分为钝性伤和穿透伤;根据损伤是否造成胸膜腔与外界沟通,可分为开放伤和闭合伤。胸部的骨性胸廓支撑保护胸腔内脏器官并参与呼吸功能。钝性伤可破坏骨性胸廓的完整性,使胸腔内心、肺发生碰撞、挤压、扭曲,造成广泛组织挫伤。穿透伤可使心脏大血管破裂并迅速致死。

Thoracic thauma

Thoracic trauma is caused by vehicle accidents, crush injuries, fall injuries and sharp injuries, including chest wall contusions, lacerations, fractures of ribs and sternum, pneumothorax, hemothorax, pulmonary contusion, trachea and main bronchus injuries, heart damage, diaphragm injuries, traumatic asphyxia, and sometimes abdominal injuries can be combined. According to the different nature of injury, chest injury can be divided into blunt trauma and penetrating injury; according to whether the injury caused the pleural cavity communicates with the outside world, it can be divided into open wound and closed injury. The bony thoracic support of the chest protects the visceral organs of the chest and participates in respiratory functions. Blunt wounds can destroy the integrity of the bony thoracic cage, causing the heart and lungs of the chest to collide, squash, and distort, causing extensive tissue bruising. Penetrating injuries can rupture the large blood vessels of the heart and quickly kill them.

【汉字知识】

部首"页"

部首"页"的意思为"额头",一般出现在汉字的右侧。以"页"为部首的汉字大都跟肉体有关。如"颈""颅""顶""额""颞""领""频""颜""顿"等。此类汉字多为形声结构,右侧的部首为形旁,左侧的部件为声旁,代表字音。

例如:颈——脖颈　颈部　颈椎
　　　颅——颅腔　颅骨　头颅

构词

——骨折　表示"由于外伤或骨组织病变,骨头折断、变成碎块或发生裂纹"。

例如:肋骨骨折、颅骨骨折。

——脉　表示"分布在人和动物全身的血管"。

例如:动脉、静脉、经脉、诊脉。

【练习】

一、选择听到的词语。

1.(　　)A.摔伤　　B.损伤　　C.裂伤　　D.挫伤

2.(　　)A.意识　　B.意思　　C.意志　　D.意义

3.(　　)A.跑步　　B.漫步　　C.初步　　D.稳步

4.(　　)A.保护　　B.保守　　C.保存　　D.保留

5.(　　)A.折扣　　B.挫折　　C.打折　　D.骨折

二、根据听到的句子排列词语和短语。

1.我　拍了　个　当地医院　胸部CT　就　去

2.才　能　根据　决定　治疗方案　检查结果

3.相关指标　也　明显　下降　各　血常规

4.据　各　系统　还　未见　异常　目前　检查　其他

5.您　要　避免　现在　特别　是　剧烈　活动　不能　胸部　随意扭动

三、仿照句子造句。

1.痛死我了。

_____死我了。

_____死我了。

2.根据检查结果才能决定治疗方案。

根据_____才能_____。

根据_____才能_____。

2.能不能先给我输点止痛药,我痛得受不了呀。

能不能先_____,我_____。

能不能先_____,我_____。

3.若能耐受手术,就急诊手术治疗吧。

若能_____,就_____。

若能_____,就_____。

四、选词填空。

明显　初步　保守　评估　沟通　稳定

1.等他病情_____后,我们再考虑搭桥手术吧。

2.术前术后的变化是很_____的,胸闷的症状基本消失了。

3.王大爷年龄大了,不建议做胸部的大手术了,还是_____治疗吧。

4.手术之前要和家属进行_____,让他们了解手术的各种风险。

5.临床医生要对患者的病情和心理状况进行正确科学的_____。

6.一般病史采集之后,先要进行_____检查,根据各项检查结果才能确诊。

五、完成下面的对话和句子。

(一)

患　者:哎哟,不能动,一动就痛得要命。

医　生:_____?

患　者:摘苹果时,我不小心从树上摔下来了。

医　生:_____。

患　者:大夫,我需不需要做手术?

医　生:_____。

(二)

1.胸部损伤是由_____、_____、_____和_____等所致的疾病。

2.根据损伤性质不同,胸部损伤可分为_____和_____;根据损伤是否造成胸膜腔与外界沟通,可分为_____和_____。

3._____可使心脏大血管破裂并迅速致死。

六、根据对话和短文内容回答问题。

1.王凯是怎么受伤的?

2.胸部 CT 显示王凯受了什么伤?

3.王医生为什么说"进行性血胸的可能性极大"?

4.根据胸部损伤分类,小车司机应属于哪一类损伤?

5.哪一类损伤可以破坏骨性胸廓的完整性?

七、交际练习。

患者 A 在高空作业时从 3 米高处坠落,左胸背先着地,伤后自行爬起,感左胸痛、明显气短、无力,被工友送往医院。医生 B 为其进行检查。

两人一组,分别扮演上述情景中的角色,组织一段 3 分钟左右的对话展现上文场景。

【补充医学词汇】

序号	词语	拼音	词义
1	闭合性气胸	bìhé xìng qìxiōng	closed pneumothorax
2	开放性气胸	kāifàng xìng qìxiōng	open pneumothorax
3	张力性气胸	zhānglì xìng qìxiōng	tension pneumothorax
4	胸腹联合伤	xiōng fù liánhé shāng	thoraco-abdominal injury
5	失血性休克	shīxuè xìng xiūkè	hemorrhagic shock

(吕兆格)

第十二单元

骨科（一）——骨折

现在不能排除骨折的可能

第十二单元
生词、对话、短文

【学习目的】

1.学会用汉语表述各类人体骨骼。

2.学会用汉语问诊典型骨折病例。

3.了解肱骨骨折的相关医学常识。

【热身】

一、给下面的词语选择对应的字母。

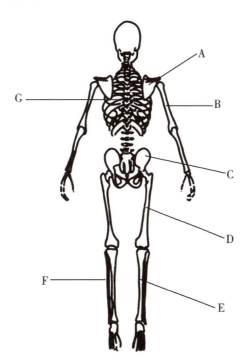

1.髂骨_____　　2.腓骨_____　　3.肩胛骨_____　　4.股骨_____

5. 胫骨_____   6. 肱骨_____   7. 胸椎_____

二、下面哪一项的脊柱各组成部分的顺序是正确的?   (   )

A. 胸椎、颈椎、腰椎、骶椎、尾椎

B. 颈椎、胸椎、腰椎、骶椎、尾椎

C. 腰椎、颈椎、胸椎、骶椎、尾椎

D. 颈椎、胸椎、腰椎、尾椎、骶椎

【会话】

场景简介:
人物:患者——于方(男,23 岁)
　　　医生——江天(男,37 岁)
　　　实习医生——穆汗默德(男,20 岁,巴基斯坦人)
地点:骨科门诊

对话一

生词

序号	词语	词性	拼音	词义
1	受限	动	shòuxiàn	be limitted
2	肱骨外科颈	名	gōnggǔ wàikē jǐng	surgical neck of humerus
3	复位	名	fùwèi	restoration

(患者因打篮球摔倒,左臂剧烈疼痛、活动受限前来就诊)

于　方:您好,医生,我今天下午打篮球时不小心摔了,之后发现左胳膊很痛,手也不能动。

江　天:当时有没有其他地方不舒服?

于　方:没有。

江　天:您的左上臂肿得很厉害,这里压着痛吗?

于　方:哎哟,好痛!

江　天:现在不能排除骨折的可能,您最好拍张 X 射线片。

(半小时后,于方拿来了 X 射线片)

江　天:从 X 射线片来看,您是左侧肱骨外科颈骨折,需要马上复位和石膏固定。

(The patient came to the clinic because of a fall while playing basketball, has severe pain in his left arm, limited mobility)

Yu Fang:Hello,doctor,I accidentally fell after playing basketball this afternoon. The left arm is very painful and my hand can not move.

Jiang Tian:Was there any other place uncomfortable at that time?

Yu Fang:No.

Jiang Tian:Your left upper arm is very swollen. Do you feel pain while pressing here?

Yu Fang:Oh,it hurts!

Jiang Tian:It is impossible to exclude the possibility of a fracture. You'd better take an X-ray.

(Half an hour later,Yu Fang took an X-ray film)

Jiang Tian:From the X-ray point of view,you have a surgical neck fracture of the left humerus and needs immediate reduction and needs plaster cast immobilization immediately.

对话二

生词

序号	词语	词性	拼音	词义
1	麻醉药	名	mázuìyào	anesthetics
2	错位	动	cuòwèi	dislocate
3	糖钳石膏	名	tángqián shígāo	forcep
4	绷带	名	bēngdài	bandage
5	悬挂	动	xuánguà	hang
6	肱骨干	名	gōnggǔ gàn	shaft of humerus
7	愈合	动	yùhé	heal
8	失用性萎缩	动	shīyòngxìng wěisuō	disuse atrophy

江 天:请坐好,我先给您注射麻醉药。

于 方:会很痛吗?

江 天:石膏固定不是很痛。但在固定前,需要对骨折进行复位,将断裂错位的骨端连接好,这时会有些痛。

(复位后,复查 X 射线片,证实复位成功)

江 天:穆罕默德,复位成功,现在用糖钳石膏来固定,用纱布绷带将前臂悬挂在脖子上,一定要使前臂和上臂呈90°功能位。

穆罕默德:老师,肱骨骨折都是这样处理吗?

江 天:肱骨骨折根据发生的部位可以分为肱骨外科颈骨折、肱骨干骨折、肱骨髁上骨折。这些部位骨折的处理,如果有移位,需要先复位,然后再固定。

于 方:医生,什么时候可以拆除石膏?

穆罕默德:于先生,一般 3~4 周来医院复查,根据 X 射线片中所示骨骼愈合情况决定拆除石膏的时间。

于 方:好的。

穆罕默德:要加强营养,及时补充蛋白质、维生素和钙。同时要注意功能锻炼,手和手指要经常活动,以免发生功能障碍和肌肉失用性萎缩。

于 方:好的,谢谢!

Jiang Tian:Please sit down. I will give you an injection of anesthesia.

Yu Fang:Will it hurt?

Jiang Tian:Plaster casts are not very painful. However,before fixation,fractures need to be positioned,the fractured and dislocated bone ends need to be connected,and then there will be some pain.

(After reduction,X-ray examination was performed to confirm that the reduction was successful)

Jiang Tian:Muhammad,the reduction is successful. Now forceps are used to fix the plaster,and gauzes are also applied. The bandage hangs the forearm on the neck and must extend both the forearm and upper arm 90° functional position.

Muhammad:Teacher,Is humeral fracture treated like this?

Jiang Tian:Tibial fractures can be divided into surgical neck fractures of the humerus,humeral shaft fracture and supracondylar fractures of the humerus according to the site of the fracture. The treatment of these fractures;If there is a displacement,it needs reduction first and then it is fixed.

Yu Fang:Doctor,when can the plaster be removed?

Muhammad:Mr. Yu,it usually takes 3－4 weeks for the hospital to review and decide the time to remove the plaster according to the bone healing condition shown on the X－ray.

Yu Fang:Okay.

Muhammad:You should strengthen nutrition and replenish protein,vitamins and calcium in time. At the same time functional exercise,hands and fingers should be constantly mobilized so as to avoid dysfunction and muscle disuse atrophy.

Yu Fang:Okay,thank you!

【短文】

生词

序号	词语	词性	拼音	词义
1	瘀斑	名	yūbān	ecchymosis
2	畸形	名	jīxíng	malformation
3	骨擦音	名	gǔcāyīn	bone crepitus
4	骨擦感	名	gǔcāgǎn	bone abrasion
5	康复	动	kāngfù	rehabilitate
6	舒缩	动	shū suō	systolic and diastolic

肱骨骨折

肱骨骨折是一种常见的上肢骨折。它的临床表现为肩部疼痛、肿胀、瘀斑等,上肢活动不顺利。多由直接暴力和间接暴力所引起,如重物撞击、挤压、打击及扑倒时手或肘部着地,暴力经前臂或肘部传至各部位。严重时可能出现休克、发热等全身症状;检查时有明显的压痛感觉,有时可能会触碰到骨折处。

如果出现畸形、活动不正常、骨擦音或骨擦感等其中一种情况,就可以诊断为骨折。对于肱骨骨折的治疗,首先要进行复位,将移位的骨折端恢复正常或近乎正常程度。接下来要固定,就是把骨骼维持到复位后的位置;之后再进行康复治疗,就是说在不影响固定的情况下,让患者进行舒缩活动,使患者肢体的软组织更早恢复。

Tibial fractures

Tibial fractures are a common upper limb fracture. Its clinical manifestations are shoulder pain,swelling,ecchymosis,etc. ,and the upper limbs activity is not smooth. It is caused by direct and indirect violence;such as hitting with heavy objects,squeezing,and throwing hands down or elbow landing. The violence effect spread to various parts through the forearm or elbow. In severe cases,there may be systemic symptoms such as shock,fever,etc. ;there is a marked feeling of tenderness during the examination,and may be severe on the area of fracture.

If one of the conditions of malformation,abnormal movement,bone crepitus or abrasion;can be diagnosed as a fracture;For the treatment of tibial fractures,a reduction must first be performed to restore the displaced fractured end to normal or nearly normal levels. The next thing to fix is to maintain the bones in a reset position；after that，they will be rehabilitated. This means that the patient will be allowed to perform systolic and diastolic activities without affecting the fixation，in order to restore the soft tissue of the patient's limbs earlier.

【汉字知识】

部首"骨"

部首"骨"的意思为"骨骼"，一般出现在汉字左侧。以"骨"为部首的汉字多与人体骨骼有关。如"骼""骸""髋""髌""髓"等。此类汉字多为形声结构，左侧的部首为形旁，右侧的部件为声旁，代表字音。

例如：骼——骨骼

　　　髓——骨髓　脊髓　脑髓

构词

——骨　表示"骨骼"。

例如：胸骨、肋骨、锁骨、肱骨、尺骨、桡骨、掌骨、腓骨、髌骨。

——椎　表示"身体椎类部位"。

例如：脊椎、腰椎、颈椎、尾椎、椎骨。

【练习】

一、选择听到的词语。

1. （　　）A. 骨折　　B. 鼓着　　C. 固执　　D. 故障

2. （　　）A. 急性　　B. 记性　　C. 畸形　　D. 机芯

3. （　　）A. 诗稿　　B. 石膏　　C. 思考　　D. 史稿

4. （　　）A. 功能　　B. 动能　　C. 高能　　D. 光能

5. （　　）A. 错位　　B. 成为　　C. 作为　　D. 座位

二、根据听到的句子排列词语和短语。

1. 打篮球　剧烈疼痛　前　来　就诊　左臂　患者　活动受限　摔了一跤　因

2. 左侧　肱骨外科颈　复位　固定　您　骨折　和　石膏　是　需要

3. 骨折　一种　常见　上肢　的　肱骨骨折　是

三、仿照句子造句。

1. 现在不能排除骨折的可能，您最好拍张 X 射线片。

现在不能排除＿＿＿＿＿＿，您最好＿＿＿＿＿＿。

现在不能排除＿＿＿＿＿＿，您最好＿＿＿＿＿＿。

2. 这里压着痛吗？

＿＿＿＿＿压着痛吗？

＿＿＿＿＿压着痛吗？

3. 严重时可出现休克、发热等全身症状。

严重时可出现＿＿＿＿＿等＿＿＿＿＿症状。

严重时可出现＿＿＿＿＿等＿＿＿＿＿症状。

四、选词填空。

麻醉药　　愈合　　骨擦音　　错位　　骨擦感　　复位　　康复　　畸形　　失用性萎缩

肱骨外科颈

1.您是左侧＿＿＿＿骨折,需要马上＿＿＿＿和石膏固定。

2.对于骨折患者,在复位和固定后,需要进行＿＿＿＿＿治疗。

3.手及手指要经常活动,以免发生功能障碍和肌肉＿＿＿＿＿。

4.如果出现＿＿＿＿、活动不正常、＿＿＿＿或＿＿＿＿等其中一种情况,就可以诊断为骨折。

5.将断裂＿＿＿＿的骨端连接好时,会有些痛。

6.请坐好,我先给您注射＿＿＿＿。

7.拆除石膏的时间需要根据骨骼＿＿＿＿情况来决定。

五、完成下面的对话和句子。

（一）

医生:您＿＿＿＿＿＿＿＿＿肿得很厉害,这里压着痛吗?

患者:哎哟,痛死了!

医生:现在不能排除＿＿＿＿＿＿＿＿的可能,最好＿＿＿＿＿＿＿。

患者:好的,谢谢!

医生:从 X 射线片来看,您是＿＿＿＿＿＿,需要＿＿＿＿＿＿和＿＿＿＿＿＿。

（二）

1.骨折是指骨的＿＿＿＿＿和(或)＿＿＿＿中断。

2.根据骨折处皮肤黏膜的完整性,分为＿＿＿＿＿骨折和＿＿＿＿骨折。

3.肱骨骨折的一般临床表现有＿＿＿＿、＿＿＿＿和＿＿＿＿＿。

六、根据对话和短文内容回答问题。

1.骨折的定义是什么?

2.肱骨骨折的临床表现是什么?

3.根据骨折处皮肤黏膜的完整性,骨折可分为哪两型?

4.骨折的一般临床表现和特有体征分别包括哪些?

5.骨折治疗的三大原则是什么?

七、交际练习。

患者 A 因打篮球摔了一跤后,左臂剧烈疼痛、活动受限,来到医院骨科门诊就诊,医生 B 接待了患者 A。医生 B 先向患者 A 询问了症状,然后要求他做一个 X 射线检查。检查结果显示为左侧肱骨外科颈骨折,医生 B 要给患者 A 进行骨折复位和固定。

两人一组,分别扮演角色 A、B,组织一段 3 分钟左右的对话展现上文场景。

【补充医学词汇】

序号	词语	拼音	词义
1	脱位	tuōwèi	dislocation
2	锁骨	suógǔ	clavicle
3	腱鞘囊肿	jiànqiào nángzhǒng	ganglion cyst
4	制动	zhìdòng	immobilize
5	支持带	zhīchí dài	retinaculum

（蒋　伟　马生元）

第十三单元

骨科（二）——腰椎间盘突出症

我弯腰的时候，突然背直不起来了

第十三单元
生词、对话、短文

【学习目的】

1. 学会用汉语表述脊柱主要关节。
2. 学会用汉语问诊典型腰椎间盘突出症病例。
3. 了解腰椎间盘突出症的相关医学常识。

【热身】

一、给下面的词语选择对应的字母。

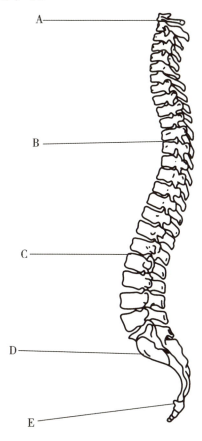

1. 胸椎＿＿＿＿＿　　2. 尾椎＿＿＿＿＿　　3. 颈椎＿＿＿＿＿　　4. 腰椎＿＿＿＿＿　　5. 骶椎＿＿＿＿＿

二、根据拼音写汉字。

1. jǐngzhuī＿＿＿＿＿＿＿＿＿＿

2. xiōngzhuī＿＿＿＿＿＿＿＿＿＿

3. dǐzhuī＿＿＿＿＿＿＿＿＿＿

4. wěizhuī＿＿＿＿＿＿＿＿＿＿

5. yāozhuī＿＿＿＿＿＿＿＿＿＿

【会话】

> 场景简介：
> 人物：患者——张明（男，43 岁）
> 　　　医生——王远（男，38 岁）
> 　　　实习医生——穆汗默德（男，20 岁，巴基斯坦人）
> 地点：骨科门诊

对话一

生词

序号	词语	词性	拼音	词义
1	背	名	bèi	human back
2	断断续续	形	duànduànxùxù	off and on
3	下腰部	名	xià yāobù	back bend
4	弯腰	动	wānyāo	stoop
5	臀部	名	túnbù	hip
6	膝盖	名	xīgài	knee
7	直腿抬高	动	zhítuǐ táigāo	straight leg raise
8	阳性	形	yángxìng	positive
9	磁共振成像	名	cígòngzhèn chéngxiàng	magnetic resonance imaging
10	扫描	动	sǎomiáo	scan
11	预约	动	yùyuē	make an appointment

（张明因 2 天前弯腰搬重物后出现腰腿痛，不能走远路，前来就诊）

王　远：您哪里不舒服？

张　明：我的后背有问题，断断续续好几年了，前两天又开始痛了。我弯腰的时候，突然背直不起来了，现在特别痛！

王　远：（指着下腰部）是这儿痛吗？

张　明：对，一直痛，而且从我的臀部右边，沿着右腿一直到膝盖都痛。

王　远：好的，我知道了。穆汗默德，你来给这位患者做直腿抬高试验。

默汗默德：请您先躺在床上。

张　明：好的。

穆汗默德：您能将腿抬到这个高度吗？

张　明：啊……只能抬这么高了，再高就痛了。

穆汗默德:您的直腿抬高试验是阳性的。好的,您现在可以站起来了。

王　远:张明,您需要做 X 射线和磁共振成像检查,了解您的背部情况。今天先拍 X 射线片,磁共振成像检查会尽快给您预约。

张　明:好的,谢谢!

(Zhang Ming suffered a low back pain after bending over two days before lifting heavy objects. He couldn't travel far to see the doctor)

Wang Yuan:Where are you uncomfortable?

Zhang Ming:I have problems with my back,I have been off and on for several years,and I started to feel pain in the past two days. When I bend down,I suddenly couldn't stand upright. Now it hurts!

Wang Yuan:(Pointing to the lower back) Is it pain here?

Zhang Ming:Yes,it hurts all the time,and my right side of the hips,along the right leg until the knee hurts.

Wang Yuan:Yes,I know. Muhammad,you are going to perform this patient a straight leg raise test.

Muhammed:Please lie in bed first.

Zhang Ming:OK.

Muhammed:Can you lift your leg to this height?

Zhang Ming:Ah…I can only lift it so high,and then I feel hurt.

Muhammed:Your straight leg raise test is positive. OK,you can stand up now.

Wang Yuan:Zhang Ming,take an X-ray and magnetic resonance imaging scan to check your back condition. Take the X-ray first today and an magnetic resonance imaging scan will be scheduled as soon as possible.

Zhang Ming:Yes,thank you!

对话二

生词

序号	词语	词性	拼音	词义
1	腰椎间盘突出症	名	yāozhuījiānpán tūchūzhèng	lumbar disc herniation
2	恶化	动	èhuà	get worse
3	理疗	名	lǐliáo	physiotherapy
4	自如	形	zìrú	free
5	强力	形	qiánglì	strong

(患者把 X 射线片和磁共振成像检查结果递给医生)

张　明:医生,我的检查结果怎么样?

王　远:看了您的检查结果后,可以确定您得了腰椎间盘突出症。

张　明:我需要做手术吗?

王　远:您这种情况已经好多年了,而且病情在恶化。我可以安排您到理疗部,他们会安排一些运动,帮助您解决这个问题,让您行动更自如。不过,建议您最好做手术。

张　明:哦,好的。

王　远:我会给您开些强力止痛药,在您的背没有好转之前,请尽可能多休息。

张　明:好的,谢谢! 我先试一试药物治疗和理疗吧。

王　远:如果非手术治疗效果仍不好的话,建议您尽快进行手术治疗。

张　明:好的,谢谢! 如果需要手术,我会来找您。

王　远:祝您早日康复!

(Patient submits X-ray and magnetic resonance imaging results to doctor)

Zhang Ming:Doctor,what's the result of my X-ray and magnetic resonance imaging?

Wang Yuan:After reading your test results,you can be sure that you have lumbar disc herniation.

Zhang Ming:Do I need surgery?

Wang Yuan:You have been in this situation for many years,and your condition is getting worse. I can arrange for you to go to the physiotherapy department. They will arrange some exercises to help you solve this problem and make you move more freely. However,it is recommended that you have the surgery.

Zhang Ming:Oh,yes.

Wang Yuan:I will give you some strong painkillers. Please rest as much as you can until your back does not improve.

Zhang Ming:Yes,thank you. I first try drug treatment and physiotherapy.

Wang Yuan:If non-surgical treatment is still not good,it is recommended that you treat as soon as possible.

Zhang Ming:OK,thank you. I'd like to try a drug treatment and a physiotherapy first.

Wang Yuan:Get well soon!

【短文】

生词

序号	词语	词性	拼音	词义
1	加剧	动	jiājù	aggravat
2	绝对	副	juéduì	absolute
3	卧床	名	wòchuáng	lie on the bed
4	佩戴	动	pèidài	wear
5	腰围保护	名	yāowéi bǎohù	waist protection
6	概率	名	gàilǜ	probability
7	推拿	动	tuīná	massage
8	手法	名	shǒufǎ	method
9	预防	动	yùfáng	prevent
10	姿势	名	zīshì	posture
11	靠背	名	kàobèi	backrest of chair
12	硬板床	名	yìngbǎnchuáng	hard bed
13	蹲	动	dūn	kneel down

腰椎间盘突出症

多数腰椎间盘突出症的患者最先出现的症状是腰痛,在打喷嚏或咳嗽的情况下,疼痛会加剧。对于年轻或者得病时间短的患者,可以采用非手术治疗。要绝对地卧床休息,3 个星期以后可以佩戴腰围保护下床活动,3 个月内不能弯腰。这个方法简单有效,但是很难坚持。腰痛缓解后,还要加强锻炼,减少复发的概率。理疗、推拿和按摩也是常见的缓解腰痛的办法,但是也应注意不正确的手法将会加重病情。

保持腰椎的正确姿势对预防腰椎间盘突出症很重要。坐的时候尽量选高而且有靠背的椅子,睡觉可以选硬板床。不要长时间保持一种姿势,久坐、长时间弯腰最容易引起腰椎间盘后突。搬重物时,应蹲下来再弯腰搬,避免直腿弯腰。

Lumbar disc herniation

The first symptom of most patients with lumbar disc herniation is low back pain. In the case of sneezing or coughing, the pain is aggravated. For young patients or patients with short duration of disease, non-surgical treatment can be used. Absolute bed rest, After 3 weeks, you can wear waist protection to get out of bed. You can't bend over for 3 months. This method is simple and effective, but it is difficult to stick to. After the back pain is relieved, exercise must be strengthened to reduce the chance of recurrence. Physiotherapy, Tui na and massage therapy are also common ways to relieve back pain, but it should also be noted that incorrect practices will worsen the condition.

Maintaining the correct posture of the lumbar spine is important for preventing lumbar disc herniation. Whenever you sit, try to choose a high chair with backrest, you can choose hard bed board for sleeping. Do not maintain a same position for a long time; sedentary position, bent over for a long time most likely to cause lumbar disc protrusion. When lifting heavy objects, kneel down and bend over to avoid bending straight legs.

【汉字知识】

部首"足(𧾷)"

部首"足"的意思为"脚",一般出现在汉字左侧。以"足"为部首的汉字多与脚或与脚有关的动作有关。如"踢""趾""跪""踝""趴""跟"等。此类汉字多为形声结构,左侧的部首为形旁,右侧的部件为声旁,代表字音。

例如:踢——踢球　踢打　踢人

　　　跟——脚后跟　鞋跟　跟从

构词

——髓　表示"骨头或其他身体器官中胶状的东西"。

例如:骨髓、精髓、脊髓、脑髓。

——骸　表示"骨头或者身体"。

例如:病骸、残骸、尸骸、遗骸、骨骸、肢骸。

【练习】

一、选择听到的词语。

1. (　　　) A. 突出　　B. 拖出　　C. 吐出　　D. 提出

2. (　　　) A. 颈椎　　B. 腰椎　　C. 骶椎　　D. 胸椎

3.（　　） A.尽力　　 B.尽量　　 C.进行　　 D.力量

4.（　　） A.按摩　　 B.按压　　 C.按照　　 D.按时

5.（　　） A.预习　　 B.预防　　 C.以防　　 D.预备

二、根据听到的句子排列词语和短语。

1.需要　您　拍　和　磁共振成像　X射线片　背部　的　情况　检查

2.之后　看了　您的　检查结果　得了　我　能　腰椎间盘突出症　确定　您

3.他们　一些运动　帮　您　安排　解决　这个问题　让　您　自如　更　行动

4.打喷嚏　咳嗽　或　在　的　情况　下　会　加剧　疼痛

三、仿照句子造句。

1.看了您的检查结果之后,我能确定您得了腰椎间盘突出症。

看了＿＿＿＿＿＿之后,我能确定您得了＿＿＿＿。

看了＿＿＿＿＿＿之后,我能确定您得了＿＿＿＿。

2.如果非手术治疗效果仍不好的话,建议您尽快手术治疗。

如果＿＿＿＿＿＿的话,建议您尽快＿＿＿＿＿＿。

如果＿＿＿＿＿＿的话,建议您尽快＿＿＿＿＿＿。

3.在您的背没有好转之前,请尽可能多休息。

在＿＿＿＿＿＿之前,请尽可能＿＿＿＿＿＿。

在＿＿＿＿＿＿之前,请尽可能＿＿＿＿＿＿。

四、选词填空。

理疗　姿势　恶化　复发　蹲

1.腰痛缓解后,还要加强锻炼,减少＿＿＿＿＿＿的概率。

2.搬重物时,＿＿＿＿＿＿下来再弯腰搬。

3.你这种情况已经好多年了,而且病情在＿＿＿＿＿＿。

4.我先试一试药物治疗和＿＿＿＿＿＿。

5.保持腰椎的正确＿＿＿＿＿＿很重要。

五、完成下面的对话和句子。

（一）

张明:我＿＿＿＿＿＿的时候,突然背直不起来了,现在特别痛!

王远:其他地方也痛吗?

张明:是的,从我的＿＿＿＿＿＿右边,沿着右腿一直到＿＿＿＿＿＿都痛。

王远:您现在走路有＿＿＿＿＿＿吗?

张明:我不能走远路。

王远:您能将腿＿＿＿＿＿吗? 能尽量抬到这个＿＿＿＿＿吗?

张明:好的……只能抬＿＿＿＿＿＿了,再高就痛了。

（二）

1.多数腰椎间盘突出症的患者最先出现的＿＿＿＿＿＿是＿＿＿＿＿＿。

2.要绝对地＿＿＿＿＿＿休息,3个星期以后可以＿＿＿＿＿＿腰围保护下床活动。

3.坐的时候尽量选高而且有＿＿＿＿＿＿的椅子,睡觉可以选＿＿＿＿＿＿。

4.不要长时间保持一种＿＿＿＿＿＿,久坐、长时间＿＿＿＿＿＿最容易引起腰椎间盘＿＿＿＿＿＿。

六、根据对话和短文内容回答问题。

1. 张明哪个地方痛?

2. 王远让张明做了什么检查?

3. 张明得了什么病?

4. 王远有什么建议?

5. 腰椎间盘突出症有哪些非手术治疗方法?

6. 如何预防腰椎间盘突出症?

七、交际练习。

患者 A 因两天前弯腰搬重物后出现腰腿痛,不能走远路而来就诊。实习医生 B 向患者 A 询问了病情。实习医生 B 要求他先做 X 射线和磁共振成像检查,检查结果显示为腰椎间盘突出症。实习医生 B 和门诊医生 C 讨论病情,医生 C 建议患者 A 进行药物治疗和理疗。

三人一组,分别扮演角色 A、B、C,组织一段 5 分钟左右的对话展现上文场景。

【补充医学词汇】

序号	词语	拼音	词义
1	牵涉痛	qiān shè tòng	referred pain
2	放射痛	fàng shè tòng	radiating pain
3	神经根	shén jīng gēn	nerve root
4	正位片	zhèng wèi piàn	frontal film
5	侧位片	cè wèi piàn	lateral film

（蒋尧传　代　晶）

第十四单元

泌尿外科——输尿管结石

第十四单元
生词、对话、短文

医生说我左侧肾有结石

【学习目的】

1. 学会用汉语表述泌尿系统主要器官的名称。
2. 学会用汉语问诊典型肾结石、输尿管结石病例。
3. 了解肾、输尿管结石的相关医学常识。

【热身】

一、给下面的词语选择对应的字母。

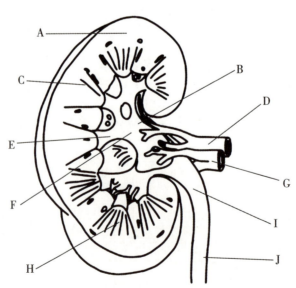

1.肾大盏_____   2.肾动脉_____   3.肾乳头_____   4.肾皮质_____   5.肾小盏_____

6.肾盂_____   7.肾静脉_____   8.肾大盏_____   9.肾锥体_____   10.输尿管_____

二、根据拼音写汉字。

1. shènzhǎn_____

2. shènyú_____

3. shūniàoguǎn_____

4. shèn dòngmài_____

5. shèn jìngmài_____

6. shèn rǔtóu_____

【会话】

场景简介:
人物:患者——丁宇(男,38岁)
　　　医生——段飞(男,40岁)
地点:泌尿外科门诊

对话一

生词

序号	词语	词性	拼音	词义
1	凌晨	名	língchén	before dawn
2	深夜	名	shēnyè	late at night
3	会阴	名	huìyīn	perineum
4	肾结石	名	shènjiéshí	renal calculus

段　飞:您好,您哪里不舒服?

丁　宇:从今天凌晨到现在一直腰痛。

段　飞:哪儿痛?您指给我看看。

丁　宇:(手扶左侧腰部)医生这儿痛。痛了差不多6个多小时,今天深夜睡觉时被痛醒了,会阴部也有疼痛的感觉。

段　飞:疼痛时有没有恶心、呕吐,是否发热?

丁　宇:昨晚痛的时候吐过2次,体温没量过,我还不知道呢。吐的都是昨晚吃的。

段　飞:以前有过这样的情况吗?

丁　宇:大概1年前好像也有过1次。

段　飞:有没有做过什么检查?吃过什么药?

丁　宇:上次痛的时候做过B超,医生说我左侧肾有结石,没吃过药。

段　飞:那我先给您检查检查,您在那儿躺下。

Duan Fei:Hello,what's troubling you?

Ding Yu:I have been suffering from back pain sincetoday's early morning.

Duan Fei:Can you show me the exact part?

Ding Yu:(Put his one hand on the left side of his waist) Doctor,it hurts here,for almost 6 hours. I was awakened,as here it hurt so badly,in the middle of the night. And the perineum part also hurts now.

Duan Fei:Any nausea or fever when it hurts?

Ding Yu:I vomited what I had eaten for two times last night,and I have no clue whether I have a fever, as I didn't take my temperature last night.

　　Duan Fei：Did you have any similar experiences before?

　　Ding Yu：I had one similar suffering about one year ago.

　　Duan Fei：Have you had any medical tests? What medicine did you eat?

　　Ding Yu：I had B-type ultrasonic examination, the last time it hurt, and the doctor told me that I had a stone in my left kidney. But I hadn't eaten any medicine.

　　Duan Fei：Okay, I see. Please lie down there, and I'll run a few tests for you first.

对话二

生词

序号	词语	词性	拼音	词义
1	肋	名	lèi	rib
2	脊	名	jǐ	costolumbar
3	叩击痛	名	kòujī tòng	percussive pain
4	轻微	形	qīngwēi	slightly
5	尿路感染	–	niàolù gǎnrǎn	urinary tract infection
6	类(似)	形	lèi(sì)	similar
7	肾上盏结石	名	shèn shàng zhǎn jiéshí	upper calyceal calculus
8	肾绞痛	名	shèn jiǎotòng	renal colic

　　(医生给患者做体格检查：左侧肋腰点及肋脊点有明显压痛，左侧输尿管走行区压痛明显，左肾区有叩击痛，体温 38 ℃)

　　段　飞：建议您做个尿常规和中下腹 CT 检查。

　　丁　宇：行。

　　段　飞：那我给您开检查单。

　　(1 小时后，检查结果出来了)

　　段　飞：您看这检查结果，尿常规提示白细胞和红细胞有轻微升高，有尿路感染的可能。CT 结果显示左肾上盏有一个 2 cm 类圆形结石，左侧输尿管上段还有一个 0.8 cm 左右的结石，您的症状主要是由输尿管结石引起的肾绞痛，建议您住院并进行手术治疗。

　　(The doctoris making a physical examination for the patient：the left costolumbar point and costovertebral point have an obvious tenderness. And the course of the urinary tract has an obvious tenderness. The left renal region has a percussive pain. The temperature is 38 degrees)

　　Duan Fei：I suggest that you take a normal urine routine and a middle or lower abdominal CT scanning.

　　Ding Yu：Okay.

　　Duan Fei：Now I will prescribe the tests.

　　(The test results came out after one hour)

　　Duan Fei：The normal urine routine result shows that white blood cells and red blood cells are slightly elevated and it means you may have urinary tract infections. The CT result shows that there is a 2 cm round stone on your left upper calyx, and there is also a stone about 0.8 cm in the upper part of the left ureter. And your symptoms are mainly renal colic caused by calculus in your left ureter. I suggest you can be hospitalized and receive a surgical treatment.

【短文】

生词

序号	词语	词性	拼音	词义
1	血尿	名	xuèniào	hematuria
2	输尿管镜	名	shūniàoguǎn jìng	ureteroscope
3	解除	动	jiěchú	get rid of
4	成分	名	chéngfèn	ingredient
5	积水	名	jīshuǐ	hydrops

肾、输尿管结石

　　肾、输尿管结石,又称为上尿路结石,多发生于中年人。肾、输尿管结石的主要症状是绞痛和血尿,常见并发症是梗阻和感染。通过病史、体检、影像学检查如 X 射线检查、CT 检查及输尿管镜或肾镜检查,多数病例可确诊。肾、输尿管结石的治疗不仅是解除疼痛,保护肾功能,而且应尽可能防止结石复发。医生会根据每个患者的身体状况、结石大小、结石成分,有无梗阻、感染、积水,肾损害程度及结石复发情况等,制定防治方案。

Renal calculus and calculus in ureter

Renalcalculus and calculus in ureter, also called upper urinary tract calculus, and the middle-aged people are the usual victims. Colic and hematuria are the main symptom of the renal calculus and calculus in ureter. And the common complications are obstruction and infection. Most cases can be diagnosed, through medical history inquiry, physical examination, imaging examinations such as X-ray examination, CT examination, and ureteroscope or nephroscope. The treatment of kidney and ureteral stones not only relieves patients' pain, protects their kidneys, but also prevents the recurrent calculus. The doctor will formulate prevention and treatment plans, according to each patient's physical condition, the size of stones, the composition of stones, whether there is obstruction, infection and hydronephrosis, the degree of kidney damage, and the recurrent calculus.

【汉字知识】

部首"尸"

　　部首"尸"的意思为"死人的身体",一般出现在汉字的左上侧。以"尸"为部首的汉字一部分与人体有关,如"尿""屎""屁""尾"等;还有一部分与房子有关,如"屋""层""局""居"等。此类汉字多为半包围结构。

　　例如:层——楼层　层次　表层
　　　　　居——居住　居民　邻居

构词

　　——感染　表示"病原体侵入机体,在体内生长繁殖引起病变"。

　　例如:尿路感染、呼吸道感染。

　　——点　表示"部分"。

例如:肋腰点、肋脊点、麦氏点。

——结石 表示"某些有空腔的器官及其导管内,由于有机物和无机盐类沉积而形成的坚硬物质"。

例如:肾结石、输尿管结石、胆结石。

【练习】

一、选择听到的词语。

1. ( ) A. 肾盏 B. 肾盂 C. 肾脏 D. 肾皮质

2. ( ) A. 早晨 B. 凌晨 C. 临床 D. 零时

3. ( ) A. 血常规 B. 大便常规 C. 尿常规 D. 小便常规

4. ( ) A. 请问 B. 轻微 C. 稍微 D. 微微

5. ( ) A. 绞痛 B. 压痛 C. 胀痛 D. 叩击痛

二、根据听到的句子排列词语和短语。

1. 睡觉 时 痛醒了 被 今天 深夜

2. 提示 升高 白细胞 轻微 尿常规 有 和 红细胞

3. 手术 治疗 进行 建议 您 住院 并

三、仿照句子造句。

1. 痛了差不多6个多小时。

_____了差不多_____。

_____了差不多_____。

2. 建议您做个尿常规和中下腹CT检查。

建议您_____。

建议您_____。

3. 由输尿管结石引起的肾绞痛。

由_____引起的_____。

由_____引起的_____。

四、选词填空。

肾绞痛 轻微 尿路 尽快 输尿管

1. 尿常规结果提示白细胞和红细胞有_____升高,有_____感染的可能。

2. 左侧_____行走区有明显压痛。

3. 这是输尿管结石引起的_____。

4. 我建议您_____入院治疗,可能还要做手术。

五、完成下面的对话和句子。

(一)

医生:您好,_____?

患者:(手扶左侧腰部)医生我这儿痛,痛了半天了。

医生:疼痛是突然_____的吗?

患者:是的,昨天深夜睡觉时被_____。

医生:_____还有哪儿痛?

患者:会阴部也有疼痛的感觉。

医生:疼痛时有没有_____、_____、_____?

患者:昨晚痛的时候＿＿＿＿＿＿＿＿,＿＿＿＿＿＿＿＿37.5 ℃。

医生:您先躺下,我给您＿＿＿＿＿＿＿＿＿＿。

(二)

1.尿常规提示＿＿＿＿＿＿和＿＿＿＿＿＿有轻微＿＿＿＿＿＿,有＿＿＿＿＿＿感染的可能。

2.肾、输尿管结石的主要症状是＿＿＿＿＿＿和＿＿＿＿＿＿,常见并发症是＿＿＿＿＿＿和感染。

3.肾、输尿管结石的治疗不仅是＿＿＿＿＿＿,保护肾＿＿＿＿＿＿,而且应尽可能防止＿＿＿＿＿＿＿＿＿＿。

六、根据对话和短文内容回答问题。

1.患者丁宇的疼痛在什么部位?

2.丁宇昨晚睡得怎么样?

3.丁宇除了左侧腰部疼痛外还有什么地方疼痛?

4.肾、输尿管结石的诊断有什么手段和方法?

5.肾、输尿管结石多发于什么群体?

七、交际练习。

患者 A 于 1 年前体检时检查出右肾结石,近 1 个月常觉得乏力,食欲、精神不佳,两天前因右侧腰部疼痛前来就诊,实习医生 B 与指导医生 C 讨论病情和进一步检查并制订治疗方案。检查后建议患者 A 住院,进行排结石手术。

三人一组,分别扮演角色 A、B、C,组织一段 5 分钟左右的对话展现上文场景。

【补充医学词汇】

序号	词语	拼音	词义
1	膀胱	pángguāng	urinary bladder
2	泌尿道	mìniàodào	urinary tract

(王　越)

第十五单元

肝胆外科——胆囊结石

您的胆囊内有一些小结石

【学习目的】

1. 学会用汉语表述肝、胆主要解剖结构的名称。
2. 学会用汉语问诊肝胆外科的典型病例。
3. 了解胆总管结石的相关医学常识。

【热身】

一、给下面的词语选择对应的字母。

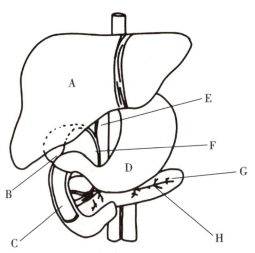

1.胰腺_____ 2.胆囊_____ 3.肝总管_____ 4.胆总管_____ 5.胃_____

6.十二指肠_____ 7.胰管_____ 8.肝_____

二、根据拼音写汉字。

1. gān_____

2. yíxiàn_____

3. yíguǎn_____

4. dǎnnáng_____

5. xiǎocháng_____

6. gānzǒngguǎn_____

7. shí'èrzhǐcháng_____

8. dǎnzǒngguǎn_____

【会话】

场景简介:
人物:患者——陈兴贵(男,46 岁)
　　　医生——邓杰(男,51 岁)
地点:外科门诊

对话一

生词

序号	词语	词性	拼音	词义
1	火锅	名	huǒguō	hot pot
2	忍受	动	rěnshòu	tolerate;endure
3	稍微	副	shāowēi	slightly
4	胆囊	名	dǎnnáng	gall bladder

陈兴贵:哎哟! 医生,我肚子痛……这里,还有这里(指着中上腹、右上腹),1 天前开始痛的。

邓　杰:腹痛前您做过些什么?

陈兴贵:腹痛前吃过火锅,还喝过半斤白酒,回到家后就开始腹痛了。一阵一阵的绞痛,刚开始还能忍受。

邓　杰:其他地方痛吗? 有腹泻吗?

陈兴贵:我感觉右肩和右腰部也有一阵一阵的疼痛。腹痛剧烈时,我呕吐过 2 次,全身无力。但呕吐之后腹痛稍微缓解了一些,没腹泻。

邓　杰:您的眼睛有点发黄。您还得过什么病吗?

陈兴贵:我身体一直都好,5 年前体检发现胆囊内有一些小结石,但不痛。

邓　杰:先量个体温,我再给您做个腹部检查。

Chen Xinggui:Ouch! I'm suffering from a stomachache! This part and that part (point to his the upper-middle abdomen and right upper abdomen). My stomachache began a day ago.

Deng Jie:Can you tell me what did you do before your stomachache?

Chen Xinggui:Well,I enjoyed a hot pot and half a kilo alcohol. And my stomachache occurred as soon as I came back home. It was a colicky pain that I could bear only at the beginning.

Deng Jie:Is it hurt in other parts of your body? Diarrhea?

Chen Xinggui:I also feel severe pains in my right shoulder and right waist. I vomited for two times, when feeling the suddenly severe abdominal pain,which made me a general weakness. And fortunately,the pain was relieved a little bit after vomiting. No diarrhea.

Deng Jie:Your eyes are a bit yellow. So,did you have any illnesses before?

Chen Xinggui:I think I'm very healthy. But five years ago,the physical examination revealed that there were some small stones in my gallbladder,but it did not hurt.

Deng Jie:First I need to take your temperature and then do a physical abdominal examination.

对话二

生词

序号	词语	词性	拼音	词义
1	胆囊结石	名	dǎnnáng jiéshí	gallstone
2	胆囊炎	名	dǎnnángyán	cholecystitis
3	肝功能	名	gāngōngnéng	liver function
4	胆红素	名	dǎnhóngsù	bilirubin
5	伴	动	bàn	and
6	黄疸	名	huángdǎn	jaundice
7	紧急	形	jǐnjí	urgent

（医生将患者搀扶至体检室,5 分钟后……）

邓　杰:根据您的病史和体格检查,我觉得可能是胆囊结石引起胆囊炎,但是您的眼睛有点黄,为了明确诊断,您还需要做血常规和肝功能检查,并再做一个腹部 B 超。做完检查后把报告拿给我看。

（30 分钟后……）

邓　杰:抽血结果提示您现在有感染,血胆红素也明显升高了,B 超提示有胆囊结石伴慢性胆囊炎、胆总管下段结石。

陈兴贵:那情况严重吗?

邓　杰:您现在有发热、腹痛、黄疸等症状,结合检查结果,我们诊断您得的是胆总管结石并急性胆管炎、胆囊结石,需要紧急处理,可能要手术治疗了。

陈兴贵:那么严重!

邓　杰:是的,我现在开住院证给您,您马上去肝胆外科住院治疗。

（The doctor carried his patient to the examination room,and after five minutes…）

Deng Jie:According to your medical history and physical examination,I think the pain may be due to cholecystitis caused by gallstones. But your eyes are a bit yellow. You also need to do blood routine and liver function test,and abdominal ultrasound,so as to confirm my diagnosis. Please show me your results after finishing these tests.

（After 30 minutes…）

Deng Jie:The results of the blood routine suggest that you have an infection,and the bilirubin is also significantly elevated. B-ultrasound suggests there are gallstones in your gall bladder,with chronic cholecystitis and segment choledochus calculi.

Chen Xinggui:Very serious?

Deng Jie:Now you have fever,abdominal pain,jaundice and other symptoms. Combined with the test results,we diagnose you with choledocholithiasis and acute cholecystitis,gallstones. You need to be treated immediately,and you may need a surgery.

Chen Xinggui:Oh,Jesus,that's so horrible!

Deng Jie:Yes,it's very serious. Now I will do the admission procedures for you,and please go to the hepatology department and get hospitalized there.

【短文】

生词

序号	词语	词性	拼音	词义
1	胆色素	名	dǎnsèsù	bile pigment
2	胆汁淤积	名	dǎnzhī yūjī	cholestasis
3	蛔虫	名	huíchóng	ascarid
4	胆固醇	名	dǎngùchún	cholesterol
5	寒战	名	hánzhàn	shivering
6	解除梗阻	–	jiěchú gěngzǔ	relieve the obstruction
7	通畅	形	tōngchàng	unobstructed

胆总管结石

　　胆总管结石是指位于胆总管内的结石,大多数为胆色素结石或以胆色素为主的混合结石,常发于胆总管下段。一般分为原发性胆总管结石和继发性胆总管结石。在胆管内形成的结石称为原发性胆总管结石,其形成与胆道感染、胆汁淤积、胆道蛔虫密切有关。胆管内结石来自胆囊者,称之为继发性胆总管结石,以胆固醇结石多见。

　　胆总管结石典型的临床表现是上腹部绞痛和对穿性背痛,寒战、高热和随后发生的黄疸三大症状;胆总管结石的外科治疗原则和目的主要是取净结石,解除梗阻,通畅胆流,防止感染。

Choledocholithiasis

　　Choledocholithiasis refers to stones in the common bile duct, and most of them are pigment gallstone or mixed stones mainly composed of pigments and can be often found in the distal common bile duct. Generally choledocholithiasis can be divided into primary choledocholith and secondary choledocholith. The stones formed in the bile ducts are called primary choledocholith and its formation is closely related to biliary infection, cholestasis, and biliary ascariasis. Stones from the gall bladder, are called secondary choledocholith, and most of them belong to cholesterol gallstone.

　　The typical clinical manifestations of choledocholithiasis are abdominal colic, back pain, chills, high fever and the subsequent three major symptoms of jaundice; the principle and purpose of surgical treatment is to ensure that stones are completely cleared, and to remove the obstruction of bile flow, and to prevent infection.

【汉字知识】

部首“石”

　　部首“石”的意思为“石头”,一般出现在汉字的左侧。以“石”为部首的汉字一般与石头有关,如“砖”“碑”“码”“硬”;还有一些与用石头加工有关,如“碎”“破”“碰”。此类汉字多为形声结构,左侧的部首为形旁,右侧的部件为声旁,代表字音。

　　例如:硬——坚硬　硬币　硬度

　　　　　破——破烂　破旧　破裂

构词

——管　表示"圆而细长中空的东西"。

例如：胆总管、气管、支气管、输尿管、毛细血管。

——膜　表示"动植物体内像薄皮的组织"。

例如：薄膜、耳膜、角膜、视网膜、细胞膜。

【练习】

一、选择听到的词语。

1. (　　) A. 胆囊　　B. 胆子　　C. 胆管　　D. 胆汁

2. (　　) A. 胆红素　B. 胆总管　C. 胆色素　D. 胆结石

3. (　　) A. 解释　　B. 结石　　C. 结实　　D. 结束

4. (　　) A. 环节　　B. 缓解　　C. 换届　　D. 暖角

5. (　　) A. 紧张　　B. 紧紧　　C. 紧急　　D. 着急

二、根据听到的句子排列词语和短语。

1. 右肩　我　感觉　一阵一阵的　也有　右腰部　和　疼痛

2. 呕吐　之后　一些　但是　缓解了　稍微　腹痛

3. 明显　血　胆红素　也　升高了

4. 胆总管结石　和　原发性胆总管结石　一般　继发性胆总管结石　分为

三、仿照句子造句。

1. 腹痛前您做过些什么？

　　＿＿＿＿＿前您＿＿＿＿＿过＿＿＿＿＿？

　　＿＿＿＿＿前您＿＿＿＿＿过＿＿＿＿＿？

2. 为了明确诊断，您还需要做血常规和肝功能检查。

　　为了明确诊断，您还需要＿＿＿＿＿＿。

　　为了明确诊断，您还需要＿＿＿＿＿＿。

四、选词填空。

　　　　　　　　结石　黄疸　忍受　缓解　紧急

1. 刚开始还能＿＿＿＿＿，可到后面越来越痛了。

2. 去年体检时邓杰说我胆囊内有一些＿＿＿＿＿。

3. 呕吐之后疼痛稍微＿＿＿＿＿了一点儿。

4. 您的情况是需要＿＿＿＿＿处理的。

5. 您现在有发热、腹痛、＿＿＿＿＿等表现，结合检查结果，诊断是胆总管结石。

五、完成下面的对话和句子。

（一）

陈兴贵：医生，我＿＿＿＿＿，1天前开始痛的。

邓　杰：腹痛前您做过些什么？

陈兴贵：腹痛前＿＿＿＿＿，还喝了半斤白酒，到家后＿＿＿＿＿。刚开始＿＿＿＿＿。

邓　杰：其他地方痛吗？

陈兴贵：我感觉＿＿＿＿＿也有一阵一阵的疼痛。腹痛剧烈时，我＿＿＿＿＿。但是呕吐之后＿＿＿＿＿。

邓　　杰:我发现您的眼睛_____。您还得过什么病吗?

陈兴贵:5 年前体检发现_____。

邓　　杰:_____。我先给您做个_____,看看您腹部的情况。

(二)

1.胆总管结石一般分为_____和_____。

2.胆总管结石典型的临床表现是_____和对穿性背痛,_____、高热和随后发生的_____三大症状。

3.胆总管结石的外科治疗原则和目的主要是_____,_____,通畅胆流,防止感染。

六、根据对话和短文内容回答问题。

1.患者陈兴贵的疼痛是什么性质的?

2.陈兴贵腹痛前吃了些什么?

3.陈兴贵的身体一直很好吗? 有没有什么病?

4.医生建议患者做哪些检查?

5.胆总管结石的治疗原则和目的是什么?

七、交际练习。

患者 A 4 年前做过胆结石手术,近 2 个月常觉得右侧腹部偶尔疼痛,不能吃油腻的东西,近 1 周乏力,疼痛加重前来就诊,实习医生 B 与副主任医生 C 讨论病情和进一步治疗方案。检查后建议患者 A 住院,再次进行取石手术。

三人一组,分别扮演角色 A,B,C,组织一段 5 分钟左右的对话展现上文场景。

【补充医学词汇】

序号	词语	拼音	词义
1	原发性结石	yuánfāxìng jiéshí	primary calculus
2	继发性结石	jìfāxìng jiéshí	secondary

(王　越)

第十六单元

妇科(一)——卵巢肿瘤

包块稳定性怎么样

【学习目的】

1. 学会用汉语表述卵巢肿瘤的常见类型。

2. 学会用汉语问诊卵巢肿瘤典型病例。

3. 了解卵巢肿瘤的相关医学常识。

【热身】

一、给下面的词语选择对应的字母。

A

B

1. 卵巢黏液性囊肿_____   2. 卵巢浆液性囊肿_____

二、根据英文写汉字。

1. ovarian epithelial tumor _____

2. serous tumor of the ovary _____

【会话】

场景简介：
人物：患者——陈兰(女,35 岁)
　　　医生——李洁(女,34 岁)
　　　实习医生——珍妮弗(女,24 岁,摩洛哥人)
地点：妇科门诊

对话一

生词

序号	词语	词性	拼音	词义
1	包块	名	bāo kuài	enclosed mass
2	婴儿	名	yīng'ér	infant
3	稳定性	名	wěndìngxìng	stability
4	月经	名	yuèjīng	menstruation
5	周期	名	zhōuqī	period
6	规律	名	guīlǜ	regular
7	腹部	名	fùbù	abdomen

珍妮弗：您好！您哪儿不舒服？

陈　兰：我感觉这 3 个月肚子里一直有个包块,最近好像长得比较大了。

珍妮弗：大概有多大？

陈　兰：一开始有橙子那么大吧,最近 1 个月长到婴儿的头那么大了。

珍妮弗：包块稳定性怎么样？是固定的还是活动的？

陈　兰：不稳定,经常动。

珍妮弗：月经周期怎么样？

陈　兰：这半年都不规律。出血量很大,经常持续十几天。有时候周期会推迟到四五十天 1 次。

珍妮弗：下腹部有没有疼痛感？

陈　兰：左边有时连续痛几分钟,像有东西在里面绞,有时候真的受不了。但过去之后就不痛了。

珍妮弗：好的,我去和医生讨论一下下一步做哪些检查。

Jennifer：Hello. How are you feeling?

Chen Lan：I have been feeling a mass on the left side of my lower abdomen for the last 3 months. It has grown bigger.

Jennifer：How big is it?

Chen Lan：When it started it was the size of an orange and became as big as the head of a newborn baby in the last 1 month.

Jennifer：What is the consistency?

Chen Lan：. It's quite movable from side to side.

Jennifer：How is your menses?

Chen Lan：My periods became irregular within the last 6 months. Bleeding became heavy and lasted up to more than 10 days; sometimes my periods were delayed 40-50 days.

Jennifer: Do you feel any pain in your abdomen?

Chen Lan: I sometimes feel pain in the lower left side of the abdomen and each attack lasts for a. few minutes and then disappears.

Jennifer: Well, Let me examine you. Briefly and then I'll talk over your problem with another doctor and decide what to do.

对话二

生词

序号	词语	词性	拼音	词义
1	卵巢囊肿	名	luǎncháo nángzhǒng	ovarian cyst
2	子宫	名	zǐgōng	uterus
3	直径	名	zhíjìng	diameter
4	入院单	名	rùyuàn dān	admission list
5	病房	名	bìngfáng	ward

李　洁：根据您的描述，可以初步判断您得的是卵巢囊肿。请到这边来，我给您检查一下。

陈　兰：好的。

李　洁：嗯，彩超显示子宫左侧确实有一个包块。直径有 12 cm 了，而且活动性很强，是个卵巢囊肿。

陈　兰：是吗？我妈以前也得过这种病。

李　洁：我用手摸的时候您觉得痛吗？

陈　兰：不痛。情况严重吗？

李　洁：这种情况需要手术了。肿瘤增长速度相当快，而且卵巢囊肿很容易发生病变。

陈　兰：那我要马上住院吗？来之前完全没有准备。

李　洁：这样，我给您开一张入院单，通知病房给您准备床位。您可以先回家准备一下，明天再过来。

陈　兰：好的，医生。太谢谢您了！

Li jie: You have an ovarian cyst, I think. Let me make a thorough examination.

Chen Lan: All right.

Li jie: You have an ovarian cyst, I think. Let me make a thorough examination. Oh, there is a mass beside` the uterus in. the left quadrant, about 12 cm in diameter, quite movable. It is an ovarian tumor.

Chen Lan: Really? My mother had this disease before.

Jennifer: Do you feel any pain when I touch it.

Chen Lan: No, I don't.

Li jie: You should be admitted to the hospital for an operation, because it may grow rather rapidly and an ovarian tumor can change quite easily in nature.

Chen Lan: Should I go to the hospital immediately? I had no preparation before coming.

Li jie: I will give you an admission slip and have a bed arranged for you. You can go home and prepare yourself. Come back tomorrow for admission.

Chen Lan: Yes, doctor. Thank you very much.

【短文】

生词

序号	词语	词性	拼音	词义
1	肿瘤	名	zhǒngliú	tumor
2	生殖	名	shēngzhí	reproduction
3	上皮性	形	shàngpíxìng	epithelial
4	浆液性	形	jiāngyèxìng	serous
5	黏液性	形	niányèxìng	mucinous
6	良性	形	liángxìng	benign
7	恶性	形	èxìng	malignant
8	复发率	名	fùfālǜ	recurrence rate
9	措施	名	cuòshī	measure
10	表现	名	biǎoxiàn	manifestation
11	妇科	名	fùkē	gynecology department
12	超声	名	chāoshēng	ultrasound

卵巢肿瘤

卵巢肿瘤是女性生殖器的常见肿瘤,包括卵巢良性、交界性和恶性肿瘤。良性肿瘤的复发率低,恶性肿瘤的复发率高。其中卵巢上皮性肿瘤是最常见的卵巢恶性肿瘤,包括浆液性和黏液性两种。目前没有预防卵巢肿瘤的有效措施。

卵巢肿瘤早期表现为肿块,往往没有症状,大多数是女性在进行妇科检查时才发现的。许多卵巢肿瘤患者在感觉不舒服去就医时,往往已经是晚期了。因此女性应该定期去医院做妇科检查,做到早诊断、早治疗。卵巢肿瘤可以通过妇科检查和超声检查发现,如果增长迅速,需要通过手术治疗以防发生病变。

Ovarian tumor

Ovarian tumors are female genital common tumors which include ovarian benign, borderline and malignant tumors. Recurrent rate of benign tumor is lower while that of malignant tumor is higher. Epithelial tumors are the most common ovarian tumor. It includes serous tumors and mucous tumors. There isn't efficient preventive method so far.

Early manifestation of ovarian tumor is mass, usually asymptomatic, usually detected during gynecology examination. In many cases, it has been in late stage when the patients feel uncomfortable and visit the hospital. It is necessary to have regular gynecology examination to get early diagnoses and treatment. Ovarian tumor can be detected by gynecology examination and ultrasound. If the tumor grows fast, surgery treatment is necessary to prevent extend of disease.

【汉字知识】

部首"女"

部首"女"的意思为"女性",一般出现在汉字的左侧。以"女"为部首的汉字多与女性有关。如"妈""奶""姥""姐""妹""婆""娶""嫁""娩""妊""娠"等。此类汉字多为形声结构,左侧的部首为形旁,右侧的部件为声旁,代表字音。

例如:妇——妇科　妇女　孕妇

　　　娩——分娩　娩出　娩怀

构词

——瘤　表示"生物体的组织细胞不正常增生而成的疙瘩"。

例如:肿瘤、肌瘤、骨肉瘤。

——率　表示"两个相关的数在一定条件下的比值"。

例如:复发率、死亡率。

【练习】

一、选择听到的词语。

1.(　　)A. 生意　　B. 繁殖　　C. 生殖　　D. 种植

2.(　　)A. 化疗　　B. 制药　　C. 治疗　　D. 放疗

3.(　　)A. 婴孩　　B. 婴儿　　C. 应该　　D. 这儿

4.(　　)A. 直径　　B. 径直　　C. 致敬　　D. 直接

5.(　　)A. 消防　　B. 预习　　C. 防疫　　D. 预防

二、根据听到的句子排列词语和短语。

1.上皮性　浆液性　黏液性　卵巢　肿瘤　恶性肿瘤　最常见的　是　两种　和　包括

2.左下腹　包块　感觉　3个月　我　最近　一个　有　一直

3.速度　肿瘤　增长　相当快　卵巢　而且　病变　发生　很容易

三、根据拼音写汉字。

fùbù(　　　　)　　yīng'ér(　　　　)　　zhōuqī(　　　　　)

bìngbiàn(　　　　)　　zhíjìng(　　　　)　　shàngpíxìng(　　　　)

zhǒngliú(　　　　)　　cuòshī(　　　　)　　èxìng(　　　　)

四、选词填空。

稳定性　直径　病房　超声　妇科

1.包块_____怎么样? 是固定的还是活动的?

2.子宫左侧确实有一个包块,_____有 12 cm 了。

3.我给您开一张入院单,通知_____给您准备床位。

4.卵巢肿瘤可以通过妇科检查和_____方式发现,如果增长迅速需要通过手术治疗以防发生病变。

5.大多数是女性在进行_____检查时才发现自己患有卵巢囊肿的。

五、完成下面的对话和句子。

(一)

医生:在您的体内有一个_____,位置在_____,是_____。

陈兰:_____?_____以前也得过这种病。

医生:我_____时候您觉得痛吗?

陈兰:_____。医生,我的情况很严重吗?

医生:这种情况需要____了。_____增长速度相当快,而且_____很容易发生病变。

陈兰:那我要马上_____吗? 我来之前_____。

（二）

1. 卵巢肿瘤是发生在女性卵巢上的肿瘤,是女性_____的常见肿瘤之一。

2. _____肿瘤的复发率低,_____肿瘤复发率高。

3. 女性应该定期去医院做妇科检查,做到早_____、早_____。

4. 卵巢肿瘤早期表现为_____,往往没有_____。

六、根据对话和短文内容回答问题。

1. 陈兰感觉哪里不舒服?

2. 包块对陈兰的月经有什么影响?

3. 根据两段对话总结描述陈兰腹部包块的特征。

4. 陈兰的疾病需要如何治疗?

5. 最常见的卵巢恶性肿瘤是什么? 分为哪些类型?

6. 简述卵巢肿瘤的主要发现方式及治疗方法。

七、交际练习。

患者常欢,女,20 岁,急诊入院。右下腹持续疼痛,伴有下腹正中疼痛,呈持续性、阵发性加剧,体位改变时腹痛加剧。恶心、呕吐 3 次,呕吐物为胃内容物。

查体结果:体温 36.3 ℃,血压 110/70 mmHg,面容痛苦,心肺正常,腹平坦,下腹部压痛、反跳痛、肌紧张,移动性浊音不明显。

肛诊结果:左侧附件可触及一肿物 6 cm×6 cm,压痛明显,张力高。

初步判断为卵巢囊肿蒂扭转。实习医生珍妮弗向患者询问病情,解释病因,并推荐治疗方案。

两人一组,分别扮演常欢和珍妮弗,根据提供的信息询问病情,解释病因,并推荐治疗方案。

【补充医学词汇】

序号	词语	拼音	词义
1	未成熟畸胎瘤	wèi chéngshú jī tāi liú	immature teratoma
2	腹膜种植	fùmó zhòngzhí	peritioneal implantation
3	附件肿块	fùjiàn zhǒngkuài	adnexal mass
4	剖腹探查	pōu fù tànchá	exploratory laparotomy
5	子宫内膜癌	zǐgōng nèimó ái	endometrial cancer
6	纤维上皮瘤	xiānwéi shàngpí liú	fibro-epithelioma

（凌 奕 刘 畅）

第十七单元

妇科(二)——子宫肌瘤

第十七单元
生词、对话、短文

您的子宫里有一些肿块

【学习目的】

1.学会用汉语介绍子宫肌瘤的主要类型。

2.学会用汉语问诊典型子宫肌瘤病例。

3.了解子宫肌瘤的相关医学常识。

【热身】

一、给下面的词语选择对应的字母。

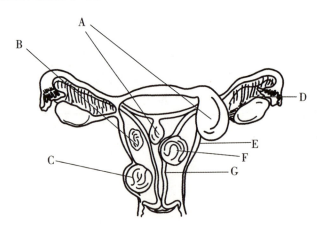

1.子宫_____ 2.卵巢_____ 3.带蒂的肌瘤_____ 4.浆膜下肌瘤_____

5.肌壁间肌瘤_____ 6.宫颈_____ 7.黏膜下肌瘤_____

二、根据汉字写英文。

1.子宫_____

2.宫颈_____

3.卵巢_____

4.浆膜下肌瘤_____

【会话】

场景简介:
人物:患者——张英(女,48 岁)
　　　医生——李洁(女,34 岁)
　　　实习医生——珍妮弗(女,24 岁,摩洛哥人)
地点:妇科门诊

对话一

生词

序号	词语	词性	拼音	词义
1	折磨	动	zhémó	torment
2	血块	名	xuèkuài	blood clot
3	痛经	名	tòngjīng	dysmenorrhea
4	同房	动	tóngfáng	intercourse
5	阴道	名	yīndào	vagina

珍妮弗:张英是吧,您哪里不舒服?
张　英:最近快被月经折磨死了。
珍妮弗:具体什么情况?
张　英:每次出血量都很大,而且很难受。
珍妮弗:周期规律吗?
张　英:还可以。
珍妮弗:我的意思是每月 1 次吗?
张　英:是的。但持续时间有点长。
珍妮弗:多长?
张　英:八九天吧。
珍妮弗:经血中有血块吗?
张　英:有,而且痛经很厉害。每次来月经我都疼得没法上班。
珍妮弗:您末次月经是什么时候?
张　英:大概两周之前。
珍妮弗:两次经期之间及同房之后有没有阴道出血的情况?
张　英:没有。我跟我家老伴儿已经不同房了。
珍妮弗:有孩子吗?
张　英:有,儿子 21 岁,女儿 17 岁。

Jennifer:Are you Zhang Ying? What's wrong with you?
Zhang Ying:It's my periods. They've been playing me up.
Jennifer:In what way are they bothering you?
Zhang Ying:They're ever so heavy and I feel so queer when I'm on.
Jennifer:Are they still regular?
Zhang Ying:Ever so regular.

Jennifer：I mean do you still see them monthly?

Zhang Ying：Yes, but they last a lot longer.

Jennifer：How long?

Zhang Ying：Eight or nine days.

Jennifer：Do you pass clots?

Zhang Ying：Yes and it really hurts. I can't go to my work each time.

Jennifer：When was your last period?

Zhang Ying：That's about two weeks ago.

Jennifer：Do you have any bleeding between the periods or after intercourse?

Zhang Ying：No, but I don't go with my husband any more.

Jennifer：Have you any children?

Zhang Ying：Yes, a boy and a girl. The boy is 21 years old and the girl is 17 years old.

对话二

生词

序号	词语	词性	拼音	词义
1	纤维	名	xiānwéi	fibrous
2	癌症	名	áizhèng	cancer
3	一旦	副	yīdàn	once

李　洁：检查发现您的子宫里有一些纤维状的肿块，就是这些肿块导致的过量出血。

张　英：这样啊，严重吗？

李　洁：目前还不太严重，但是也必须治疗，建议您住院手术。

张　英：药物能治疗吗？

李　洁：可能性不大。手术是目前唯一的治疗方式。

张　英：天哪！是癌症吗？

李　洁：放心，不是癌症。手术之后就不会再大量出血了。

张　英：我相信您，医生，但我就是害怕手术和住院。

李　洁：我了解您的感受，但有时这是没法避免的。而且您只需要住几天院，手术一旦完成，您就会感觉好很多。

张　英：那好吧。

李　洁：住院期间您可以请病假吧。

张　英：可以。手术之前我会把这些问题处理好。

Li Jie：We find some lumps of fibrous tissue on the womb which are causing the bleeding.

Zhang Ying：Oh. Is that serious?

Li Jie：No. It's not now. But treatment is still necessary. I'd recommend you to come in and we'll deal with the situation by operation.

Zhang Ying：Couldn't the lumps be melted away by medicine?

Li Jie：Sorry. I don't think so. An operation is the only way to stop this problem at present.

Zhang Ying：Oh dear! It's not cancer, is it?

Li Jie：No. It's not cancer but I think you won't bleed heavily after operation.

Zhang Ying：I suppose you know best but I'm frightened of operation and hospitals.

Li Jie：I know but hospitals are useful places to turn to when you need them. You'll only be in for several days or so and once the operation is over,you'll feel so much better.

Zhang Ying：OK.

Li Jie：Is that all right for your holidays?

Zhang Ying：Yes. I'll get it over with before then.

【短文】

生词

序号	词语	词性	拼音	词义
1	肌瘤	名	jīliú	leiomyomata
2	确切	形	quèqiè	definite
3	明确	形	míngquè	explicite
4	监控	动	jiānkòng	monitor
5	恶变	动	èbiàn	degenerate
6	骨盆	名	gǔpén	pelvis
7	膀胱	名	pángguāng	bladder
8	直肠	名	zhícháng	rectum
9	规则	形	guīzé	regular
10	宫颈	名	gōngjǐng	cervix
11	生育	名	shēngyù	bearing

子宫肌瘤

子宫肌瘤是常见的肿瘤,发病率可达25%,伴有多种临床表现。最常见的临床表现为月经过多或经期失血过多。引发出血的确切原因尚不明确。许多子宫肌瘤没有临床症状,只需要监控观察。快速增长是其恶变的危险因素之一,但恶变情况极少。如果子宫肌瘤足够大,患者可能会有骨盆、膀胱或直肠的压迫感。

典型的子宫肌瘤体检表现为不规则、居骨盆中位、质硬、无压痛的包块,与宫颈相连并可移动。通常根据肌瘤的大小、有无临床症状及生育要求等因素决定是否手术。对于有临床症状且不再有生育要求的患者,通常采取子宫切除术进行治疗。

Uterine leiomyomata

Uterine leiomyomatas are common tumors. They occur in up to 25% of women and have a variety of clinical presentations. The most common clinical manifestation is menorrhagia,or excessive bleeding during menses. The exact mechanism is unclear at present. Many uterine fibroids are asymptomatatic and only require monitoring. Very rarely,uterine fibroids degenerate with rapid growth as one of the dangerous elements. If the uterine leiomyomata are sufficiently large,patients may also complain of pressure to the pelvis, bladder,or rectum.

The physical examination typical of uterine leiomyomata is an irregular,in the middle of pelvis,firm, nontender mass that moves contiguously with the cervix. Whether to perform an operation depend on the size of the uterine leiomyomata, clinical symptoms, bearing requirement, etc. Hysterectomy is considered the proven treatment for symptomatica uterine fibroids when pregnancy is undesired.

【汉字知识】

部首"宀"

部首"宀"像房屋的形状,一般出现在汉字的顶部。以"宀"为部首的大都跟房屋有关。如"宫""室""家""宿""宅""寓"等。

例如:宫——子宫 宫殿 皇宫
　　　室——教室 寝室 手术室

构词

——关节 表示"骨头与骨头之间相连接的地方"。

例如:膝关节、踝关节、肩关节。

宫——表示"子宫"。

例如:宫颈、宫口、宫缩、宫高、宫外孕。

【练习】

一、选择听到的词语。

1.(　　)A.肌肉　　B.肌瘤　　C.肿瘤　　D.滞留

2.(　　)A.症状　　B.正装　　C.整装　　D.告状

3.(　　)A.阴道　　B.应到　　C.引导　　D.音调

4.(　　)A.手续　　B.手术　　C.技术　　D.美术

5.(　　)A.生于　　B.声乐　　C.生育　　D.剩余

二、根据听到的句子排列词语和短语。

1.临床　月经　失血　最常见的　表现　过多　为　或　过多　经期

2.肿瘤　肌瘤　子宫　常见的　是　25%　发病率　可　达

3.发现　肿块　您　的　子宫里　一些　我们　纤维状的　有

4.经期　同房　及　两次　之间　之后　情况　有没有　出血　阴道　的

三、根据汉语拼音写汉字。

xiānwéi(　　　　)　　áizhèng(　　　　)　　jīliú(　　　　)

qiēchú(　　　　)　　gǔpén(　　　　)　　gōngjǐng(　　　　)

shēngyù(　　　　)　　tòngjīng(　　　　)　　yīndào(　　　　)

四、选词填空。

同房　折磨　明确　生育　恶变

1.引发出血的确切原因尚不＿＿＿＿＿＿＿。

2.快速增长是其＿＿＿＿＿＿＿的危险因素之一。

3.对于有临床症状且不再有＿＿＿＿＿＿＿要求的患者,通常采取子宫切除术进行治疗。

4.我最近快被月经＿＿＿＿＿＿＿死了。

5.你和你爱人最近＿＿＿＿＿＿＿过吗?

五、完成下面的对话和句子。

（一）

张英:可以通过_____吗?

医生:我觉得_____。_____是目前_____。

张英:我的天哪! 这是_____吗?

医生:放心,_____。_____之后就_____了。

张英:我相信您,医生,但我就是_____。

医生:我了解您的感受,但有时_____。而且您只需要_____,_____一旦_____,您就会_____。

张英:那好吧。

（二）

1.许多子宫肌瘤没有_____,只需要_____。

2.如果子宫肌瘤足够大,患者可能会有_____、_____或直肠的_____感。

3.典型的子宫肌瘤体检表现为_____、_____、_____、无压痛的包块,与_____相连并可移动。

4.通常根据子宫肌瘤的_____、有无_____及_____等因素决定是否手术。

六、根据对话和短文内容回答问题。

1.张英感觉哪里不舒服?

2.张英目前的月经状况如何?

3.张英的检查结果是什么?

4.张英对治疗方案表示不安时,医生是如何安慰她的?

5.如果子宫肌瘤足够大,患者可能会有哪些感觉?

6.根据哪些因素决定是否对子宫肌瘤进行手术?

七、交际练习。

患者,江雪,35 岁,孕 1 产 0,因月经过多,继发性贫血前来妇科就诊。患者近半年以来月经周期规律,但经期延长,经量增多,为之前经量的 2 倍多。时有痛经,白带增多。B 超检查发现子宫内有一实性团块,直径 4 cm。实习医生珍妮弗向患者询问病情,解释病因,并推荐治疗方案。

两人一组,分别扮演江雪和珍妮弗,根据提供的信息询问病情,解释病因,并推荐治疗方案,对话时长在 3 分钟左右。

【补充医学词汇】

序号	词语	拼音	词义
1	玻璃样变	bōli yàng biàn	hyaline change
2	囊性变	náng xìng biàn	cystic change
3	红色样变	hóngsè yàng biàn	red degeration
4	肉瘤样变	ròu liú yàng biàn	sarcomatous change
5	宫颈脱垂	gōngjǐng tuō chuí	the cervical prolapse
6	子宫动脉栓塞术	zǐgōng dòngmài shuānsè shù	uterine arterial embolization

（凌 奕 刘 畅）

第十八单元

产科（一）——产前检查

我怀孕了

【学习目的】

1. 会用汉语表达孕期妇女生殖器官及孕期子宫的主要解剖结构。

2. 会用汉语问诊典型产检病例。

3. 了解产前检查的相关医学常识。

【热身】

一、给下面的词语选择对应的字母。

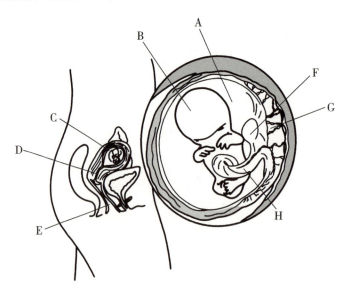

1. 脐带_____ 2. 羊水_____ 3. 胎盘_____ 4. 子宫_____ 5. 阴道_____

6. 胚胎_____ 7. 宫颈_____ 8. 卵黄囊_____

二、连线题。

1. 子宫　　　　　　　A. embryo

2. 宫颈　　　　　　　B. uterus

3. 阴道　　　　　　　C. cervix

4. 胚胎　　　　　　　D. amniotic fluid

5. 羊水　　　　　　　E. umbilical cord

6. 胎盘　　　　　　　F. placenta

7. 脐带　　　　　　　G. vagina

【会话】

场景简介：

人物：患者——高虹(女,28 岁,怀孕 12 周)

　　　医生——李洁(女,34 岁)

　　　实习医生——珍妮弗(女,24 岁)

地点：产科门诊

对话一

生词

序号	词语	词性	拼音	词义
1	怀孕	动	huáiyùn	be pregnant
2	产前检查	名	chǎnqián jiǎnchá	antenatal examination
3	体重	名	tǐzhòng	body weight
4	宫高	名	gōnggāo	fundal height
5	腹围	名	fùwéi	abdominal perimeter
6	预产期	名	yùchǎnqī	expected date of confinement
7	胃口	名	wèikǒu	appetite
8	营养	名	yíngyǎng	nutrition

高　虹：医生您好！我怀孕了,想做个产前检查。

珍妮弗：好的,请到这边称下体重,量一下宫高和腹围,再测个血压。

(检查结束)

珍妮弗：您的末次月经是哪天？

高　虹：7 月 14 号。

珍妮弗：平常月经周期规律吗？

高　虹：挺规律的,30 天左右。

珍妮弗：那您的预产期在明年 4 月 21 号。有没有不舒服？

高　虹：我最近胃口不太好,前 2 个月饭后经常恶心想吐。不过最近好多了。

珍妮弗：那没关系。怀孕之前没生过病吧？

高　虹：没有,我身体一直不错。

珍妮弗：您怀孕 3 个月了,要加强营养,适当锻炼,注意休息。我请其他医生帮您看看还需要做哪些检查。

高　虹：好的，谢谢！

Gao Hong：Good morning，doctor. I think I'm pregnant. Would you give me an antenatal examination？

Jennifer：OK. Please come here and I'll weigh and measure you. We'll take the blood pressure then.

（Examination is completed）

Jennifer：When was your last menstruation？

Gao Hong：It was on July 14ᵗʰ.

Jennifer：Are your menstrual cycles regular？

Gao Hong：Yes，they are. 30 days approximately.

Jennifer：Then，your due date will be April 21ˢᵗ next year. What problem have you had during this pregnancy？

Gao Hong：I have had a poor appetite and have been vomiting after meals during the first 2 months. But it's much better now.

Jennifer：It doesn't matter. Did you have any illnesses before pregnancy？

Gao Hong：No，I'm quite healthy.

Jennifer：You have been pregnant for 3 months. It's necessary to strengthen nutrition，do appropriate physical exercise，and have a good rest. I'll ask other doctors what other examinations you need to take.

Gao Hong：OK. Thanks a lot.

对话二

生词

序号	词语	词性	拼音	词义
1	目前	形	mùqián	at present
2	双胞胎	名	shuāngbāotāi	twins
3	多胎妊娠	名	duōtāi rènshēn	multiple pregnancy
4	家族病	名	jiāzúbìng	hereditary disease
5	去世	动	qùshì	die

李　洁：目前看来您的情况还不错。孕期有过阴道流血、流水，下腹或者腿疼痛的情况吗？

高　虹：一累就腿部疼痛，其他情况没有过。

李　洁：有高血压、糖尿病、多胎妊娠或者家族病史吗？

高　虹：我有个双胞胎妹妹，她和我妈都是因为生孩子大出血去世的。

李　洁：我知道了。请到这边来做一个骨盆检查。

高　虹：好的。

李　洁：嗯，您的骨盆情况还不错，足够大。再去做一些抽血检查，做完我帮您看结果。

高　虹：好的医生。

李　洁：以后要定期产检。前6个月每月1次，接下来的3个月每2周1次，最后1个月每周1次。前3个月和最后1个月不要同房。

高　虹：好的，我会按您说的做。

Li Jie：Your condition is quite good at present. Have you had bleeding，watery discharge，pain in your lower abdomen and legs？

Gao Hong：I do have some pain in my legs when I'm tired. There's no other problem.

Li Jie：Is there any hypertension，diabetes，multiple pregnancy，or hereditary disease in your family？

Gao Hong：I was one of a pair of twins，my mother and younger sister died during the delivery because of profuse bleeding.

Li Jie：I know about it now. Please come here to take a pelvis examination.

Gao Hong：OK.

Li Jie：Well，the condition of your pelvis is big enough. Then take some examination of your blood. I'll help you to analyse the results.

Gao Hong：OK，doctor.

Li Jie：Please come and take examination regularly afterwards. Every two weeks for the next three months；and once a week in the last month. You should avoid sexual relations in the first three months and the last month of pregnancy.

Gao Hong：All right. I will do as your advise.

【短文】

生词

序号	词语	词性	拼音	词义
1	改善	动	gǎishàn	ameliorate
2	监测	动	jiāncè	monitor
3	促进	动	cùjìn	promote
4	胎儿	名	tāi'ér	fetal
5	分娩	动	fēnmiǎn	childbirth；delivery
6	询问	动	xúnwèn	inquire
7	盆腔	名	pénqiāng	pelvis
8	血栓病	名	xuèshuānbìng	thrombus
9	化验	动	huàyàn	test

产前检查

产前检查的目的是发现孕妇疾病，改善孕期不适症状，监测和促进胎儿健康，帮助孕妇做好分娩准备。初次产检非常重要，内容也很详细，通常在妊娠12周之前预约。

产前检查主要包括初次的病史询问，包括月经史、避孕史、用药史、盆腔及腹部手术史、孕产史、家族病史、糖尿病及高血压病史、多胎妊娠史、血栓病病史等。还需进行全面的血液、尿液化验。期间应根据需要做好腹部超声检查和心肺、血压、体重、宫高、腹围增长等各项身体检查，有时还需采集宫颈涂片。最后还要根据检查结果对已发现的孕妇和胎儿的问题进行指导，并对下次产检提出建议。

Antenatal examination

The aims of antenatal examination are to detect any disease in the mother，ameliorate the discomforts of pregnancy，monitor and promote fetal well–being，prepare mothers for childbirth. The 1st antenatal visit is very important and comprehensive. It should be booked within 12 weeks.

Antenatal examination consists of inquiring of medical history during the 1st visit which include history of menstruation, contraception, drugs, surgery to abdomen or pelvis, outcome and complications of past pregnancies, family disease, diabetes and hypertension, multiple pregnancy, thrombus, etc. Comprehensive tests of blood and urine are also necessary. Body check on heart, lungs, blood pressure, weight, fundal height and abdominal girth should be taken during the pregnancy as needed. Sometime a cervical smear needs to be gathered. Guidance to the problems of gravida and fetal should be given according to the results. Suggestion for the examination of next time is also needed.

【汉字知识】

部首"子（孑）"

部首"子"像小孩子的形状，以"子"为部首的汉字多与小孩子有关。"子"在一部分汉字中位于左侧，写作"孑"，如"孙""孩""孤"等；也有在汉字底部的情况，如"孕""孝""孪"等。

例如：孩——男孩　女孩　小孩
　　　孕——怀孕　孕育　孕妇

【构词】

——史　表示"历史"。
例如：流产史、月经史、避孕史、用药史、孕产史、家族史。
——期　表示"规定的时间或一段时间"。
例如：预产期、月经期、急性期、初发期。

【练习】

一、选择听到的词语。

1. (　) A. 怀孕　　B. 怀疑　　C. 好运　　D. 怀念
2. (　) A. 宫缩　　B. 身高　　C. 宫高　　D. 宫颈
3. (　) A. 温馨　　B. 恶心　　C. 开心　　D. 恶化
4. (　) A. 盆腔　　B. 喷枪　　C. 宫腔　　D. 盆地
5. (　) A. 人参　　B. 人生　　C. 认真　　D. 妊娠

二、根据听到的句子排列词语和短语。

1. 重要　产检　初次　非常　内容　详细　通常　很　也　在　妊娠12周　预约　之前

2. 胃口　最近　不太好　我　饭后　前2个月　想吐　恶心　经常

3. 妹妹　双胞胎　我　个　有　她　因为　是　去世　大出血　生孩子　的

三、根据汉语拼音写汉字。

fùwéi(　　)　　　yùchǎnqī(　　　)　　　pénqiāng(　　　)

fēnmiǎn(　　)　　duōtāi rènshēn(　　　)　　shuāngbāotāi(　　　)

tāi'ér(　　)　　　huáiyùn(　　　)　　　gōnggāo(　　)

四、选词填空。

怀孕　分娩　双胞胎　预产期　营养　胎儿

1. 您的_____快到了，可以考虑谁来照顾产妇和宝宝了。
2. 您_____了，不能做太累的工作了，要注意休息。
3. 鱼虾的_____很丰富，孕妇可以适当多吃一些。
4. 产前检查可以监测和促进_____健康，帮助孕妇做好_____准备。
5. 恭喜您！您怀的是_____。

五、完成下面的对话和句子。

（一）

珍妮弗：您是哪天_____？

高虹：_____月_____号。

珍妮弗：平常_____吗？

高虹：_____的，_____左右。

珍妮弗：那您的_____在_____。有没有_____？

高虹：我最近胃口不太好，前 2 个月_____。不过_____。

珍妮弗：那_____。_____没生过病吧？

高虹：没有，我_____。

珍妮弗：您_____了，要加强_____，适当_____，注意_____。我请其他医生_____
_____。

（二）

1. 产前检查主要包括初次的_____，包括_____史、_____史、_____史、_____史、
_____史、_____史、_____及_____史、_____史、_____史等。

2. 应根据需要做好_____检查和_____、血压、_____、宫高、腹围增长等各项身体检查，
有时还需采集_____。

3. 最后还要根据检查结果对已发现的_____和_____的问题进行指导，并对下次产检提出
建议。

六、根据对话和短文内容回答问题。

1. 初次产检通常在什么时候预约？

2. 初次产检的检查项目主要有哪些？

3. 高虹怀孕之后有没有不舒服？

4. 怀孕 3 个月有哪些注意事项？

5. 高虹的妈妈和妹妹是什么原因去世的？

6. 产前检查的时间有哪些注意事项？

七、交际练习。

孕妇李佳，28 岁，停经 6 周，无孕产史。近期时常有晨吐反映，自行用试纸测出已怀孕，前来医院
产科做检查。实习医生珍妮弗向其询问病史并做初步检查。

两人一组，分别扮演角色孕妇和医生，组织一段 3 分钟左右的对话展现上文场景。

【补充医学词汇】

序号	词语	拼音	词义
1	瘢痕子宫	bān hén zǐ gōng	scar uterus
2	初产妇	chū chǎn fù	primipara
3	子痫	zǐ xián	eclampsia
4	复发性流产	fù fā xìng liú chǎn	recurrent spontaneous abortion
5	异位妊娠	yì wèi rèn shēn	ectopic pregnancy

（凌　奕　刘　畅）

第十九单元

产科(二)——前置胎盘

医生,我的阴道流血了

【学习目的】

1.学会用汉语表达前置胎盘的常见类型。

2.学会用汉语问诊典型前置胎盘病例。

3.了解前置胎盘的相关医学常识。

【热身】

一、给下面的词语选择对应的字母。

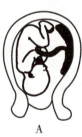   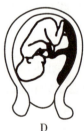 

A   B   C   D   E

1.低置胎盘_____ 2.部分性前置胎盘_____ 3.正常胎盘_____

4.完全性前置胎盘_____ 5.边缘性前置胎盘_____

二、根据英文写汉字。

1. placenta praevia _____

2. partial placenta praevia _____

3. total placenta praevia _____

4. low-lying placenta _____

5. marginal placenta praevia _____

6. normal placenta _____

【会话】

场景简介:
人物:患者——高虹(女,28 岁,怀孕 36 周)
　　　实习医生——珍妮弗(女,18 岁,摩洛哥人)
地点:产科门诊

对话一

生词

序号	词语	词性	拼音	词义
1	卫生巾	名	wèishēngjīn	sanitary towel
2	流	动	liú	flow
3	虚	形	xū	deficient
4	浑身	副	húnshēn	from head to foot
5	之前	副	zhīqián	before
6	胎动	名	tāidòng	fetal movement
7	处理	动	chǔlǐ	deal with

珍妮弗:高虹对吗? 我记得您两周前来过。现在哪里不舒服吗?

高　虹:昨天晚上我忽然阴道出血了。

珍妮弗:用了多少卫生巾?

高　虹:用完 1 盒了,后来只能用毛巾。我以为一会儿能停,但还是一直流。所以今天一早就过来了。

珍妮弗:出血过程中觉得痛吗?

高　虹:不痛,就是有点虚,浑身没力气。

珍妮弗:现在还流血吗?

高　虹:之前停过一会儿,但是后来又流了。

珍妮弗:预产期还有 1 个月,对吧?

高　虹:是的。

珍妮弗:还能感觉到胎动吗?

高　虹:没有之前那么频繁了。

珍妮弗:我先给您初步检查下,再和其他医生讨论怎么处理。

高　虹:好的。

Jennifer:Hi,Gao Hong,I remember that you have been here two weeks ago. How are you feeling?

Gao Hong:Last night I began to bleed,and I'm really worried about it.

Jennifer:How many pads did you have to use?

Gao Hong:I used up an entire box,and then I had to use a towel. I thought it would go away,but it didn't,so I decided to come and see you.

Jennifer:Was there any pain associated with this?

Gao Hong:No,no pain,just weakness,I have no strength.

Jennifer: Are you still bleeding?

Gao Hong: Well, it stopped for a while, but then it started up again.

Jennifer: Let's see. You're not due for another month, are you?

Gao Hong: No, I'm not.

Jennifer: Have you felt your baby moving around?

Gao Hong: Not as frequent as before.

Jennifer: Well, let me examine you briefly, then I'll discuss with other doctors about what to do.

Gao Hong: All right.

对话二

生词

序号	词语	词性	拼音	词义
1	前置胎盘	名	qiánzhì tāipán	placenta praevia
2	流产	名	liúchǎn	abortion
3	剖宫产	名	pōugōngchǎn	caesarean section
4	彩超	名	cǎichāo	color ultrasound
5	属于	动	shǔyú	be belong to
6	边缘性	名	biānyuánxìng	marginality
7	耽误	动	dānwu	delay

（初步检查后）

珍妮弗：我刚才和代教医生讨论了您的情况，可能是前置胎盘导致的出血。您有过流产或者剖宫产的经历吗？

高　虹：我儿子是 3 年前剖宫产的，没流过产。

珍妮弗：那您先做个腹部彩超吧，确定下胎盘位置。这是检查单。

高　虹：好的。

（检查结果出来后）

珍妮弗：从检查结果来看，您属于边缘性前置胎盘的情况，妊娠晚期出血很常见。

高　虹：这样啊，情况严重吗？

珍妮弗：现在还不好说，不过为了您和宝宝的安全，最好能住院观察一段时间。

高　虹：好吧。但我还有孩子要照顾，我想先回家安排一下。

珍妮弗：可以，不过您最好尽快过来办理住院手续，不要耽误太久。

（After the examination）

Jennifer: I have discussed your problem with the attending doctor. The bleeding is probably caused by placenta previa. Have you had abortion or ceserean?

Gao Hong: I had ceserean dilivery my son three years ago. No abortion.

Jennifer: This is your sheet. Please have an color doppler ultrasound scan to exam the location od placenta first.

Gao Hong: All right.

（After the check result comes out）

Jennifer: According to the result, it is marginal placenta previa which can often cause bleeding in late pregnancy.

Gao Hong：I see，is it serious？

Jennifer：It is hard to say by now. For the savety of you ang the baby，you'd better stay in the hospital for a brief period of observation.

Gao Hong：OK. But I have to take care of my children at home，I have to go home and make arrange-ment.

Jennifer：All right. You'd better to admit to the hospital as soon as possible，don't delay for too long time.

【短文】

生词

序号	词语	词性	拼音	词义
1	位于	动	wèiyú	locate
2	前后壁	名	qián hòu bì	anterior（posterior）wall
3	宫颈口	名	gōngjǐngkǒu	cervix
4	类	名	lèi	kind；category
5	覆盖	动	fùgài	cover
6	整个	形	zhěnggè	whole
7	内口	名	nèikǒu	internal opening
8	部分性	名	bùfenxìng	partial seizures
9	低置	动	dīzhì	locate in a low position
10	附着	动	fùzhuó	adhere to
11	接近	动	jiējìn	be close to
12	精确	形	jīngquè	precise
13	定位	动	dìngwèi	orient
14	反复	副	fǎnfù	repeatedly
15	先兆	名	xiānzhào	foreboding
16	终止	动	zhōngzhǐ	end

前置胎盘

正常的胎盘位于子宫前后壁、两侧壁和宫底。如果胎盘离宫颈口很近，称为前置胎盘。这种情况可分为4类：第一类是完全性前置胎盘，覆盖了整个宫颈内口；第二类是部分性前置胎盘，覆盖部分宫颈内口；第三类是边缘性前置胎盘，位于宫颈内口的边缘；第四类是低置胎盘，附着于子宫下段，接近宫颈内口。腹部超声是最简单、精确、安全的胎盘定位方法。

前置胎盘的典型症状为妊娠晚期或临产时出现反复、无先兆、无痛性阴道出血。若出血量大，可能需要剖宫产提前终止妊娠。分娩后也可能有大量出血。有剖宫产史、流产史，多胎及高龄孕妇要注意胎盘前置情况。

Placenta praevia

Normal placenta locates on the anterial, posteria, biletaral and fudus of the uterus. If it located very near to the internal os of the cervix. It can be devided into 4 classifications:①total placenta previa, the internal cervical os is covered completely by placenta;②partial placenta previa, the internal os is partially covered by placenta;③marginal placenta previa, the edge of the placenta is at the margin of the internal os;④low-lying placenta, the placenta is implanted in the lower uterine segment such that the placenta edge actually does not reach the internal os but is in close proximity to it.

The classic symptom is recurrent asymtomatic vaginal bleeding on third trimester and during delivery. If there is massive bleeding, cesarean is needed to terminate the pregnancy. Postpartum hemorrhagerate is also increased. High risk factors including:Prior cesarean delivery or abortion, multiparity, advancing maternal age.

【汉字知识】

部首"皿"

部首"皿"的形状和意思为"容器,器皿",一般出现在汉字的底部。以"皿"为部首的汉字大都跟容器有关。如"盆""盘""盒""盛""盥"等。此类汉字多为形声结构,底部的部首为形旁,顶部的部件为声旁,代表字音。

例如:盆——骨盆　盆腔炎　脸盆
　　　盘——胎盘　椎间盘　光盘

构词

胎——表示"胎儿"。

例如:胎盘、胎心、胎芽、胎动、胎毛、胎膜、胎位。

——检查　表示"为了发现问题而用心查看"。

例如:产前检查。

【练习】

一、选择听到的词语。

1. (　　　) A. 胎儿　　B. 光盘　　C. 胎盘　　D. 胎动

2. (　　　) A. 卫生间　B. 卫生局　C. 卫生员　D. 卫生巾

3. (　　　) A. 频繁　　B. 麻烦　　C. 贫穷　　D. 平凡

4. (　　　) A. 流血　　B. 流产　　C. 流水　　D. 流畅

5. (　　　) A. 种植　　B. 总之　　C. 终止　　D. 种子

二、根据听到的句子排列词语和短语。

1. 前后壁　胎盘　正常的　子宫　位于　宫底　和　两侧壁

2. 能　停　我　一会儿　以为　一直　但　流　还是

3. 我　初步　先　检查　给　您　下　医生　其他　处理　怎么　讨论　和　再

4. 剖宫产　流产　您　经历　有过　吗　或者　的

三、根据汉语拼音写汉字。

pínfán tāidòng(　　　　)　　qiánzhì tāipán (　　　　　)　　liúchǎn (　　　　　)

biānyuánxìng (　　　　)　　gōngjǐngkǒu (　　　　)　　rènshēn (　　　　)

wèiyú (　　　　)　　　　　dīzhì (　　　　)　　　　fùzhuó (　　　　　)

四、选词填空。

定位　剖宫产　耽误　边缘性　精确　胎动

1. 腹部超声是最简单、_____、安全的胎盘_____方法。

2. 有_____史、流产史,多胎及高龄孕妇要注意胎盘前置情况。

3. 一般来说,怀孕 4~5 个月就能感觉到_____了。

4. 您确实属于前置胎盘的情况,是_____前置胎盘。

5. 不过您最好尽快过来办理住院手续,不要_____太久。

五、完成下面的对话和句子。

(一)

高　虹:昨天晚上我忽然_____了。

珍妮弗:用了多少_____?

高　虹:用完 1 盒了,后来只能用_____。

珍妮弗:出血过程中觉得痛吗?

高　虹:不痛,就是_____,_____没力气。

珍妮弗:现在还流血吗?

高　虹:之前停过一会儿,但是后来又流了。

珍妮弗:_____还有 1 个月,对吧?

高　虹:是的。

珍妮弗:还能感觉到__吗?

高　虹:没有之前那么_____了。

(二)

1. 前置胎盘可分为 4 类:第一类是_____前置胎盘,_____了整个_____。

2. 第四类是_____,_____于子宫下段,接近宫颈内口。

3. 前置胎盘的_____症状为_____期或临产时出现反复、无_____、无痛性_____。

4. 若出血量大,可能需要_____提前_____妊娠。

六、根据对话和短文内容回答问题。

1. 高虹的出血状况如何? 她感觉痛吗?

2. 这是高虹第一次生孩子吗?

3. 高虹还有多久才到预产期?

4. 高虹的胎盘属于什么类型的胎盘?

5. 四类前置胎盘的特点分别是什么?

6. 前置胎盘有什么样的典型症状?

七、交际练习。

患者王红,42 岁,初产妇,怀孕 23 周,近期时常感觉精神不佳,腹部隐痛。昨天夜里忽然阴道流血,今早前来产科就诊。实习医生珍妮弗为其做了病情询问和初步检查,并与产科医生李洁讨论病情。珍妮弗和王红商量后决定先让其住院观察。

三人一组,分别扮演角色王红、珍妮弗、李洁,组织一段 3 分钟左右的对话展现上文场景。

【补充医学词汇】

序号	词语	拼音	词义
1	产褥热	chǎnrùrè	childbed fever
2	会阴侧切术	huìyīn cèqiēshù	lateral episiotomy
3	缩宫素	suōgōngsù	pitocin
4	羊水栓塞	yángshuǐ shuānsè	amniotic fluid embolism
5	产后抑郁症	chǎn hòu yìyùzhèng	postnatal depression

（凌　奕　刘　畅）

第二十单元

新生儿科（一）——早产儿

生产时有些缺氧

【学习目的】

1. 学会用汉语表述评估胎儿发育情况的相关指标。
2. 学会用汉语问诊典型早产儿病例。
3. 了解早产儿的相关医学常识。

【热身】

一、给下面的词语选择对应的字母。

A   B   C

D   E

1. 股骨长_____   2. 双顶径_____   3. 枕额径_____   4. 头围_____   5. 腹围_____

二、根据拼音写汉字。

1. shuāngdǐngjìng_____

2. gǔgǔ cháng_____

3. tóuwéi_____

4. fùwéi_____

5. zhěnéjìng_____

【会话】

场景简介：
人物：患者——胡丽(女,9 分钟)
　　　患者家属——刘小燕(女,24 岁)
　　　医生——廖小妹(女,39 岁)
　　　实习医生——珍妮弗(女,18 岁,摩洛哥人)
地点：产科、新生儿科住院部

对话一

生词

序号	词语	词性	拼音	词义
1	恭喜	动	gōngxǐ	congratulations
2	阿氏评分	名	āshìpíngfēn	Apgar scores
3	肌张力	名	jīzhānglì	muscle tension
4	喉反射	名	hóufǎnshè	laryngeal reflex
5	缺氧	动	quēyǎng	hypoxia

（产科）

珍妮弗：您好！恭喜您添了一个女儿。

刘小燕：谢谢,她好吗？

珍妮弗：还好,出生时阿氏评分 1 分钟、5 分钟评分均为 10 分。

刘小燕：什么是阿氏评分？

珍妮弗：阿氏评分是用来评价新生儿出生时有无窒息及窒息严重程度的一个简单方法。在婴儿出生后 1、5、10 分钟分别对呼吸、心率、肌张力、皮肤颜色、喉反射等 5 项指标评分,每项 0～2 分,共 10 分。您的孩子的评分是 10 分。但是……

刘小燕：但是什么？

珍妮弗：但是生产时有些缺氧,体重太轻了。

刘小燕：多重？

珍妮弗：1.1 kg。廖医生说您的妊娠期才 32 周零 6 天,孩子是早产儿,属于极低出生体重,需要入院治疗。您需要给她办下住院手续。

刘小燕：好的。我让她爸爸去办。

（Obstetrical department）

Jennifer：Hello! Congratulations you gave birth to a daughter.

Liu Xiaoyan：Thank you, is she fine?

Jennifer:It's good,She got 10 points at 1 and 5 minutes after birth by the Apgar scores.

Liu Xiaoyan:What is the Apgar scores?

Jennifer:The Apgar score is a simple method for assessing whether a newborn suffer from asphyxia or not and severity of asphyxia. Each of the five indicators of respiratory rate,heart rate,muscle tension,skin color,and laryngeal reflex was scored at 1,5,and 10 minutes after birth. Your child's score is 10 points. but…

Liu Xiaoyan:But what?

Jennifer:But at the time of birth there was lack of oxygen,and a very low birth weight.

Liu Xiaoyan:How heavy?

Jennifer:1.1 kilograms. Dr. Liao said that your pregnancy is only 32 weeks and 6 days. It is a premature baby,belongs to a very low birth weight and needs hospitalization. You need to get her hospitalized.

Liu Xiaoyan:Yes. I let her father do it.

对话二

生词

序号	词语	词性	拼音	词义
1	极	副	jí	pole
2	浅促	形	qiǎncù	shortness of breath
3	痰鸣音	名	tánmíngyīn	spittle sound
4	调节	动	tiáojié	adjust
5	完善	形	wánshàn	perfect
6	采取	动	cǎiqǔ	take
7	暖箱	名	nuǎnxiāng	warm box
8	保温	动	bǎowēn	insulation
9	辅助	形	fǔzhù	aid
10	通气	动	tōngqì	ventilate

（新生儿科）

廖小妹:你去看过刚从产科转过来的 35 床女婴了吗?

珍妮弗:看了。18:46 剖腹生产,10 分钟前转过来的。

廖小妹:情况怎么样?

珍妮弗:体温 36.1 ℃,脉搏 126 次/分,呼吸 60 次/分。体温和脉搏都正常,呼吸较快。可是体重只有 1.1 kg,太轻了,是个极轻早产儿。

廖小妹:给她做听诊了吗?

珍妮弗:做了,呼吸浅促,双侧呼吸音弱,有一点痰鸣音。

廖小妹:早产儿的呼吸系统、消化系统、体温调节功能等常常不完善,需要采取措施帮助他们调节呼吸、体温等。

珍妮弗:是不是可以采取暖箱保温措施?

廖小妹:嗯,可以。必要时还需要采用呼吸机辅助通气。

（Neonatal department）

Liao Xiaomei：Have you seen the infant girlof bed No. 35，who just shifted from obstetrics?

Jennifer：Yes. She was born by Caesarean section at 18：46 and shifted 10 minutes ago.

Liao Xiaomei：How is the situation?

Jennifer：Body temperature 36. 1 ℃，pulse rate 126 beats per minute，breathing 60 breaths per minute. Body temperature and pulse rate are normal，breathing is fast. However，it weighs only 1. 1 kg and is extremely low weight preterm infant.

Liao Xiaomei：Did you auscultate her?

Jennifer：Yes，I did. She has a shallow breathing，bilateral breath weak sounds，and a little phlegm sound.

Liao Xiaomei：The respiratory system，digestive system，and body temperature regulation function of preterm infants are often imperfect and measures need to be taken to help them regulate their breathing and body temperature.

Jennifer：Is it possible to take incubator insulation?

Liao Xiaomei：Em，yes. Ventilator-assisted ventilation is also needed if necessary.

【短文】

生词

序号	词语	词性	拼音	词义
1	胎龄	名	tāilíng	gestational age
2	超	副	chāo	ultra
3	薄	形	báo	thin
4	趾甲	名	zhǐjiǎ	nail
5	端	名	duān	end
6	适应	动	shìyìng	adapt
7	呼吸窘迫综合征	名	hūxī jiǒngpò zōnghézhēng	respiratory distress syndrome

早产儿

正常新生儿的胎龄是 37～42 周。临床上把胎龄小于 37 周的新生儿叫作早产儿。其中，胎龄小于 28 周的早产儿叫作超早产儿。胎龄是 28～32 周的早产儿叫作极早产儿，胎龄是 32～34 周的叫作中期早产儿，胎龄是 34～36 周的早产儿叫作晚期早产儿。

早产儿体重常常小于 2 500 g。出生体重是 1 000～1 499 g 的，称为极低出生体重儿，出生体重小于 1 000 g 的，称为超低出生体重。

从外观上看，早产儿皮肤薄嫩，毛发稀疏、柔软，手脚趾甲未达到趾端。早产儿因为胎龄小、体重低，对外界的适应能力差，所以容易发生各种并发症。如早产儿容易出现进行性呼吸困难，临床上称为早产儿呼吸窘迫综合征。

在我国，减少使用辅助生育技术生育双胎或多胎，孕期保持良好心态，避免高龄怀孕，加强孕期产检，可降低早产儿的发生率。

Premature baby

The gestational age of normal newborns is 37–42 weeks. Newborns with a gestational age of less than 37 weeks are clinically called premature infants. Among them, preterm infants whose gestational age is less than 28 weeks are called super premature infants. Preterm infants with a gestational age of 28–32 weeks are called extremely preterm infants. The gestational age is 32–34 weeks for midterm preterm infants. The preterm infants whose gestational age is 34–36 weeks are called late preterm infants.

Preterm children often weigh less than 2 500 grams. The birth weight is 1 000–1 499 grams, which is called a very low birth weight infant. The birth weight is less than 1 000 grams, which is called ultra-low birth weight.

In terms of appearance, premature babies have thin skin, sparse and soft hair, and thenails do not reach the toes. Because of the small gestational age and low body weight, premature infants have poor adaptability to the outside world, and are prone to various complications. Premature babies are prone to progressive dyspnea, they are clinically referred to as respiratory distress syndrome in preterm infants.

In China, reducing the use of assisted reproductive technology for the birth of twins or multiple births, maintaining a goodmood during pregnancy, avoiding older age pregnancy and strengthening prenatal maternity checkups are helpful for reducing the incidence rate of preterm infants.

【汉字知识】

部首"穴"

部首"穴"的意思为"洞穴"，一般出现在汉字的顶部。以"穴"为部首的汉字大都跟洞穴和房屋有关。如"窒""空""窄""穿""穷""窗""窘"等。

例如：窗——窗户　窗帘　关窗
　　　窘——窘迫　窘态　窘境

构词

——系统　表示"人体的不同系统"。

例如：消化系统、呼吸系统、循环系统、免疫系统。

——径　表示"两点之间的直线距离"。

例如：前后径、上下径、左右径、双顶径。

【练习】

一、选择听到的词语。

1. (　　) A.恭喜　　B.欢喜　　C.空喜　　D.烘洗
2. (　　) A.浅促　　B.前足　　C.煎煮　　D.兼职
3. (　　) A.保温　　B.气温　　C.泡面　　D.饱含
4. (　　) A.适龄　　B.适应　　C.十里　　D.湿润
5. (　　) A.胎龄　　B.台铃　　C.呆气　　D.带子

二、根据听到的句子排列词语和短语。

1. 孩子　您　的　体重　极低　出生时　入院　治疗　需要

2. 调节　常常　体温　措施　早产儿　需要　采取　帮助　他们　呼吸　等

3. 是　严重　新生儿　阿氏评分　程度　评价　出生时　有无　窒息　及　一种　方法　窒息　的

4. 通气　必要时　呼吸机　我们　会　辅助　采用　早产儿

三、根据拼音写汉字。

hóufǎnshè（　　　）　　　　nuǎnxiāng（　　　）　　　　tāilíng（　　　）

zhǐjiǎ（　　　）　　　　tōngqì（　　　）　　　　āshìpíngfēn（　　　）

quēyǎng（　　　）　　　　hūxī jiǒngpò zōnghézhēng（　　　）

四、选词填空。

调节　辅助　指标　浅促　窒息

1. 新生儿体温_____能力较弱,需要注意防寒保暖。

2. 她的各项检查_____都正常,明天可以出院了。

3. 医生给她做听诊时,发现她呼吸_____,双侧呼吸音很弱。

4. 大部分鱼类如果离开水,就会因缺氧_____而死。

5. 必要时,我们会采用呼吸机_____她呼吸。

五、完成下面的对话和句子。

（一）

护士:您好,恭喜您! 您生了个女孩。

产妇:_____。让我看看。

护士:您的孩子很可爱,就是_____。

产妇:她有多重?

护士:_____。

产妇:嗯,_____?

护士:医生说她需要立即转入新生儿科入院治疗。

产妇:_____。

（二）

1. 临床上常常把_____叫作早产儿。

2. 早产儿_____、_____,因此对外界的_____差。

3. 皮肤非常_____,毛发非常_____、_____,手脚趾甲未达到_____。

4. 早产儿容易发生各个脏器的_____。

六、根据对话和短文内容回答问题。

1. 刘小燕的女儿出生时阿氏评分分值是多少?

2. 刘小燕的女儿出生时体重是多少?

3. 刘小燕是剖宫产还是自然生产?

4. 刘小燕的女儿的呼吸系统怎么样?

5. 正常的新生儿胎龄是多少周?

6. 早产儿有什么特点?

七、交际练习。

男婴 A,34 周多 3 天剖宫产出生,体重 2 310 g,出生时 Apgar 评分分别为 9 分、10 分、10 分。由产科转入新生儿科,医生 B 为其检查,发现其反应好,面色红润,呼吸稍促,四肢肌张力正常,腹胀。吩咐护士 C 立即给以保暖、心电监护、禁食、静脉输液等处理。同时为其做血常规、大小便常规和肝功能等检查。

请根据此情况编写对话,并展示出来。

【补充医学词汇】

序号	词语	拼音	词义
1	足月儿	zúyuè ér	term infant
2	过期产儿	guòqī chǎn ér	post-term infant
3	产卵期	chǎnluǎn qī	ovulation period
4	胚胎期	pēitāi qī	embryonic period
5	新生儿期	xīn shēng ér qī	neonatal period

（姜冬梅　张　帆）

第二十一单元

新生儿科(二)——新生儿黄疸

孩子的黄疸消退了

【学习目的】

1. 学会用汉语表述常见新生儿黄疸类型。

2. 学会用汉语问诊典型新生儿黄疸病例。

3. 了解新生儿黄疸的相关医学知识。

【热身】

一、给下面的词语选择对应的字母。

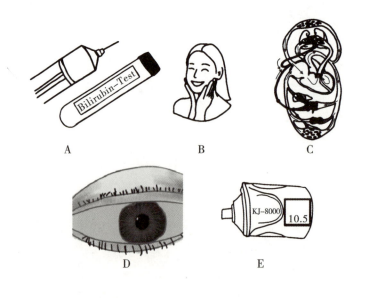

A   B   C

D   E

1. 巩膜_____   2. 血液循环_____   3. 经皮黄疸仪_____

4. 胆红素检测_____   5. 皮肤_____

二、根据英文写汉字。

1. hepatocellular jaundice _____

2. obstructive jaundice _____

3. breast milk jaundice _____

4. hemolytic jaundice _____

5. physiologic jaundice _____

6. pathologic jaundice _____

【会话】

场景简介:
人物:患者——李少芳(女,1 天)
　　　医生——张明(男,37 岁)
　　　实习医生——爱丽丝(女,18 岁,纳米比亚人)
地点:新生儿科住院部

对话一

生词

序号	词语	词性	拼音	词义
1	黄染	形	huángrǎn	yellow dye
2	顺产	动	shùnchǎn	natural labor
3	巩膜	名	gǒngmó	sclera
4	吸吮	动	xīshǔn	sucking
5	烦躁	形	fánzào	irritability
6	新生儿高胆红素血症	名	xīnshēng'ér gāo dǎnhóngsù xuèzhèng	neonatal hyperbilirubinemia

爱丽丝:张医生,昨天晚上产科又转来一个新生儿患者,安排在 15 床。

张　明:嗯。什么时候出生的? 顺产还是剖宫产?

爱丽丝:昨天 20:43 出生,顺产。

张　明:情况怎么样?

爱丽丝:出生时 1 分钟、5 分钟阿氏评分均正常。但脸部皮肤出现黄染,向胸腹部、四肢蔓延。今天黄染又加重了,巩膜也很黄。

张　明:母亲开始喂奶了吗?

爱丽丝:昨天生产后就开始喂了,小孩吸吮有力。

张　明:大、小便是什么颜色?

爱丽丝:小便和大便都是黄色。

张　明:有没有发热、抽搐、烦躁不安等症状。

爱丽丝:没有。

张　明:皮测胆红素(经皮黄疸仪)值是多少?

爱丽丝:249.66 μmol/L,277.02 μmol/L,225.72 μmol/L。

张　明:这个数值比较高,可能是新生儿高胆红素血症。让母亲继续母乳喂养,加上其他支持治疗,考虑蓝光退黄治疗。现在给她做进一步检查。

Alice:Dr. Zhang,The neonate patient transferred from obstetrics department last night was arranged in bed No. 15.

Zhang Ming: Oh. What time was he born, a natural labor or a cesarean section?

Alice: A natural labor at 20:43 yesterday.

Zhang Ming: How is the patient?

Alice: The Apgar scoring at 1 minute and 5 minutes after birth, was normal. However, Her face was stained yellow, then the chest, abdomen and limbs, which has exacerbated today, the sclera is also very yellow.

Zhang Ming: Did the mother start breastfeeding?

Alice: She began to feed after the birth yesterday, and the child vigorously sucked himself.

Zhang Ming: What are the color of the stool and urine?

Alice: Both are yellow.

Zhang Ming: Are there any symptoms such as fever, convulsions, and restlessness?

Alice: No.

Zhang Ming: What is the value of skin test bilirubin (percutaneous jaundice meter)?

Alice: 249.66 μmol/L, 277.02 μmol/L, 225.72 μmol/L。

Zhang Ming: This value is relatively high, it may be neonatal hyperbilirubinemia. Let the mother continue breast feeding, and provide other supportive treatment, consider the blue light yellow treatment. Now give her further examination for the diagnosis.

对话二

序号	词语	词性	拼音	词义
1	淋巴细胞	名	línbā xìbāo	lymphocyte
2	百分数	名	bǎifēnshù	percentage
3	生理性	形	shēnglǐxìng	physiological
4	病理性	形	bìnglǐxìng	pathological
5	进展	动	jìnzhǎn	progress
6	重度	形	zhòngdù	severe

张　明：爱丽丝，你去看了15床的患者没有，情况怎么样？

爱丽丝：看了，15床患者全身及巩膜的黄疸消退了些，经皮测黄疸均值49.59 μmol/L。

张　明：效果还可以，其他辅助检查情况怎么样？

爱丽丝：血常规检查结果是白细胞 $7.98×10^9/L$，血红蛋白 180 g/L，血小板 $312×10^9/L$，淋巴细胞百分比41.9%，中性粒细胞百分比46.9%，基本正常。医生，我知道黄疸有生理性的和病理性的，这个患者有没有可能是生理性黄疸？

张　明：嗯，黄疸有生理性的和病理性的。但他们出现的时间、病情进展、黄染程度都会不同。这个新生儿患者出生后不久就出现了黄疸，黄疸进展快，大小便均为黄色，属重度黄染。应做病理性黄疸处理。

爱丽丝：哦，我知道了。谢谢张医生。

Zhang Ming: Alice, did you go to see the patient of bed 15? What's she doing?

Alice: Yes, I did. The 15-bed patient's whole body and sclera jaundice disappeared a little, and the mean value of jaundice percutaneous was 49.59 μmol/L.

Zhang Ming：The effect is still OK. What about other auxiliary inspections?

Alice：The results of routine blood tests werealmost normal，with white blood cell 7. 98×10^9/L，hemoglobin 180 g/L，platelet 312×10^9/L，lymphocyte percentage 41. 9%，percentage of neutrophils 46. 9%. Doctor，I know that the jaundice can be physiological and pathological. Is this patient likely to be a physiological jaundice?

Zhang Ming：Well，Jaundicecan be physiological and pathological. However，the time they appear，the progress of the disease，and the degree of stained yellow will be different. The jaundice of this neonate appeared shortly after birth and the progressed rapidly with yellow urine and stool. It was so severely yellow stained that it should be treated as pathological jaundice.

Alice：Oh，I know. Thank you，Dr. Zhang.

【短文】

生词

序号	词语	词性	拼音	词义
1	满月	名	mǎnyuè	a baby's completion of its first month of life
2	浓度	名	nóngdù	concentration
3	自然	形	zìrán	natural

新生儿黄疸

医学上把未满月(出生 28 天)新生儿出现的黄疸，称为新生儿黄疸。新生儿黄疸是新生儿时期最常见的一种临床表现。主要是因为新生儿早期胆红素生成过多，肝发育不完善，胆红素代谢能力差，血中的胆红素浓度升高所导致的。有黄疸的新生儿常常表现为面部、四肢、身体皮肤，巩膜、黏膜呈浅黄色和深黄色。大约 60% 足月儿和 80% 的早产儿会出现黄疸。

大部分新生儿黄疸是新生儿发育过程中的一个正常生理现象。一般在出生后 2~3 天出现。多母乳喂养、多晒太阳有助于黄疸自然消退，不需要特殊处理。但如果新生儿在出生后 24 小时内出现黄疸，胆红素水平过高，就有可能损害神经系统，需要及时治疗。

新生儿出生后 1 周内，每天的胆红素水平都在上升，需要严密监测胆红素水平，预防严重的高胆红素血症。

Neonatal jaundice

In medicine，the jaundice that appears in newbornsless than one month（28 days after birth）is called neonatal jaundice. Neonatal jaundice is the most common clinical manifestation of the neonatal period. It is mainly because that the early neonatal has too much bilirubin in the blood，poor liver development and bilirubin metabolism capability，which leads to the build-up of bilirubin in the blood. Newborns with jaundice often show facial，limb，and body skin，and the sclera and mucous membranes are light yellow and dark yellow. About 60% of term infants and 80% of preterm infants have jaundice.

Most neonatal jaundice is a normal physiological phenomenon during neonatal development. It usually appears 2-3 days after birth. More breastfeeding and more sun exposure help the jaundice to subside naturally and does not require special treatment. However，if newborns develop jaundice within 24 hours of birth and the bilirubin levels are too high, they may damage the nervous system and require timely treatment.

Within one week after birth, the level of bilirubin rises everyday, and bilirubin levels need to be closely monitored to prevent severe hyperbilirubinemia.

【汉字知识】

部首"米"

部首"米"的意思为"米、粟米、谷物和其他植物去壳后的子实",一般出现在汉字的左侧。以"米"为部首的汉字大都跟米或者粮食有关。如"粒""精""粘""粉""糊"等。此类汉字多为形声结构,左侧的部首为形旁,右侧的部件为声旁,代表字音。

例如:粉——淀粉　花粉　药粉

　　　粘——粘贴　粘连

构词

——区　表示"人体某区域"。

例如:胸前区、胸后区、顶叶区、枕叶区、颞叶区、额叶区。

——窦　表示"人体某些器官或组织的内部凹陷的部分"。

例如:额窦、蝶窦、鼻窦、颌窦。

【练习】

一、选择听到的词语。

1. (　　) A. 纠住　　B. 秋树　　C. 抽搐　　D. 吃住
2. (　　) A. 环绕　　B. 饭少　　C. 繁琐　　D. 烦躁
3. (　　) A. 黄染　　B. 黄疸　　C. 花王　　D. 坏蛋
4. (　　) A. 成就　　B. 程度　　C. 陈醋　　D. 层浪
5. (　　) A. 吸引　　B. 集体　　C. 吸吮　　D. 聚会

二、根据听到的句子排列词语和短语。

1. 安排　15床　患者　从产科　昨晚　转来的　在

2. 生理性黄疸　黄疸　病理性黄疸　新生儿　可　分为　和

3. 肝　发育　不完善　胆红素　新生儿　能力　差　代谢　的

4. 生理现象　生理性黄疸　治疗　是　新生儿　的　不需要　正常　常常　特殊

三、根据拼音写汉字。

huángrǎn(　　　)　　　dǎnhóngsù(　　　)　　　huángda(　　　)

zhōngxìnglì xìbāo (　　　)　　bìnglǐxìng(　　　)　　mǎnyuè(　　　)

dàixiè(　　　)　　　　shēnglǐxìng(　　　)

四、选词填空。

黄疸　抽搐　进展　烦躁　重度

1. 一会儿,白鼠全身_____,眼睛发红,体温骤升。
2. 有_____的婴儿常常面部、四肢、身体皮肤和眼球呈黄色。
3. 最近几天,北京的天气质量出现_____污染。
4. 当你_____不安时,到公园或海边看看蓝色的大海,心情会很快好起来。
5. 近年来,心理治疗事业在我国已有了很大的_____,但仍存在不少问题。

五、完成下面的对话和句子。

（一）

张　明:是什么情况?

爱丽丝:出生后不久脸部皮肤出现_____,向_____。

张　明:大、小便什么颜色?

爱丽丝:_____。

张　明:皮测胆红素值是多少?

爱丽丝:_____。

（二）

1.新生儿黄疸是新生儿的_____发育不完善,_____代谢异常,血中的胆红素_____升高引起的一种疾病。

2.大约_____足月儿和_____早产儿会出现黄疸。

3.胆红素水平_____有可能损害神经系统。

4.新生儿出后_____,每天的胆红素水平都在上升,需要严密监测胆红素水平。

六、根据对话和短文内容回答问题。

1.15 床患者什么时间出生的?

2.15 床患者有什么症状?

3.治疗后,15 床患者经皮测黄疸均值是多少?

4.15 床患者的症状是生理性的还是病理性的?

5.黄疸是怎么引起的?

6.生理性黄疸需要特殊治疗吗?

七、根据课文内容补充病历信息。

姓名:_____　　　　性别:_____

年龄:_____　　　　就诊时间:_____

主诉:母孕38^{+4}周,生后_____天,皮肤黄染_____天。

现病史:母孕38^{+4}周,_____年_____月_____日在我院产科_____出生。出生时1分钟、5分钟_____评分均正常。生后当天开奶,_____有力。1 天前出现_____皮肤黄染,向_____、_____蔓延,伴_____大便及_____尿。皮肤黄染进行加重。

既往史:无。

辅助检查:_____249.66 μmol/L,277.02 μmol/L,225.72 μmol/L。

初步诊断:新生儿高胆红素血症

医生签名:张明

(改编自医院病历)

八、交际练习。

新生儿 A,出生后 12 小时出现皮肤轻微黄染,逐渐加深,遍布全身,反应弱、拒奶。父母心情紧张,带其前来医院就诊。医生 B 接诊,询问后得知 A 是足月儿,第 1 胎第 1 产,剖宫产,出生时 Apgar 评分:1 分钟 9 分,5 分钟 10 分。检查后发现其精神差、反应弱,但没有发热、抽搐等症状,大小便均为黄色。医生 B 初步诊断为新生儿高胆红素血症,要求其父母为其进一步检查及化验,并入院治疗。

根据以上情况编写对话并展示出来。

【补充医学词汇】

序号	词语	拼音	词义
1	母乳喂养	mǔrǔ wèiyǎng	breast feeding
2	人工喂养	réngōng wèiyǎng	bottle feeding
3	混合喂养	hùnhé wèiyǎng	mixed feeding
4	断奶	duàn nǎi	wean
5	新生儿	xīnshēng ér	newborn baby

（姜冬梅　张　帆）

儿科——手足口病

她的嘴里好像有疱疹

第二十二单元
生词、对话、短文

【学习目的】

1. 用汉语表述儿科的常见疾病和症状。
2. 学会用汉语问诊典型手足口病病例。
3. 学会用汉语表述儿科的主要特点。

【热身】

一、给下面的词语选择对应的字母。

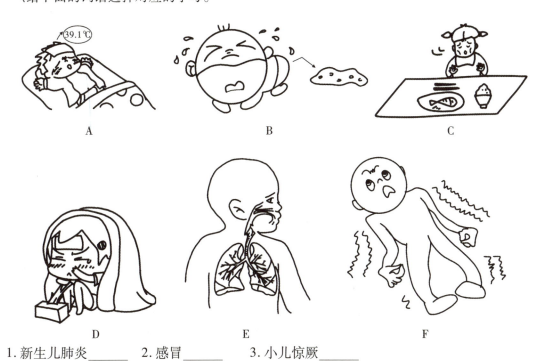

A   B   C

D   E   F

1. 新生儿肺炎_____ 2. 感冒_____ 3. 小儿惊厥_____

4. 小儿高热_____ 5. 水样便_____ 6. 纳差/食欲减退_____

二、根据英文写汉字。

1. hand-foot-and-mouth disease _____

2. febrile convulsion _____

3. neonatal pneumonia _____

4. attention deficit hyperactivity disorder(ADHD) _____

【会话】

场景简介：

人物：患者——王晓红(女,2 岁零 6 个月)

患者母亲——李晓雨(女,32 岁)

医生——张琪(女,42 岁)

实习医生——马克(男,21 岁,黎巴嫩人)

地点：儿科住院部 23 床

对话一

生词

序号	词语	词性	拼音	词义
1	详细	形/副	xiángxì	particular;in detail
2	疱疹	名	pàozhěn	herpes
3	疹子	名	zhěnzi	measles
4	水疱	名	shuǐpào	blister
5	温的	形	wēnde	warm

李晓雨：张医生,您好! 您找我吗?

张　琪：您是 23 床的家属吗?

李晓雨：是的。

张　琪：您请坐。我叫您来是因为想跟您详细了解一下您女儿的病情。方便我们进行进一步治疗。

李晓雨：好的。我一定配合。

张　琪：您女儿是什么时候不舒服的?

李晓雨：昨天晚上,她不想吃东西,还老流口水。到了半夜,她发热厉害,我们就赶紧上医院来了。

张　琪：当时还有别的症状吗?

李晓雨：有。她的嘴里好像有疱疹,手上也有不少红色的疹子和水疱。痛得她直哭。张医生,我的孩子到底怎么了? 严不严重啊? 看着她那么痛苦,我心里更痛啊。

张　琪：您放心,我们会尽力的。您先回去照顾孩子吧。只能让她吃一些温的流质食物。

Li Xiaoyu：Hello! Doctor Zhang. You wanted to see me?

Zhang Qi：Are you families of the 23rd bed?

Li Xiaoyu：Yes.

Zhang Qi：Please have a seat. I asked you to come because I wanted to know more about your daughter's illness. It is convenient for us to carry out further treatment.

Li Xiaoyu：OK. I will cooperate.

Zhang Qi：When was your daughter uncomfortable?

Li Xiaoyu：Last night，she didn't want to eat，and she was drooling. In the middle of the night，she had a fever，and we hurried to the hospital.

Zhang Qi：Were there any other symptoms？

Li Xiaoyu：Yes. Her mouth seemed to have some herpes，and she had a lot of red rashes and blisters on her hands. The pain made her cry. Doctor Zhang，what's wrong with my child？ Is that serious？ It hurt me more to watch her suffer.

Zhang Qi：You can rest assured that we will try our best. You go back to take care of the children first. Only let her eat some warm liquid food.

对话二

生词

序号	词语	词性	拼音	词义
1	惊厥	名	jīngjué	convulsions
2	红晕	名	hóngyùn	flush
3	口腔黏膜	名	kǒuqiāng niánmó	mucous membrane of mouth
4	发绀	名	fāgàn	cyanosis
5	手足口病	名	shǒuzúkǒubìng	hand-foot-and-mouth disease

张　琪：马克，23 床患者住院后的情况怎么样？

（张医生一边听马克描述病情，一边给 23 床做检查）

马　克：她还在发热，体温是 38.8 ℃。精神不太好，食欲也不好，伴有咳嗽、呕吐、惊厥和抽搐。手、脚、臀部出现散在的红色斑点和疱疹，疱疹周围有炎性红晕。舌头和口腔黏膜上也有散在疱疹。

张　琪：她的疱疹数量有变化吗？

马　克：比刚来的时候多了不少。

张　琪：血常规结果怎么样？

马　克：有炎症反映，白细胞总数升高。

张　琪：你看，她的口唇发绀。刚才我给她做了心肺听诊，心音有力，无杂音；双肺呼吸音浅促，有湿啰音。我怀疑是重症手足口病。

马　克：重症手足口病？

张　琪：走，我们去办公室讨论一下治疗方案。

Zhang Qi：Mark，how about 23ʳᵈ bed patient after admitted in hospital？

（Doctor Zhang listens to Mark's description，and checks 23ʳᵈ bed patient. ）

Mark：She's still running a fever，and her temperature is 38. 8 degree Celsius. She is quiet inactive，and her appetite also is bad，accompanied by coughing，vomiting，convulsions and tic. The hands，feet，and buttocks skin are scattered on red spots and herpes，and there is an inflammatory halo around herpes. The tongue and oral mucosa are also scattered on herpes.

Zhang Qi：Is there any change in the number of herpes？

Mark：It was a lot more than when I first came here.

Zhang Qi：How about the result of routine blood test？

Mark：There is an inflammatory response，and the total number of white cells is elevated.

Zhang Qi：Look，her lips are cyanotic. Just now I gave her cardiopulmonary auscultation，the heart sound is powerful, with no murmurs; Rapid breath sounds and rales were heard un two lungs. I suspect she got a severe hand-foot-mouth disease.

Mark: Severe hand-foot-mouth disease?

Zhang Qi: Let's go to the office and discuss the treatment plan.

【短文】

生词

序号	词语	词性	拼音	词义
1	全面	形	quánmiàn	comprehensive
2	身心	名	shēnxīn	mind and body
3	发育	名/动	fāyù	growth; grow
4	保健	名	bǎojiàn	health and fitness
5	范围	名	fànwéi	scope
6	脐	名	qí	funicle
7	随着	动	suízhe	along with
8	先天性	形	xiāntiānxìng	congenital
9	感染性	形	gǎnrǎnxìng	infectious

儿科

儿科是全面研究小儿时期身心发育、保健及疾病防治的综合医学科学。世界各国的儿科范围年龄各有不同，在中国从出生断脐到14周岁末为儿科范围。

儿科是一个非常复杂的医学科学。小儿在成长过程中，身体特征、生理生化正常值等都会随着年龄增长而发生变化。小儿疾病临床表现与成人差别比较大，其先天性、遗传性、感染性疾病多见。另外，小儿免疫力低下，调节和适应能力均差，短期内可有重大病情变化，且易发生各种并发症。所以，在给小儿患者诊断时，应注意考虑年龄因素，留心观察治疗效果。

Pediatrics

Paediatrics is a comprehensive medical science of comprehensively study in children's physical and mental development, health care and disease prevention and treatment. There are different age ranges of paediatrics around the world, it ranges from the birth to the end of 14 years in China.

Pediatrics is a very complicated medical science. As children grow up, their physical characteristics and normal values of physiological and biochemical change with age. The clinical manifestation of pediatric diseases is quite different from adults, congenital, hereditary and infectious diseases are more common. In addition, because children's immunity is low, and their adjustment and adaptation ability is poor, significant changes in the disease could occur in short term, and complications can occur easily. Therefore, in the diagnosis of pediatric patients, the age factor should be considered, meanwhile, therapeutic effect should be continuously observed.

【汉字知识】

部首"忄"

部首"忄"由"心"演变而来，一般出现在汉字的左侧。以"忄"为部首的汉字大都跟心理活动有关。

如"悸""惊""情"等。此类汉字多为形声结构,左侧的部首为形旁,右部的部件为声旁,代表字音。

例如:悸——心悸　发悸　悲悸

惊——惊人　惊吓　惊叫

构词

——酸　表示"关节或肌肉疲劳酸痛"。

例如:腰酸、腿酸、胳膊酸、臀大肌酸。

——组织　表示"在医学中,机体中构成器官的单位,是由形态和功能相同的细胞按一定方式结合而成的"。

例如:肌肉组织、神经组织、上皮组织、结缔组织。

【练习】

一、选择听到的词语。

1. (　　　) A. 氧气　　　　B. 详细　　　　C. 洋气　　　　D. 养鸡

2. (　　　) A. 溃疡　　　　B. 惊厥　　　　C. 抽搐　　　　D. 绞痛

3. (　　　) A. 水疱　　　　B. 水杯　　　　C. 水样　　　　D. 水桶

4. (　　　) A. 黏膜　　　　B. 模样　　　　C. 粘住　　　　D. 恋爱

5. (　　　) A. 手忙脚乱　B. 手下留情　C. 手足口病　D. 手足无措

二、根据听到的句子排列词语和短语。

1. 想　我　跟　了解　患者　一下　详细　病情　您　的

2. 不太　患者　咳嗽　好　呕吐　食欲　惊厥　精神　抽搐　和　都　伴有　和

3. 全面　保健　综合　儿科　是　身心发育　防治　研究　及　疾病　的　医学科学　小儿时期

4. 免疫力　小儿　能力　差　低下　和　调节　适应

三、根据拼音写汉字。

shēnxīn(　　　　　)　　　　kǒuqiāng niánmó(　　　　　)　　　zhěnzi(　　　　　)

xiāntiānxìng(　　　　　)　　　quánmiàn(　　　　　)　　　　shǒuzúkǒubìng(　　　　　)

shuǐpào(　　　　　)

四、选词填空。

详细　复杂　溃疡　流质食物　红晕　发绀

1. 儿科是一个非常_____的医学学科。

2. 疱疹周围有炎性_____。

3. 20 床的患者嘴里有_____,只能吃一些_____。

4. 马克,你去_____了解一下 20 床患者的情况。

5. 张老师,您看,20 床的患者口唇_____。

五、完成下面的对话和句子。

(一)

医生:您的女儿_____?

患者家属:昨天晚上开始不舒服的。食欲_____,老流_____,发热。

医生:还有别的症状吗?

患者家属:_____。

(二)

医生:20 床的患者现在的情况怎么样?

实习医生:她还在_____,体温是_____。精神和食欲也_____,伴有_____。手、脚、臀部出现_____,疱疹周围有_____。舌头和_____上也有散在疱疹。

医生:她的疱疹数量有变化吗?

实习医生:_____。

医生:她口唇颜色如何?

实习医生:_____。

医生:我怀疑是_____。

(三)

1. 小儿在成长过程中,_____、_____等都会随着_____增长而发生变化。

2. 小儿疾病临床表现与成人差别_____,其_____、_____、_____疾病多见。

3. 在给小儿患者诊断时,应注意考虑_____,留心观察_____。

六、根据对话和短文内容回答问题。

1. 李晓雨的女儿是什么时候不舒服的?

2. 张医生找患者的妈妈做什么?

3. 入院后 23 床患者的情况怎么样?

4. 张医生怀疑 23 床患者得了什么病?

5. 中国的儿科范围是什么?

6. 在给小儿患者诊断时要注意什么?

七、根据课文内容补充病历信息。

姓名:____王晓红____   性别:_____

年龄:_____   婚姻状况:_____否_____

职业:____无____   入院时间:2019 年 7 月 3 日 02:15

病史陈述者:患者母亲,李晓雨

主诉:(患者母亲代述)纳差,流口水,_____,口腔溃疡,手足皮肤有_____。

现病史:患者母亲述患者 1 天前_____差,流口水,口腔黏膜有少量_____,手部皮肤有少量_____,无瘙痒和疼痛,半夜发热不退到我院就诊。

既往史:患者既往体健,为第 1 胎第 1 产,足月顺产。无外伤、输血及手术史,无药物过敏史。预防接种按国际计划进行。

体格检查:T 37.9 ℃,R 24 次/分,P 110 次/分,BP 90/50 mmHg,W 14.15 kg。发育正常,营养中等;神志清醒。精神差,_____,伴有_____、呕吐、惊厥和_____。手、脚、臀部出现散在的红色斑点和疱疹,疱疹周围有_____。舌头和_____上也有散在疱疹。双肺呼吸音浅促,有_____。

辅助检查:血常规示 WBC 11.84×10^9/L,N 0.30,Hb 107 g/L,PLT 178×10^9/L。

入院诊断:_____

医生签名:张琪

(改编自医院病历)

八、交际练习。

　　患者母亲 A 带女儿就诊,患儿食欲差,流口水,发热,手部皮肤有红疹。儿科医生 B 和实习医生 C 为其做了病情询问和初步检查,并告知患者病情。

　　三人一组,分别扮演角色 A、B、C,组织一段 5 分钟左右的对话展现上文场景。

【补充医学词汇】

序号	词语	拼音	词义
1	疝气	shànqì	hernia
2	维生素 A 缺乏病	wéishēngsù A quēfá bìng	vitamin A deficiency

（张　勇）

第二十三单元

耳鼻喉科——分泌性中耳炎

第二十三单元
生词、对话、短文

您应该是得了分泌性中耳炎

【学习目的】

1. 学会用汉语表述耳朵的内部结构。
2. 学会用汉语问诊典型分泌性中耳炎病例。
3. 了解分泌性中耳炎的相关医学常识。

【热身】

一、给下面的词语选择对应的字母。

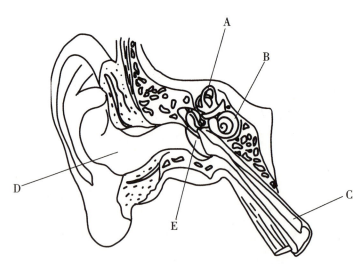

1. 耳蜗_____ 2. 咽鼓管_____ 3. 鼓膜_____ 4. 半规管_____ 5. 外耳道_____

二、根据拼音写汉字。

1. ěrwō_____

2. bànguīguǎn_____

3. wàiěrdào_____

4. nèiěr＿＿＿＿＿＿＿＿

5. gǔmó＿＿＿＿＿＿＿＿

6. zhōngěr＿＿＿＿＿＿＿＿

7. yāngǔguǎn＿＿＿＿＿＿＿＿

【会话】

场景简介：

人物：患者——张伟（男，23 岁）

　　　医生——陈丽（女，40 岁）

　　　实习医生——穆汗默德（男，20 岁，巴基斯坦人）

地点：耳鼻喉科门诊

对话一

生词

序号	词语	词性	拼音	词义
1	耳鸣	动	ěrmíng	tinnitus
2	密封	形	mìfēng	sealed
3	舱	名	cāng	cabin
4	似的	助	shìde	rather like
5	鼓膜	名	gǔmó	tympanic membrane
6	分泌物	名	fēnmìwù	secretions
7	流动	动	liúdòng	flow
8	响	动	xiǎng	loud
9	嘈杂	形	cáozá	noisy
10	中耳炎	名	zhōng'ěryán	otitis media
11	化脓性	形	huànóngxìng	purulent infection
12	黏液	名	niányè	mucus
13	诊疗室	名	zhěnliáoshì	clinic
14	鼓室腔	名	gǔshìqiāng	tympanic cavity
15	抽	动	chōu	take out
16	穿刺	动	chuāncì	puncture
17	分泌性	形	fēnmìxìng	secretory

穆汗默德：您哪里不舒服？

　张　伟：我的耳朵感觉堵住了，而且不停地耳鸣，已经 3 天了。听声音的时候，就好像自己被关在一个密封的小舱里似的。

穆罕默德：我先给您检查一下。

（检查后）

穆汗默德：您的鼓膜那里有一个液体的阴影,这说明鼓膜的后面有分泌物。

张　伟：我起床坐起来或者突然移动头部时,能听到有水在我耳朵里流动的声音。外面的声音听不清楚,但是当我自己说话的时候却有很响的嘈杂声。

穆汗默德：您应该是分泌性中耳炎。

张　伟：啊? 分泌性中耳炎?

穆汗默德：这是一种中耳的非化脓性感染,有黏液但是没有化脓。陈医生,您看……

陈　丽：张伟,我给您开个单子,您去交费然后到诊疗室把鼓室腔内的液体抽出来,要做鼓膜穿刺。我再给您开一些消炎药。

张　伟：好的,谢谢医生。

Muhammed:Where are you feeling uncomfortable?

Zhang Wei:I think my ears are blocked. and I have nonstop tinnitus for three days. when I listen to voice,it feels as if I am locked in a sealed cabin.

Muhamed:I'll check it for you first.

(After examination)

Muhammed:There is a liquid shadow in your tympanic membrane,which indicates that there are secretions at the back of the tympanic membrane.

Zhang Wei:When I get up and sit up or suddenly move my head,I can hear the sound of water flowing in my ears. Sound from outside is not heard clearly,but when I speak,I have a very loud noise.

Muhammed:You should have secretory otitis media.

Zhang Wei:Ah? Secretory otitis media?

Muhammed:This is a non purulent infection of the middle ear. It has mucus but no pus. Doctor Chen, you see…

Chen Li:Zhang Wei,I'll give you a list. You pay the bill and then go to the clinic to remove the fluid from the tympanic cavity and make tympanic membrane puncture. I'll give you some anti inflammatory drugs.

Zhang Wei:OK,thank you,doctor.

对话二

生词

序号	词语	词性	拼音	词义
1	发闷	动	fāmen	stuffy
2	积液	名	jīyè	effusion
3	恢复	动	huīfù	get well
4	咽鼓管吹张	动	yāngǔguǎn chuīzhāng	eustachian tube insufflation
5	鼓气	动	gǔqì	blow air
6	捏	动	niē	hold between fingers
7	保养	动	bǎoyǎng	maintenance
8	辛辣	形	xīnlà	spicy

（张伟做完鼓膜穿刺抽液,1个星期后前来复查）

陈　丽:张伟,最近还有耳鸣吗?

张　伟:断断续续会耳鸣,而且耳朵有点儿发闷。

陈　丽:消炎药一直在吃吗?

张　伟:一直在吃。

陈　丽:我再给您检查一下。

（检查后）

陈　丽:耳朵里还是有积液,不过不算太多。您上周做的穿刺,鼓膜还没有恢复,这个星期先药物加咽鼓管吹张保守治疗。

张　伟:好的。

陈　丽:我再给您开一些消炎药。回去以后,每天捏住鼻子鼓气,一次坚持5秒。刚开始鼓气的时候,耳朵可能会听不到声音,后面就会好一点儿了。

张　伟:我知道了,陈医生。

陈　丽:中耳炎恢复需要一个过程,所以平常一定要注意保养,避免感冒,不要吃辛辣食物。1个星期后再来复查。

张　伟:好,谢谢您。

（Zhang Wei finished the tympanic membrane aspiration and a week later,come to the clinic）

Chen Li:Zhang Wei,are there any tinnitus recently?

Zhang Wei:I have intermittent tinnitus,and my ears are a bit stuffy.

Chen Li:Should you eat anti-inflammatory drugs all the time?

Zhang Wei:Yes.

Chen Li:I'll check it for you again.

（After examination）

Chen Li:There are still some effusions in the ears,but not too much. The puncture made last week in the tympanic membrane have not been restored. This week,the medicine and the conservative treatment for eustachian tube firstly.

Zhang Wei:All right.

Chen Li:I'll give you some more anti-inflammatory drugs. After going back,hold your nose up every day and pump up for 5 seconds at a time. When you start to breathe,your ears may not hear your voice,and you will get better later.

Zhang Wei:I see,Dr. Chen.

Chen Li:Recovery of otitis media needs a process,so you must always pay attention to maintenance, avoid catching cold,and don't eat spicy food. Come back after a week for follow up.

Zhang Wei:OK,thank you.

【短文】

生词

序号	词语	词性	拼音	词义
1	中耳腔	名	zhōng'ěrqiāng	middle ear cavity
2	穿孔	动	chuānkǒng	perforation
3	聚集	动	jùjí	accumulate

序号	词语	词性	拼音	词义
4	蒙	动	méng	imprison
5	鼓	名	gǔ	drum
6	黏液促排剂	名	niányè cùpáijì	mucus promoting agents
7	腺样体	名	xiànyàngtǐ	adenoid
8	肥大	形	féidà	hypertrophy
9	抗	动	kàng	anti-
10	嚼	动	jiáo	chew
11	口香糖	名	kǒuxiāngtáng	chewing gum

分泌性中耳炎

大多数人都认为耳朵流脓了是中耳炎,那么耳朵不流脓是不是就不会得中耳炎了?错!只要是发生在鼓膜以内中耳腔的炎症,都叫中耳炎。如果鼓膜穿孔、流脓,是化脓性中耳炎。如果鼓膜完整,分泌物聚集在中耳腔,就是分泌性中耳炎。

分泌性中耳炎患者最先感觉到的就是耳闷和听力下降。自己讲话像被蒙在鼓里,声音很大却出不去,听别人讲话又听不清楚,需要别人大声说话或重复讲才能听清。

如果是炎症引起的分泌性中耳炎,可以用消炎药、黏液促排剂消炎、排出分泌物;如果是腺样体肥大引起的,要治疗腺样体;如果是肿瘤引起的,就要抗肿瘤治疗了。分泌性中耳炎患者要戒烟酒,注意保暖,避免感冒。如果能吹吹气球、嚼嚼口香糖、捏鼻子鼓鼓气,那最好不过了,这些动作能有效促进咽鼓管开放,有利于患者康复。

Secretory otitis media

Most people think that the pus in ear is otitis media, so if the ears does not have pus, will not get otitis media? Wrong! As long as it occurs in the middle ear cavity, inflammation in the tympanic membrane, it is called otitis media. If tympanic membrane perforation, pus, is suppurative otitis media. If the tympanic membrane is intact, secretions accumulate in the middle ear cavity, which is secretory otitis media.

The first sensation of secretory otitis media is ear stuffiness and hearing loss. Own speech is like being imprisoned in a drum. unable to get out loud sound. Other people's speech is also not clearly heard. Only heard when spoken in loud voice.

If it is the secretory otitis media caused by inflammation, we can use anti-inflammatory drugs, mucus promoting agents to eliminate inflammation and discharge secretions; if is caused by adenoid hypertrophy, we should treat adenoids; if is caused by the tumor, it is necessary to treat the tumor. Patients with secretory otitis media should give up smoking, keep warm and avoid catching cold. If you can blow up the balloon, chew chewing gum, and pinch the nose and drum, it is best. These actions can effectively promote the opening of the eustachian tube and help the patients to recover.

【汉字知识】

部首"耳"

部首"耳"的意思为"耳朵",一般出现在汉字的左侧或下部。以"耳"为部首的汉字大都跟耳朵有关。如"聋""聪""职""取""联"等。此类汉字多为形声结构,左侧或下部的部首为形旁,右部或上部的部件为声旁,代表字音。

　　例如:聪——失聪　聪明　聪慧

　　　　　取——听取　争取　获取

构词

发——表示"产生某种现象或发生某种情况"。

例如:发闷、发热、发冷、发炎、发火、发呆、发疯。

耳——表示"与耳朵有关的东西或者耳朵出现某种情况"。

例如:耳窝、耳道、耳鸣、耳聋、耳痛、耳闷。

【练习】

一、选择听到的词语。

1.(　　　)A.耳道　　　B.耳朵　　　C.耳痛　　　D.耳鸣

2.(　　　)A.分开　　　B.分离　　　C.分泌　　　D.分数

3.(　　　)A.改善　　　B.改正　　　C.改革　　　D.改错

4.(　　　)A.积液　　　B.技术　　　C.积累　　　D.液体

5.(　　　)A.穿衣　　　B.穿刺　　　C.穿过　　　D.穿越

二、根据听到的句子排列词语和短语。

1.自己　被　好像　关在　一个　小舱里　密封的　似的　听　时候　的　声音

2.一种　非化脓性　这是　感染　中耳的　但是　有　黏液　没有　化脓

3.中耳炎　患者　分泌性　感觉到的　最先　就是　和　听力　耳闷　下降

三、根据拼音写汉字。

ěrmíng (　　　　　)　　　　gǔmó (　　　　　)　　　　fēnmìwù (　　　　　)

gǔshìqiāng(　　　　)　　　kāngfù(　　　　)　　　　jīyè (　　　　)

zhōngěrqiāng (　　　　)　　kǒuxiāngtáng(　　　　　)　　xīnlà (　　　　)

四、选词填空。

　　　　　　　　　嚼嚼　鼓室腔　分泌性　鼓膜　咽鼓管

1.您应该是_____中耳炎。

2.要尽快把_____内的液体抽出来,要做鼓膜穿刺。

3.只要是发生在_____以内中耳腔的炎症,都叫中耳炎。

4.这个星期先药物加_____吹张保守治疗。

5.如果能吹吹气球、_____口香糖、捏鼻子鼓鼓气,那最好不过了。

五、完成下面的对话和句子。

(一)

张　伟:我听声音的时候,好像自己被关在一个_____的_____里似的。

穆罕默德:我先给您检查一下。

穆汗默德:您的_____那里有一个液体的_____,这说明鼓膜的后面有_____。

张　伟:外面的声音听不清楚,但是当我自己说话的时候却有很响的_____。

穆汗默德:您应该是_____。

张　伟:啊?分泌性中耳炎?

穆汗默德:这是一种中耳的_____,有_____但是没有_____。

（二）

1. 如果鼓膜完整,分泌物_____在中耳腔,就是分泌性中耳炎。

2. 自己讲话像被_____在_____里,声音很大却出不去。

3. 如果是_____引起的,就要_____肿瘤治疗了。

4. 如果能吹吹气球、嚼嚼_____、_____鼻子鼓鼓气,那最好不过了。

5. 这些动作能有效_____咽鼓管开放,有利于患者_____。

六、根据对话和短文内容回答问题。

1. 张伟哪里不舒服?

2. 张伟得了什么病?

3. 张伟复查的时候,陈丽怎么给张伟治疗的?

4. 张伟平时要注意什么?

5. 导致分泌性中耳炎的原因有哪些?

6. 怎么治疗分泌性中耳炎?

七、根据课文内容补充病历信息。

姓名:_____　　　性别:_____

年龄:_____　　　就诊时间:_____

主诉:因_____,听力_____前来就诊。

现病史:3 天前出现_____,听力下降,_____耳鸣。

既往史:平素体健。

体格检查:透过鼓膜可见_____。

辅助检查:无。

初步诊断:_____中耳炎

医生签名:陈丽

（改编自医院病历）

八、交际练习。

患者 A 因耳朵堵塞、耳鸣 3 天来到耳鼻喉门诊就诊,医生 B 接待了患者 A。医生 B 向患者 A 询问了症状。医生 B 给他先检查鼓膜、透过鼓膜见到液平面,医生 B 要给患者 A 进行鼓膜穿刺抽液的治疗。

两人一组,分别扮演角色 A、B,组织一段 3 分钟左右的对话展现上文场景。

【补充医学词汇】

序号	词语	拼音	词义
1	鼓窦	gǔdòu	tympanic antrum
2	半规管	bànguīguǎn	semicircular canal
3	声导体	shēng dǎotǐ	acoustic conductor
4	胶耳	jiāo'ěr	glue ear
5	中耳负压	zhōng'ěr fùyā	negative pressure in middle-ear

（张均智　代　晶）

第二十四单元

眼科（一）——继发性青光眼

她需要植入人工晶状体

第二十四单元
生词、对话、短文

【学习目的】

1. 学会用汉语表述人体眼球的基本结构。
2. 学会用汉语问诊典型青光眼病例。
3. 了解青光眼的相关医学知识。

【热身】

一、给下面的词语选择对应的字母。

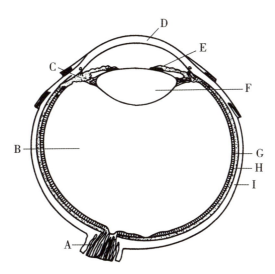

1. 玻璃体_____   2. 视神经_____   3. 视网膜_____

4. 脉络膜_____   5. 巩　膜_____   6. 角　膜_____

7. 晶状体_____   8. 虹　膜_____   9. 睫状体_____

二、根据拼音写汉字。

1. jiǎomó_____

2. tóngkǒng_____

3. shìwǎngmó_____

4. shìshénjīng_____

5. gǒngmó_____

6. jīngzhuàngtǐ_____

7. màiluòmó_____

8. bōlitǐ_____

9. hóngmó_____

【会话】

场景简介:
人物:患者——吴琼艳(女,57岁)
　　　患者家属——张文章(男,62岁)
　　　医生——陈雪(女,37岁)
　　　实习医生——马克(男,21岁,黎巴嫩人)
地点:眼科门诊,住院部

对话一

生词

序号	词语	词性	拼音	词义
1	木屑	名	mùxiè	sawdust
2	视力	名	shìlì	vision
3	眼压	名	yǎnyā	intraocular pressure
4	角膜	名	jiǎomó	cornea
5	透明	形	tòumíng	transparent
6	虹膜	名	hóngmó	iris
7	纹理	名	wénlǐ	texture
8	瞳孔	名	tóngkǒng	pupil
9	反射	动	fǎnshè	reflection
10	灵敏	形	língmǐn	sensitivity
11	晶状体	名	jīngzhuàngtǐ	lens
12	裂伤	名	lièshāng	laceration
13	迟钝	形	chídùn	slow
14	混浊	形	húnzhuó	turbid

(眼科门诊)
张文章:医生,我老婆的眼睛受伤了。
陈　雪:怎么受伤的?
张文章:她昨天上山砍木材的时候,一个木屑击伤了她的左眼。现在眼睛痛得睁不开了。
陈　雪:哦,我来给她检查一下。
张文章:好的。

陈 雪:(用一只手指在患者左眼前面晃动)您能看到前面有什么东西吗?

吴琼艳:你的手指。其他的看不清。

陈 雪:(对患者家属)她的左眼很红,还在流眼泪。您带她进来,我再给她检查一下。(检查后)右眼不错,视力 0.6,眼压 16.0 mmHg,角膜透明,虹膜纹理清楚,瞳孔大小约 3.0 mm×3.0 mm,对光反射灵敏,晶状体较透明。左眼不太好,眼压很高,28.0 mmHg,角膜 3:00~5:00 有裂伤,瞳孔大小约 4.5 mm×4.0 mm,对光反射迟钝,晶状体混浊。

张文章:严重吗?需不需要住院?

陈 雪:比较严重。我先给她做个手术再转到住院部去继续治疗。

(Ophthalmology clinic)

Zhang Wenzhang:Doctor,my wife's eye got hurt.

Chen Xue:How was it hurt?

Zhang Wenzhang:When she cut wood on the mountain yesterday,a piece of wood hit her left eye. Now her eye is so painful that it can't open up.

Chen Xue:Oh,I'll check it forher.

Zhang Wenzhang:Okay.

Chen Xue:(With one finger waving in front of the patient's left eye) Can you see what is in front of you?

Wu Qiongyan:Your finger. Nothing else.

Chen Xue:(To family members) Her left eye is red and is still tearing. Bring her in and let me give her another checkup. (After examination) The right eye is good,with visual acuity 0.6,intraocular pressure of 16.0 mmHg,cornea transparent,iris texture clear,pupil size about 3.0 mm×3.0 mm. The pupil is sensitive to light reflection,and the lens is transparent. But the left eye is not very good,with a high intraocular pressure of 28.0 mmHg,and a laceration at the place from 3:00 to 5:00 of the cornea. the pupil size is about 4.5 mm×4.0 mm,the light reflex is dull,and the lens is cloudy.

Zhang Wenzhang:Is itserious? Does she need to be hospitalized?

Chen Xue:It's quite serious. I will first give her an operation and go to the inpatient department for further treatment.

对话二

生词

序号	词语	词性	拼音	词义
1	骤降	动	zhòujiàng	sudden drop
2	畏光	形	wèiguāng	photophobia
3	角膜穿通伤	名	jiǎomó chuāntōngshāng	corneal penetrating injury
4	继发性青光眼	名	jìfāxìng qīngguāngyǎn	secondary glaucoma
5	外伤性白内障	名	wàishāngxìng báinèizhàng	traumatic cataract
6	摘除术	名	zhāichúshù	excision
7	植入	动	zhírù	implant

（住院部）

陈　雪：(对马克)5床的病历你看了没有？

马　克：看了，她砍树时左眼被木屑击伤了。门诊检查结果显示，她的左眼被击伤了。左眼视力骤降，仅有手动，伴畏光、流泪、眼红、眼痛等不适。初步诊断为左眼角膜穿通伤，左眼继发性青光眼，左眼外伤性白内障。

陈　雪：对，她已经在门诊做了左眼晶状体摘除术。你先给她复查下左眼。

（复查后）

马　克：陈医生，我检查完了。左眼视力0.05，眼压12 mmHg，瞳孔3.0 mm×3.0 mm，虹膜平坦，纹理清楚。

陈　雪：还不错。

马　克：陈医生，这个患者好像没有晶状体了？

陈　雪：对啊，她的晶状体已经被摘除了。没有晶状体，她就看不清了。

马　克：哦，那下一步还需要做什么处理？

陈　雪：还需要植入一个人工晶状体。

（Inpatient department）

Chen Xue：(To Mark) Did you read the medical records of bed No. 5?

Mark：Yes, I did. When she cut the tree, her left eye was hit by wood chips. Outpatient examination results showed that her left eye was wounded. The left eye has a sudden drop in vision, only manual, with tears of photophobia, eye redness, eye pain and other discomfort. The initial diagnosis was left corneal penetrating injury, secondary glaucoma in the left eye, and traumatic cataract in the left eye.

Chen Xue：Yes, she has done a left eye lens removal at the clinic. You first examine her left eye.

（After examination）

Mark：Dr. Chen, I checked it out. Left eyehas visual acuity 0.05 and intraocular pressure 12 mmHg, pupil is 3.0 mm×3.0 mm, iris is flat, texture is clear.

Chen Xue：Not bad.

Mark：Dr. Chen, this patient does not seem to have a lens?

Chen Xue：Yes, her lens has been removed. Without lens, she can not see well.

Mark：Oh, what elseshall we need to do next?

Chen Xue：It is necessary to implant an artificial lens.

【短文】

生词

序号	词语	词性	拼音	词义
1	致盲	动	zhìmáng	cause of blindness
2	推测	动	tuīcè	speculated
3	急剧	形	jíjù	sudden drop
4	下降	动	xiàjiàng	fall

青光眼

青光眼是一种以眼内压增高、视神经和视功能损害为主要症状的一组眼病,是我国当前主要致盲眼病之一。据世界卫生组织统计,2005 年青光眼是全球第二位致盲因素,仅次于白内障。因青光眼导致失明的人占全球盲人的 50%。据推测,2020 年我国原发性青光眼(不明原因的青光眼)患者可达到 1 120 万。

青光眼可分为急性青光眼和慢性青光眼。急性青光眼患者会突然出现眼睛痛,同时伴有头痛、恶心、呕吐、视力急剧下降等症状。但大多数慢性青光眼患者早期没有任何症状。有家族史、高度近视或远视,高眼压、高血压、高血糖、高年龄者较容易患青光眼。

现代社会,人们用电脑、手机的机会增多,年轻人患青光眼的概率也越来越大,医生建议人们定期去医院检查,预防青光眼。

Glaucoma

Glaucoma is a group of eye diseases whose main symptoms are increased intraocular pressure, optic nerve and visual function impairment, and is one of the major cause of blindness in China. According to statistics of the World Health Organization, in 2005 glaucoma was the second cause of blindness in the world, second only to cataracts. People who suffer from blindness due to glaucoma account for 50% of the global blindness. It is speculated that in China in 2020, the number of primary glaucoma patients (unexplained glaucoma) will reach 11. 2 million.

Glaucoma can be divided into acute glaucoma and chronic glaucoma. Acute glaucoma patients experience sudden eye pain, headaches, nausea, vomiting, and a sharp drop in vision. However, most patients with chronic glaucoma do not have any of these early symptoms. Family history, high myopia or hyperopia, high intraocular pressure, high blood pressure, high blood sugar, and older age are more likely to suffer from glaucoma.

In this modern society, people have more opportunities to use computers and mobile phones. Hence the probability that young people suffer from glaucoma is also increasing. Doctors advise people to go to hospitals regularly to check and prevent glaucoma.

【汉字知识】

部首"目"

部首"目"的意思为"眼睛",一般出现在汉字的左侧。以"目"为部首的汉字大都跟眼睛、视力有关。如"眼""睛""瞳"等。此类汉字多为形声结构,左侧的部首为形旁,右侧的部件为声旁,代表字音。

例如:眼——眼睛　眼睑　眼球
　　　盲——盲区　盲人　盲文

构词

——体　表示"某些人体器官"。
例如:玻璃体、脑垂体、扁桃体。
眼——表示"眼睛的不同组成部位"。
例如:眼球、眼睑、眼眶。

【练习】

一、选择听到的词语。

1.（　　　）A. 尿湿　　　B. 凉干　　　C. 裂伤　　　D. 捏伤

2.（　　　）A. 杂志　　　B. 切除　　　C. 猜出　　　D. 摘除

3.（　　　）A. 继发　　　B. 急切　　　C. 激发　　　D. 秩序

4.（　　　）A. 呼啸　　　B. 木屑　　　C. 木梢　　　D. 互相

5.（　　　）A. 膨胀　　　B. 盆腔　　　C. 膀胱　　　D. 盘子

二、根据听到的句子排列词语和短语。

1. 这边　您　住院部　需要　手术　先　在　做个　再　转到　去

2. 击伤　检查　左眼　结果　门诊　显示　她的　被

3. 致盲　青光眼　之一　是　我国　主要　原因

4. 伴有　突然　眼睛痛　同时　呕吐　急性青光眼　患者　会　视力急剧下降　出现　头痛　恶心　等　症状

三、根据拼音写汉字。

jīngzhuàngtǐ（　　　　　）　　　mùxiè（　　　　　）　　　yǎnyā（　　　　　）

tóngkǒng（　　　　　）　　　wèiguāng（　　　　　）　　　báinèizhàng（　　　　　）

zhìmáng（　　　　　）　　　tuīcè（　　　　　）　　　yùfáng（　　　　　）

四、选词填空。

骤降　畏光　摘除术　处理　致盲　推测　预防

1. 上午我先_____一些公事,下午再去你家玩吧。

2. 2月26日,海南的天气说变就变,气温_____至15 ℃以下。

3. 因为海拔高,紫外线照射强烈,西藏白内障_____发病率比其他地区高一些。

4. 据专家_____,2000年我国旅游人数将达5亿人次。

5. 我爷爷做完白内障_____,视力就恢复了。

6. 医学心理学研究疾病的诊断、治疗、护理、_____中的心理学问题。

7. 姑娘的视力逐渐下降,还出现了_____、流泪等症状。

五、完成下面的对话和句子。

（一）

患　者:哎哟,好痛啊!

医　生:_____?

患　者:我上山砍树时左眼被木屑击伤了。

医　生:_____。

患　者:严重吗? 需不需要住院?

医　生:_____。

（二）

1. _____是我国主要致盲原因之一。

2. 青光眼可分为_____和_____。

3. 有_____、高度近视或远视,高_____、高_____、高_____、高_____者都较容易患青光眼。

六、根据对话和短文内容回答问题。

1. 吴琼艳为什么来医院看病?

2. 医生初步诊断吴琼艳患了什么病?

3. 医生下一步打算给吴琼艳做什么处理?

4. 急性青光眼患者会有什么症状?

5. 什么样的人群较容易患青光眼?

七、根据课文内容补充病历信息。

门诊病历

姓名: **吴琼艳**   性别: _____

年龄: _____   婚姻状况: **已婚**

职业: **农民**   就诊时间:**2017 年 12 月 8 日**

主诉: _____ 被木材 _____ 视力下降伴胀痛 1 天。

现病史:患者 1 天前砍树时左眼被木击伤,视力下降,仅有手动,伴_____、_____、

眼红、眼痛等不适。

既往史:体健。

专科检查:

	右眼	左眼
视力		
眼压		
角膜		
瞳孔		
晶状体		

初步诊断: _____

医生签名: _____

(改编自医院病历)

八、交际练习。

患者 A,女,71 岁。10 小时前无明显原因出现右眼红、胀痛,伴视力剧降。右眼红痛逐渐加重,并伴头晕、恶心、呕吐,前来就诊。医生 B 为其检查,结果为眼压右眼 42 mmHg,左眼 17 mmHg,瞳孔呈竖椭圆形,4 mm×5 mm,对光反应消失,初步诊断为急性闭角型青光眼。医生 B 要求其立即住院治疗。

根据以上内容编写对话并展示出来。

【补充医学词汇】

序号	词语	拼音	词义
1	原发性青光眼	yuánfāxìng qīngguāngyǎn	primary glaucoma
2	继发性青光眼	jìfāxìng qīngguāngyǎn	secondary glaucoma
3	先天性青光眼	xiāntiānxìng qīngguāngyǎn	congenital glaucoma
4	闭角型青光眼	bìjiǎoxíng qīngguāngyǎn	angle-closure glaucoma
5	开角型青光眼	kāijiǎoxíng qīngguāngyǎn	open-angle glausoma
6	低眼压性青光眼	dīyǎnyāxìng qīngguāngyǎn	normal-tension glaucoma

（姜冬梅　金心怡）

第二十五单元

眼科(二)——老年性白内障

他的两只眼睛都看不清楚

第二十五单元
生词、对话、短文

【学习目的】

1. 学会用汉语表述皮质性白内障的 4 个分期。
2. 学会用汉语问诊典型老年性白内障病例。
3. 了解白内障的相关医学知识。

【热身】

一、给下面的词语选择对应的字母。

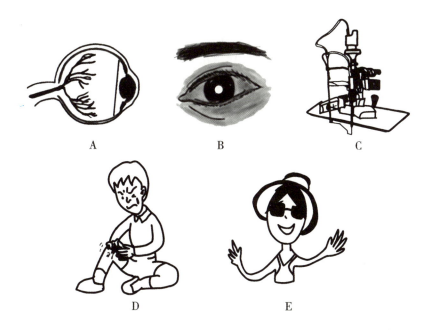

A   B   C

D   E

1. 日晒_____   2. 晶状体_____   3. 裂隙灯显微镜_____

4. 白内障_____   5. 外伤_____

二、根据英文写汉字。

1. incipient stage _____

2. immature stage _____

3. mature stage _____

4. hypermature stage _____

【会话】

场景简介:

人物:患者——吴朝阳(男,65 岁)

　　　医生——陈雪(女,37 岁)

　　　实习医生——穆汗默德(男,20 岁,巴基斯坦人)

地点:眼科住院部

对话一

生词

序号	词语	词性	拼音	词义
1	乳白色	名	rǔbáisè	milky
2	逐年	副	zhúnián	year by year
3	人工	名	réngōng	artificial

陈　雪:穆汗默德,你去给 9 床患者做个眼部检查。

穆汗默德:好的。

……

穆汗默德:陈医生,检查完了。9 床患者叫吴朝阳,男,65 岁。他的视力不好,右眼 0.2,左眼 0.02。双眼眼压正常,左眼是 12.0 mmHg,右眼是 13.0 mmHg。两只眼睛的巩膜都正常,无黄染。瞳孔大小正常,都是 3 mm×3 mm,对光反射也很灵敏。但两只眼睛的晶状体都呈乳白色,很混浊。

陈　雪:很好。他哪儿不舒服?

穆汗默德:他说看不清东西,感觉不舒服。没有别的不舒服。

陈　雪:这种情况有多久了?

穆汗默德:3 年了,视力逐年下降,2 个月前左眼有加重趋势。陈医生,他是不是患了白内障?

陈　雪:嗯,是老年性白内障。

穆汗默德:这种情况应该怎么处理?

陈　雪:最有效的办法是手术。就是先把病变的晶状体取出来,再植入人工晶状体。几分钟就能做完。

穆汗默德:知道了。

Chen Xue:Muhammad,you go to examine the eye of bed No.9 patient.

Muhammad:Okay.

…

Muhammad:Dr. Chen,check it out. The patient of bed No.9 is Wu Chaoyang,male,65 years old. His vision is not good,0.2 in his right eye and 0.02 in his left eye. The binocular intraocular pressure was normal,with the left eye being 12.0 mmHg,and the right 13.0 mmHg. Both eyes had normal sclera and no yellow stain. Both of the two pupils are normal-sized,3 mm×3 mm,and sensitive to light. However,the lenses of both eyes are milky white and very cloudy.

Chen Xue:Very good. Where is he uncomfortable?

Muhammad:He said he couldn't see anything and felt uncomfortable. No other discomfort.

Chen Xue:How long has he been like this?

Muhammad:For three years,vision has been declining year by year,and there has been an increase in the left eye two months ago. Dr. Chen,is he suffering from cataract?

Chen Xue:Well,it is senile cataract.

Muhammad:How to deal with this problem?

Chen Xue:The most effective method is surgery. It is to take out the diseased lens and implant the intraocular lens. It can be done in minutes.

Muhammad:I know.

对话二

生词

序号	词语	词性	拼音	词义
1	挡住	动	dǎngzhù	block
2	换	动	huàn	change
3	裂隙灯显微镜检查	名	lièxìdēng xiǎnwēijìng jiǎnchá	slit lamp microscope test
4	请示	动	qǐngshì	consult

穆汗默德:大叔,听说您的左眼上次做了白内障手术,现在感觉怎么样?

吴朝阳:比以前看得清楚多了,感觉很舒服。

穆汗默德:好啊。我先给您复查一下左眼。陈医生会给您安排右眼的手术。

吴朝阳:好的。

穆汗默德:请跟我来,我先测下您的眼压。嗯,右眼是 17 mmHg,左眼是 15 mmHg,都正常。请坐到这张椅子上来,我给您测下视力。先把右眼挡住,然后再换左眼。

(检查后)

穆汗默德:左眼视力是 1.0,右眼是 0.12。左眼视力恢复得很好,手术效果不错。我再给您做个裂隙灯显微镜检查。

吴朝阳:谢谢医生。什么时候可以帮我安排右眼的手术?

穆汗默德:我先请示下陈医生。

吴朝阳:好的。

Muhammad:Sir,I heard that your left eye had a cataract surgery done last time. How do you feel now?

Wu Chaoyang:I have seen more clearly than before and I feel very comfortable.

Muhammad:OK. I will first review your left eye. Dr. Chen will arrange your right eye surgery.

Wu Chaoyang:Yes.

Muhammad:Please come with me. I will measure your intraocular pressure first. Well,the right eye is 17 mmHg and the left eye is 15 mmHg,both are normal. Please sit down in this chair and I will measure your vision. Block your right eye first,then change to left.

（After inspection）

Muhammad：The left eye has a visual acuity of 1.0 and the right eye has an acuity of 0.12. Left visual acuity is restored very well and the operation was a success. I will give you a slit lamp microscope test.

Wu Chaoyang：Thank you, doctor. When will the surgery for my right eye be arranged？

Muhammad：Let me first consult Dr. Chen.

Wu Chaoyang：Okay.

【短文】

序号	词语	词性	拼音	词义
1	眼球	名	yǎnqiú	eyeball
2	凸面	名	tūmiàn	convex
3	镜头	名	jìngtóu	lens
4	屈光的	形	qūguāngde	refractive
5	会聚	动	huìjù	converge
6	外界	名	wàijiè	outside
7	紫外线	名	zǐwàixiàn	ultraviolet
8	全球	形	quánqiú	global
9	日晒	名	rìshài	exposure to the sun
10	发病率	名	fābìnglǜ	incidentce rate

白内障

人体眼球前部有一个双凸面透明的组织,就像照相机的镜头一样,叫作晶状体。晶状体有屈光作用,将光线会聚到视网膜上,帮助人们看清外界的物体。同时也能过滤部分紫外线,保护视网膜。

如果晶状体发生混浊,变成乳白色,光线不能正常通过晶状体,导致视力下降,看不清东西,我们把这种病变叫作白内障。

白内障是目前全球范围内第一大致盲眼病,与年龄、日晒、遗传、外伤等因素有关。白内障会导致视力下降、视物模糊。老年性白内障是其中最常见的一种。随着年龄的增长,白内障的发病率会上升。因年龄增长导致的白内障,也叫"年龄相关性白内障",有些患者在中年就出现了白内障。目前医学上治疗白内障最有效的方法是手术,就是把变混浊、不透明的晶状体取出来,换成人工晶状体,叫作人工晶状体植入术。

Cataract

There is a bi-convex transparent tissue, like a camera lens, in front of the human eye, called the lens. The lens has a refractive effect that collects light on the retina and helps people see things outside. At the same time it can also filter part of the UV hence protecting the retina.

If the lens becomes turbid and becomes milky white, the light does not pass through properly, it will result in decreased vision and inability to see anything. We call this lesion a cataract.

Cataract is the first cause of blindness in the world at present, which is related to factors such as age, sun exposure, heredity and trauma. Cataracts can cause vision loss and blurred vision. Age-related cataracts are the most common ones. The incidence of cataract increases with age. Cataracts caused by an increase of age are also called "age-related cataracts", and some patients even develop cataracts in the middle age. At present, the most effective method for treating cataracts in medicine is surgery. It is to remove the cloudy and opaque crystal and replace it with an artificial lens called intraocular lens implantation.

【汉字知识】

部首"艹"

部首"艹"意思为"植物",一般出现在汉字的顶部。以"艹"为部首的汉字大都跟植物有关。如"药""菜""菌"等。此类汉字多为形声结构,顶部的部首为形旁,底部的部件为声旁,代表字音。

例如:药——西药　中药　药丸
　　　菌——菌类　细菌　病菌

构词

——伤　表示"各种类型的创伤"。

例如:钝伤、挫伤、穿通伤、刀伤。

——腔　表示"人体中空的部分"。

例如:鼻腔、口腔、胸腔、腹腔。

【练习】

一、选择听到的词语。

1. (　　) A. 猪年　　　B. 去年　　　C. 逐年　　　D. 前年
2. (　　) A. 护栏　　　B. 负责　　　C. 复杂　　　D. 复查
3. (　　) A. 请示　　　B. 情绪　　　C. 轻视　　　D. 请吃
4. (　　) A. 并不　　　B. 病变　　　C. 兵变　　　D. 方便

二、根据听到的句子排列词语和短语。

1. 晶状体　病变的　取出来　人工晶状体　需要　先　把　再　植入

2. 前部　透明的　双凸面　晶状体　组织　人体　叫作　眼球　有　一个

3. 白内障　最常见的　白内障　老年性　是　一种

4. 有关　第一大　致盲　日晒　与　目前　遗传　白内障　是　全球范围内　眼病　年龄　外伤　等　因素

三、根据拼音写汉字。

rǔbáisè(　　　　)　　　huìjù(　　　　)　　　báinèizhàng(　　　　)

tūmiàn(　　　　)　　　qūguāngde(　　　　)　　　zǐwàixiàn(　　　　)

guòlǜ(　　　　)　　　fābìnglǜ(　　　　)

四、选词填空。

范围　逐年　会聚　挡住　过滤

1. 政府表示将从下个月开始在全国_____进行食品药品安全检查。
2. 我国居民中高血压患病率呈_____上升趋势。
3. 晶状体有屈光作用,将光线_____到视网膜上。
4. 通常情况下,人的鼻腔、肺等器官对尘埃有_____作用。
5. 前面的那栋高楼_____了我们的视线。

五、完成下面的对话和句子。

（一）

陈医生：你检查 9 床患者有什么异常？

穆汗默德：他的双眼晶状体_____。

陈医生：_____？

穆汗默德：双眼看不清东西。

陈医生：_____？

穆汗默德：3 年了。陈医生，他患的是什么病？

陈医生：_____。

穆汗默德：需要怎么处理？

陈医生：_____。

（二）

1. 晶状体有_____作用，将光线_____到视网膜上，也有过滤部分紫外线，保护_____的作用。

2. _____是最常见的一种白内障。

3. 目前医学上治疗白内障最有效的方法是_____。

4. 人工晶状体植入术就是把_____、_____的晶状体取出来，换成_____。

六、根据对话和短文内容回答问题。

1. 9 床患者哪儿不舒服？

2. 治疗白内障最有效的方法是什么？

3. 9 床患者手术后的视力恢复得怎么样？

4. 晶状体有什么作用？

5. 什么是人工晶状体植入术？

七、根据课文内容补充病历信息。

姓名：__吴朝阳__		性别：___男___
年龄：__65 岁__		婚姻状况：__已婚__
职业：_____		就诊时间：__2017 年 12 月 11 日__

主诉：双眼渐进性_____年余，左眼加重_____个月余。

现病史：患者于 3 年前无明显诱因双眼_____，呈渐进性发展，2 个月前左眼_____。

既往史：体健。

专科检查：

	右眼	左眼
视力		
眼压		
巩膜		
瞳孔		
晶状体		

初步诊断：_____

医生签名：陈雪

（改编自医院病历）

八、交际练习。

患者 A,男性,78 岁,因家人突然发现其左眼球表面有一白色不明物体,前来就诊。医生 B 询问其病情并为其检查,发现其左眼视力差,视野模糊,初步诊断为老年性白内障,要求其住院手术治疗。

根据以上内容编写对话并展示出来。

【补充医学词汇】

序号	词语	拼音	词义
1	先天性白内障	xiāntiānxìng báinèizhàng	congenital cataract
2	代谢性白内障	dàixièxìng báinèizhàng	metabolic cataract
3	并发性白内障	bìngfāxìng báinèizhàng	complicated cataract
4	外伤性白内障	wàishāngxìng báinèizhàng	traumatic cataract
5	辐射性白内障	fúshèxìng báinèizhàng	irradiation cataract
6	后发性白内障	hòufāxìng báinèizhàng	after-cataract

（姜冬梅　金心怡）

第二十六单元

中医科（一）——感冒

第二十六单元
生词、对话、短文

我感冒4天了

【学习目的】

1. 学会用汉语表述中医的4种诊断方法。
2. 学会用汉语在中医科问诊典型感冒病例。
3. 用汉语了解中医的诊断方法。

【热身】

一、给下面的词语选择对应的字母。

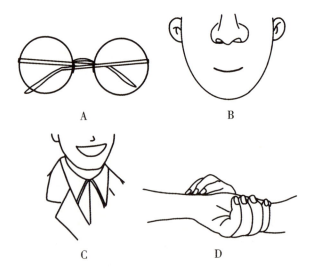

1. 望诊＿＿＿＿＿   2. 闻诊＿＿＿＿＿   3. 问诊＿＿＿＿＿   4. 切诊＿＿＿＿＿

二、连线题。

1. 望诊　　　　A. wèn zhěn

2. 切诊　　　　B. wàng zhěn

3. 问诊　　　　C. wén zhěn

4. 闻诊　　　　D. qiè zhěn

【会话】

> 场景简介：
>
> 人物：患者——李华(男,24 岁)
>
> 　　　医生——王桂香(女,45 岁)
>
> 　　　实习医生——韩汉(男,30 岁,韩国人)
>
> 地点：中医科门诊

对话一

生词

序号	词语	词性	拼音	词义
1	鼻涕	名	bítì	rhinorrhea
2	打喷嚏	动	dǎ pēntì	sneeze
3	鼻塞	名	bísè	nasal obstruction
4	蔬菜	名	shūcài	vegetables
5	舌头	名	shétou	tongue
6	舌苔	名	shétāi	coating on the tongue
7	把脉	动	bǎmài	feel the pulse
8	病毒	名	bìngdú	virus
9	外感	形	wàigǎn	exogenous
10	保持	动	bǎochí	maintain
11	畅通	形	chàngtōng	unobstructed
12	中药	名	zhōngyào	traditional Chinese herb

王桂香：请问您哪里不舒服？

李　华：我感冒 4 天了,一直不好。

王桂香：有什么症状呢？

李　华：我一直流鼻涕、打喷嚏,还有点咳嗽。

王桂香：那发热吗？

李　华：不发热。

王桂香：您的大便怎么样？

李　华：大便比较干,一两天 1 次。

王桂香：平时吃水果、蔬菜多吗？

李　华：不多,我不爱吃这些。

王桂香：这个习惯不太好。来,张开嘴,伸出舌头。（检查后）您的舌头有点红,舌苔有点厚。来,把手放这,给您把把脉。感冒一般是由病毒感染引起的常见外感疾病。可能会引发鼻塞、打喷嚏、头痛、咳嗽、发热等症状。平日注意预防,多喝水,多吃水果、蔬菜,保持大便畅通。给您开点中药。

李　华:好的,谢谢医生。

Wang Guixiang:What's the matter with you?

Li Hua:I have had a cold for four days.

Wang Guixiang:What's the symptom?

Li Hua:I have a sneezing and runny nose,and a little cough.

Wang Guixiang:Is there a fever?

Li Hua:No.

Wang Guixiang:How are your stool?

Li Hua:My stool is dry. The defecation happens once or twice a day.

Wang Guixiang:Do you usually eat more fruits and vegetables?

Li Hua:Not much,I don't like to eat these.

Wang Guixiang:This is not a good habit. Please open your mouth and show your tongue out. (After check) Your tongue is a little red. Here,put your hands here and I can feel you your pulse. Usually caused by viruses,cold is one of the common exogenous diseases. It may cause nasal congestion,sneezing,headaches,coughing,fever and other symptoms. Prevent from getting cold by drinking plenty of water,eating more fruits and vegetables,and keeping the feces smooth. I'll give you some Chinese medicine herb.

Li Hua:OK. Thank you,Doctor.

对话二

生词

序号	词语	词性	拼音	词义
1	复诊	名	fùzhěn	further consultation（with a doctor）
2	增强	动	zēngqiáng	strengthen;enhance
3	素质	名	sùzhì	quality
4	流通	动	liútōng	circulate

(复诊)

王桂香:韩汉,现在你当医生,试着问一下患者情况。

韩　汉:(对王桂香)好的,王医生。(对患者)请问您感冒好些了吗?

李　华:好多了,谢谢。基本上不咳嗽了,但是还流鼻涕。

韩　汉:大便怎么样?

李　华:不干了。

韩　汉:(对王桂香)患者感冒复诊,咳嗽得到缓解,但是还存在轻微流鼻涕的症状,大便正常。

王桂香:(对韩汉)好的,谢谢。(对患者)来,把舌头伸出来。(检查后)很好,舌头没有那么红了。来,把把脉。

李　华:王医生,我这几天喝水很多,也吃水果、蔬菜。一天一个苹果,医生远离我!

王桂香:非常好,您要坚持下去。另外,还要注意锻炼,增强身体素质。在季节气候变换的时候要注意预防感冒,尽量不要去人口密集的场所,室内注意空气流通。

李　华:谢谢医生。

王桂香:不客气。

（Further visit）

Wang Guixiang：Han Han，you are the doctor now. Please ask the patient.

Han Han：（To Wang Guixiang）Yes，Dr. Wang.（To the patient）Do you feel better?

Li Hua：Much better，thank you. Basically no cough，but I still have a runny nose.

Han Han：How about your stool?

Li Hua：Not dry anymore.

Han Han：（To Wang Guixiang）It's the second visit for the patients with cold. Her cough is relieved，but she still has a slight runny nose. Her stool is normal.

Wang Guixiang：（To Hanhan）OK，thank you.（To the patient）Show your tongue please. The tongue is not so red. Let me take your pulse.

Li Hua：Doctor Wang，I drunk a lot of water these days，also ate fruits and vegetables. An apple a day keeps the doctor away！

Wang Guixiang：Very good，you have to stick to it. You also have to enhance the physique by exercise. Prevent the disease when seasons or weather changes. Try not to go to a densely populated area. Make sure the room well ventilated.

Li Hua：OK. Thank you，Doctor.

Wang Guixiang：You're welcome.

【短文】

生词

序号	词语	词性	拼音	词义
1	望闻问切	动	wàng-wén-wèn-qiè	inspect，listen-smell，question and take the pulse
2	四诊合参	名	sìzhěn hécān	comprehensive analysis by the four examination methods
3	视觉	名	shìjué	sense of sight
4	神态	名	shéntài	expression；manner
5	排出物	名	páichūwù	discharge
6	听觉	名	tīngjué	sense of hearing
7	嗅觉	名	xiùjué	sense of smell
8	气味	名	qìwèi	smell；odour；flavour
9	触按	动	chuàn	touch and press
10	脉搏	名	màibó	pulse
11	肌肤	名	jīfū	skin
12	脉象	名	màixiàng	pulse condition
13	本质	名	běnzhì	essence

中医诊断方法

中医是一门研究人体生命、健康和疾病的科学。中医科医生通过"望闻问切"四诊合参的方法来检查病情，诊断疾病。"望诊"是医生用视觉观察患者的神态、舌头、皮肤及排出物等，了解患者的健康或疾病状态。"闻诊"是医生通过听觉听声音和通过嗅觉闻气味,观察患者的语言、咳嗽等声音的变化和排出物的气味变化。"问诊"是医生询问患者或家属,了解疾病的发生、发展、治疗经过、现在的症状等。"切诊"主要是医生用手触按患者的动脉脉搏和触按患者的肌肤、手足等部位,了解脉象变化及有关异常情况。在实际临床中,4 种诊断方法没有严格分开,往往在望的时候问,在问的时候闻等。中医科医生通过四诊合参的方法来综合收集病情,了解患者的身体状态,抓住疾病的本质,对病症作出正确判断。

Diagnostic method of traditional Chinese medicine

Traditional Chinese medicine is a scientific study of human life, health and disease. TCM doctors check and diagnosis the disease through the "inspect, listen-smell, question and take the pulse" four-diagnosis method. "Inspection" refers to that the doctor observes the patient's manner, tongue, skin and discharge, etc., in order to know the patient's health or disease status. "Listen-smell" refers to that the doctor listens sound and smells odour, in order to observe the changes in the voice of the patient's language, the sound of coughs, and the smell of odour. "Question" refers to that the doctor understands the occurrence of disease, development, treatment, and present symptoms by asking the patient or family members. "Pulse-taking" refers to that the doctor touches and feels the patient's artery pulse and touches the patient's skin, feet and other parts, in order to understand the pulse changes and related abnormalities. In clinical practice, four kinds of diagnostic methods are not separated strictly. Traditional Chinese medicine doctors often ask when inspecting, and smell when ask. Through the four-diagnosis method, traditional Chinese medicine doctors can obtain information about patient's condition, know the patient's body state, and grasp the nature of the disease to make correct judgments.

【汉字知识】

部首"身"
部首"身"的意思为"身体",一般出现在汉字的左侧。以"身"为部首的汉字多与身体有关。如"躺""躯""射"等。此类汉字多为形声结构,左侧的部首为形旁,右侧的部件为声旁,代表字音。

例如:躺——躺下　平躺　躺椅
　　　躯——躯体　躯干　身躯

构词
——觉　表示"感觉器官"。
例如:听觉、嗅觉、视觉。
——度　表示"程度"。
例如:高度、速度、强度。

【练习】
一、选择听到的词语。
1. (　　) A. 中国　　B. 中药　　C. 中医　　D. 终于
2. (　　) A. 感冒　　B. 发热　　C. 咳嗽　　D. 喷嚏
3. (　　) A. 听觉　　B. 嗅觉　　C. 触觉　　D. 味觉
4. (　　) A. 舌苔　　B. 手指　　C. 舌面　　D. 舌头
5. (　　) A. 卖力　　B. 脉搏　　C. 把脉　　D. 把握

二、根据听到的句子排列词语和短语。

1.大便　水　畅通　多喝　保持　多吃　蔬菜　水果

2.感冒　变换　季节　在　气候　要　注意　的　时候　预防

3.中医　健康　人体　研究　一门　是　科学　生命　疾病　的

4.望闻问切　中医　四诊合参　疾病　病情　的　方法　通过　来　诊断　检查

三、选词填空。

嗅觉　舌苔　增强　视觉　打喷嚏

1.我一直流鼻涕，＿＿＿＿＿＿＿，还有点咳嗽。

2.您的舌头有点红，＿＿＿＿＿＿＿有点厚。

3.要注意锻炼，＿＿＿＿＿＿＿身体素质。

4.“望诊”是医生用＿＿＿＿＿＿＿观察患者的神态、舌头、皮肤及排出物等，了解患者的健康或疾病状态。

5.“闻诊”是医生通过听觉听声音和通过＿＿＿＿＿＿＿闻气味，观察患者的语言、咳嗽等声音的变化和排出物的气味变化。

四、完成下面的对话和句子。

(一)

医生:感冒好些了吗?

患者:好多了。基本不打＿＿＿＿＿＿＿了,但是还会流＿＿＿＿＿＿＿。

医生:＿＿＿＿＿＿＿怎么样?

患者:不干了。

医生:要坚持喝水,吃蔬菜＿＿＿＿＿＿＿。注意＿＿＿＿＿＿＿,增强身体素质。

患者:好的,谢谢医生。

(二)

1.中医是一门研究人体＿＿＿＿＿＿＿、＿＿＿＿＿＿＿和＿＿＿＿＿＿＿的科学。

2.中医通过“＿＿＿＿＿＿＿”四诊合参的方法来检查病情,诊断疾病。

3.“问诊”是医生询问患者或＿＿＿＿＿＿＿,了解疾病的发生、发展、治疗经过、现在的＿＿＿＿＿＿＿等。

4.“切诊”主要是医生用手触按患者的＿＿＿＿＿＿＿脉搏和触按患者的肌肤、手足等部位,了解脉象变化及有关异常情况。

五、用下列词语造句。

1.保持

2.缓解

3.预防

六、根据对话和短文内容回答问题。

1.李华感冒有什么症状?

2.李华以前爱吃蔬菜吗?

3.复诊时李华感冒好些了吗?

4.中医诊断有哪4种方法?

5.医生问李华问题属于中医哪种诊断方法?

6.医生给李华把脉属于中医哪种诊断方法?

七、根据课文内容补充病历信息。

姓名:＿＿＿＿＿＿　　　性别:＿＿＿＿＿＿＿＿＿＿

年龄:＿＿＿＿＿＿　　　就诊时间:＿＿＿＿＿＿＿＿

主诉:患感冒＿＿＿＿＿＿天。

现病史:患者一直流＿＿＿,打＿＿＿,还有点＿＿＿,不发热。大便比较＿＿＿,一两天
1次。＿＿＿偏红、＿＿＿偏厚。

既往史:平素体健。

辅助检查:无。

初步诊断:感冒。

医生签名:王桂香

（改编自医院病历）

八、交际练习。

患者 A,男,24 岁,因感冒来到医院中医科,医生 B 和实习医生 C 接待了患者 A。患者 A 诉流鼻涕、打喷嚏、咳嗽,不发热,感冒 4 天了还是不好,所以前来医院就诊。医生 B 为其进行了"望闻问切"诊断病情,并给患者 A 开了中药。建议他多吃水果、蔬菜,多喝水,加强锻炼。

三人一组,分别扮演角色 A、B、C,组织一段 3 分钟左右的对话展现上文场景。

【补充医学词汇】

序号	词语	拼音	词义
1	辨证	biànzhèng	syndrome differentiation
2	五脏	wǔzàng	five internal organs
3	六腑	liùfǔ	the six hollow organs
4	经络	jīngluò	main and collateral channels
5	精	jīng	essence
6	气	qì	qi;vital energy
7	神	shén	spirit

（尹忠慧）

第二十七单元

中医科(二)——失眠

我晚上睡不着觉

第二十七单元
生词、对话、短文

【学习目的】

1. 学会用汉语表述中医的主要治疗方法。
2. 理解"阴阳"和"五行"的含义。
3. 学会用汉语表述中医科的常见疾病、主要症状和预防措施。

【热身】

一、给下面的词语选择对应的字母。

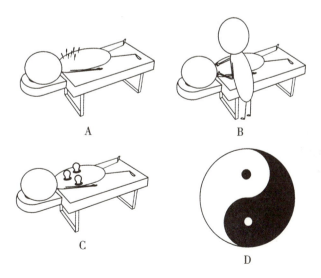

1. 阴阳_____   2. 针灸_____   3. 拔罐_____   4. 推拿_____

二、连线题。

1. 拔罐   A. tuīná

2. 针灸   B. báguàn

3. 推拿   C. zhēnjiǔ

4. 阴阳   D. yīnyáng

【会话】

> 场景简介：
> 人物：患者——张真（女,50 岁）
>   医生——王桂香（女,45 岁）
>   实习医生——韩汉（男,30 岁,韩国人）
> 地点：中医科门诊

对话一

生词

序号	词语	词性	拼音	词义
1	失眠	名	shīmián	insomnia；sleeplessness
2	降压药	名	jiàngyāyào	hypotensor
3	过度	形	guòdù	excessive
4	急躁	形	jízào	irritable；impatient
5	忧郁	形	yōuyù	gloomy
6	愤怒	形	fènnù	wrathful

（中医科门诊,患者张真因失眠前来就诊）

王桂香：请问您哪里不舒服？

张　真：我晚上睡不着觉,半夜经常醒好几次,醒了就睡不着。浑身没有力气,烦躁,也不愿意吃饭。

王桂香：大便怎么样？

张　真：还行,1 天 1 次,有点干。

王桂香：头痛吗？

张　真：嗯,睡不着的时候头痛。

王桂香：伸出舌头看看。（检查后）舌头有些红,舌苔偏少。手放这,我把把脉。血压是不是有点高？

张　真：是,我吃着降压药呢。

王桂香：平时几点睡觉？

张　真：一般在 12 点以后。

王桂香：您需要喝几副中药。以后要早点睡。平时不要有过度紧张、急躁、忧郁、愤怒等负面情绪,要保持精神舒畅。

张　真：好的,谢谢医生。

王桂香：不客气。

（At traditional Chinese medicine clinic,patient Zhang Zhen come to visit the doctor because of insomnia）

Wang Guixiang:Excuse me,what's the matter with you?

Zhang Zhen:I can't sleep at night. I always wake up several times in the middle of the night and it's hard to sleep again. I have no strength. I'm irritable,and not want to eat.

Wang Guixiang:How about your stool?

Zhang Zhen:once a day,a little dry.

Wang Guixiang:Do have a headache?

Zhang Zhen:Well,I have a headache when I can't sleep.

Wang Guixiang:Please show your tongue out. (After check) The tongue is a little red and the coating amount is less. Put your hands here,and I'll take your pulse. Is your blood pressure a little high?

Zhang Zhen:Yes,I'm eating antihypertensive drugs.

Wang Guixiang:What time do you usually go to bed?

Zhang Zhen:Usually after 12 o'clock.

Wang Guixiang:You have to take some Chinese medicine. Go to bed early. Generally,you should not have negative emotions of excessive tension,impatience,depression,anger and so on,and you have to keep happy.

Zhang Zhen:OK,thank you,doctor.

Wang Guixiang:You're welcome.

对话二

生词

序号	词语	词性	拼音	词义
1	伴随	动	bànsuí	accompany;follow
2	缺乏	动	quēfá	be short of;lack
3	精力	名	jīnglì	energy;vigour
4	舒畅	形	shūchàng	entirely free from worry
5	气血	名	qìxuè	vital energy and blood
6	阴阳	名	yīnyáng	(in Chinese philosophy,medicine, etc.) yin and yang,the two opposing principles in nature,the former feminine and negative,the latter masculine and positive
7	平衡	名	pínghéng	balance

(患者复诊。韩汉在带教医生王桂香的指导下对患者进行简单提问)

韩　汉:最近感觉怎么样?

张　真:晚上能睡一会儿了,但是醒了不容易再入睡。

韩　汉:还头痛吗? 吃饭怎么样?

张　真:不头痛了。最近吃饭有点胃口了。

韩　汉:大便怎么样?

张　真:正常,还是1天1次,没那么干了。

王桂香:好,您的情况我了解了,把舌头伸出来看看。(检查后)舌头不像以前那么红了。来,把手放这,我给您把把脉。

张　真：好。

王桂香：失眠常伴随头痛、健忘、缺乏精力、多梦等症状。您平时一定要加强锻炼，增强体质，晚餐要清淡，不要吃太饱，早点睡觉，养成良好的睡眠习惯。保持精神舒畅，血压还需要控制。再吃上几副中药，调整下气血阴阳平衡。

张　真：谢谢医生。

王桂香：不客气。

（Patient's second visit. Han Han asked the patient some simple questions under the guidance of doctor Wang Guixiang）

Han Han：How are you feeling lately?

Zhang Zhen：I can sleep for a while nowadays. But it is still not easy to sleep again after waking up.

Han Han：Do you have a headache? And how about your appetite?

Zhang Zhen：No. I have a little appetite for dinner nowadays.

Han Han：How about your stool?

Zhang Zhen：It's normal, once a day as usual. It's not dry.

Wang Guixiang：OK, I know your condition. Please show your tongue out. (After examination) The tongue is not as red as it used to be. Put your hands here, and I'll take your pulse.

Zhang Zhen：Alright.

Wang Guixiang：Insomnia is often accompanied by headaches, forgetfulness, energy lacking, more dreams and other symptoms. You must strengthen exercise to enhance physique. The dinner should be light. Don't eat too full, and go to bed early. Try to develop a good sleep habit. Keep your mind relaxed. Your blood pressure still needs to be controlled. Then eat a few pairs of traditional Chinese herb, and adjust the balance of qi, blood, yin and yang.

Zhang Zhen：OK. Thank you, doctor.

Wang Guixiang：You're welcome.

【短文】

生词

序号	词语	词性	拼音	词义
1	五行	名	wǔxíng	the five elements (metal, wood, water, fire and earth, held by the ancients to compose the physical universe and later used in traditional Chinese medicine to explain various physiological and pathological phenomena)
2	针灸	名	zhēnjiǔ	acupuncture and moxibustion
3	拔罐	名	báguàn	cupping
4	古代	形	gǔdài	ancient
5	哲学	名	zhéxué	philosophy
6	范畴	名	fànchóu	category
7	对立	动	duìlì	oppose
8	依赖	动	yīlài	rely on

序号	词语	词性	拼音	词义
9	湿润	形	shīrùn	moist
10	物质	名	wùzhì	material
11	方式	名	fāngshì	way;pattern
12	寻找	动	xúnzhǎo	seek;look for
13	探索	动	tànsuǒ	explore;probe
14	宇宙	名	yǔzhòu	universe;cosmos
15	颈椎病	名	jǐngzhuībìng	cervical spondylosis
16	脾胃病	名	píwèibìng	spleen and stomach diseases

中医

中医以阴阳、五行作为基础,运用中药、针灸、推拿、拔罐等多种治疗方法,使人体达到阴阳平衡,保证身体健康。

阴阳和五行都是中国古代哲学的范畴。在自然界中几乎所有的事物和现象都有阴阳两个方面,阴和阳相互对立又相互依赖。凡是运动的、向上的、干燥的都属阳;比较静的、下降的、湿润的属阴。如头属阳,脚属阴;气属阳,血属阴。五行,指金、木、水、火、土这5种物质及其运动方式。中国古代人民用五行的关系来寻找各种事物和现象的发生、发展、变化的规律,来认识世界、解释世界并探索宇宙变化等。人体中肝属木、心属火、脾属土、肺属金、肾属水。

中医可以设立内科、外科、妇科、儿科、眼科、耳鼻喉科、皮肤科等,对颈椎病、高血压、糖尿病、脾胃病、冠心病、感冒、失眠症等疾病都有很好的治疗效果。

Traditional Chinese medicine

Based on yin and yang and five elements, traditional Chinese medicine doctors use treating methods such as traditional Chinese herb, acupuncture, massage and cupping to ensure the human body balance between yin and yang for a good health.

Yin and yang and five elements belong to the categories of ancient Chinese philosophy. In nature, almost all things and phenomena have two aspects of yin and yang. They are two opposing and relying principles in nature. All moving, upward and dry objects belong to yang; All relatively static, falling, moist objects belong to yin. For example, the head belongs to Yang, but the foot belongs to yin; the qi is Yang, but the blood is yin. Five elements, refers to five kinds of substances metal, wood, water, fire and earth, and their movement. The ancient Chinese people used the relationship of five elements to find the law of occurrence, development and change of various things and phenomena, in order to understand the world, explain the world and explore the change of the universe. In the human body, the liver belongs to the wood, the heart belongs to the fire, the spleen belongs to the soil, the lung belongs to the gold and the kidney belongs to water.

Traditional Chinese medicine department can set up internal medicine, surgery, gynecology, pediatrics, ophthalmology, otolaryngology, dermatology and so on. Traditional Chinese medicine applys good therapeutic effect on cervical spondylosis, hypertension, diabetes, spleen and stomach disease, coronary heart disease, colds, insomnia and other diseases.

【汉字知识】

部首"扌"

部首"扌"的意思为"手",一般出现在汉字的左侧。以"扌"为部首的汉字多与手有关,如"把""打""搬"等。此类汉字多为形声结构,左侧的部首为形旁,右侧的部件为声旁,代表字音。

例如:打——打架　打扫　打针
　　　搬——搬家　搬迁　搬运

构词

——腹　表示"腹部"。

例如:上腹、下腹、左下腹。

——液　表示"液体"。

例如:体液、细胞液。

【练习】

一、选择听到的词语。

1. (　　　) A. 阴阳　　B. 五行　　C. 流行　　D. 进行

2. (　　　) A. 针灸　　B. 推拿　　C. 中药　　D. 拔罐

3. (　　　) A. 水平　　B. 平衡　　C. 平时　　D. 公平

4. (　　　) A. 金　　　B. 木　　　C. 水　　　D. 土

5. (　　　) A. 高血压　B. 糖尿病　C. 颈椎病　D. 脾胃病

二、根据听到的句子排列词语和短语。

1. 不要　紧张　急躁　忧郁　愤怒　等　保持　平时　有　负面情绪　精神舒畅　要　过度

2. 多梦　症状　失眠　头痛　常　伴随　健忘　缺乏　精力　等

3. 中国　阴阳　范畴　和　都是　五行　的　古代　哲学

4. 指　金　方式　火　土　水　这　5种　木　物质　五行　及其　运动

三、选词填空。

颈椎病　五行　古代　对立　湿润

1. 再吃上几副中药,调整下气血阴阳_____。

2. 阴阳和五行都是中国_____哲学的范畴。

3. 阴和阳相互_____又相互依赖。

4. 比较静的、下降的、_____的属阴。

5. 中医对_____、高血压、糖尿病等疾病都有很好的治疗效果。

四、完成下面的对话和句子。

(一)

医生:还头痛吗? 吃饭怎么样?

患者:不_____了,吃饭有点_____了。

医生:平时一定要加强_____,增强_____,晚餐要清淡,不要吃太饱,早点睡觉,养成良好的睡眠习惯。

患者:好的,谢谢医生。

(二)

1. 中医以阴阳、五行作为基础,运用＿＿＿＿＿＿＿、＿＿＿＿＿＿＿、＿＿＿＿＿＿＿、＿＿＿＿＿＿＿等多种治疗方法,使人体达到阴阳平衡,保证身体健康。

2. 凡是运动的、向上的、干燥的都属＿＿＿＿＿＿＿。

3. 比较静的、下降的、湿润的属＿＿＿＿＿＿＿。

4. ＿＿＿＿＿＿＿,指金、木、水、火、土这 5 种物质及其运动方式。

5. 中医对颈椎病、＿＿＿＿＿＿＿、糖尿病、脾胃病、感冒、失眠症等疾病都有很好的治疗效果。

五、用下列词语造句。

1. 失眠

2. 缺乏

3. 探索

六、根据对话和短文内容回答问题。

1. 张真血压高吗?

2. 张真晚上一般几点睡觉?

3. 复诊时张真吃饭怎么样?

4. 中医的主要治疗方法有哪些?

5. "五行"指哪 5 种物质及运动方式?

6. 中医科的常见疾病主要有哪些?

七、根据课文内容补充病历信息。

姓名:＿＿＿＿＿＿＿　　　　性别:＿＿＿＿＿＿＿

年龄:＿＿＿＿＿＿＿　　　　就诊时间:＿＿＿＿＿＿＿

主诉:失眠 1 个月。

现病史:患者晚上入睡＿＿＿＿＿＿＿,半夜易＿＿＿＿＿＿＿,醒后再睡困难。倦怠乏力,情绪＿＿＿＿＿＿＿,吃饭没有胃口。大便比较＿＿＿＿＿＿＿,＿＿＿＿＿＿＿偏红,＿＿＿＿＿＿＿偏少。

既往史:有＿＿＿＿＿＿＿病史。

辅助检查:无。

初步诊断:失眠

医生签名:王桂香

(改编自医院病历)

八、交际练习。

患者 A,女,50 岁,因患失眠症来到医院中医科,医生 B 和实习医生 C 接待了患者 A。患者 A 自述晚上睡不着,容易醒,醒后难以入睡;头痛,浑身无力,不愿意吃饭。医生 B 通过"望闻问切"为其诊断病情,并给患者 A 开了中药。建议她加强锻炼,晚餐要清淡,不要吃太饱,早点睡觉,保持精神舒畅。

三人一组,分别扮演角色 A、B、C,组织一段 3 分钟左右的对话展现上文场景。

【补充医学词汇】

序号	词语	拼音	词义
1	治未病	zhì wèi bìng	preventive treatment of disease
2	养生	yǎngshēng	keep in good health
3	伤寒	shānghán	typhia
4	虚	xū	asthenia
5	实	shí	sthenia
6	津液	jīnyè	body fluid

（尹忠慧）

皮肤科——皮肤过敏、带状疱疹

可能是化妆品过敏引起的皮疹

第二十八单元
生词、对话、短文

【学习目的】

1.用汉语表述皮肤的组成结构。

2.学会用汉语问诊典型皮肤过敏、带状疱疹病例。

3.学会用汉语表述皮肤科的常见疾病、主要症状、体征、常规检查和预防措施。

【热身】

一、给下面的词语选择对应的字母。

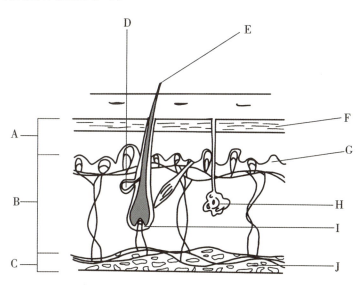

1.毛发_____   2.毛囊_____   3.皮脂腺_____   4.汗腺_____   5.表皮_____

6.真皮_____   7.角质层_____   8.皮下组织_____   9.真皮乳头_____   10.脂肪细胞_____

二、判断以下各题的说法是否正确,正确的打"√",错误的打"×"。

1.皮肤覆盖人体全身表面。   (　　　)

2.肺是人体面积最大的器官。 （　　　）

3.皮肤由表皮、真皮和皮下组织构成,并含有附属器官(毛、汗腺、皮脂腺、指甲等)及血管、淋巴管、神经和肌肉等。 （　　　）

4.皮肤的主要功能是排汗、调节体温、感知压力等,但不能隔离有害物质、保护身体。 （　　　）

5.正常皮肤表面 pH 值(氢离子浓度指数 Hydrogen ion concentration)为 5.0~7.0,呈弱酸性。

（　　　）

【会话】

对话一

场景简介:
人物:患者——李小妹(女,22 岁)
　　　医生——王魏娜(女,37 岁)
地点:皮肤科门诊

生词

序号	词语	词性	拼音	词义
1	疙瘩	名	gēda	pimple;knot
2	痒	形	yǎng	itching
3	变应原	名	biànyìngyuán	allergen
4	式	名	shì	type;style;mode
5	花粉	名	huāfěn	pollen
6	粉尘	名	fěnchén	dust
7	皮屑	名	píxiè	scuff;dander
8	链霉素	名	liànméisù	streptomycin
9	自身组织抗原	名	zìshēn zǔzhī kàngyuán	self tissue antigens

王魏娜:请坐,您有什么不舒服的?

李小妹:医生,我身上起了很多小疙瘩,又红又痒。

王魏娜:我看看……哦,我怀疑是皮肤过敏了。您以前有过敏史吗?

李小妹:我吃太多海鲜会过敏,但是我这几天都没有吃过海鲜或者高蛋白的食物。

王魏娜:那你想一想,最近有没有吃过或者接触过什么特别的东西?

李小妹:没有啊。

王魏娜:造成皮肤过敏的变应原有很多种,一般有吸入式变应原,如花粉、粉尘、动物皮屑等;食入式变应原,如海鲜、药物、部分水果等;接触式变应原,如紫外线、化妆品等;注射式变应原,如青霉素、链霉素等;有时候精神太紧张也会引起自身组织抗原。您好好回想一下,有没有这些情况?

李小妹:哦,我想起来了,昨天我的妈妈给我买了一盒新的面膜,昨天晚上睡觉前我敷过面膜。

王魏娜:那可能是化妆品过敏引起的皮疹,您不要再用那个面膜了。我给您开点儿抗过敏的药,记住多喝水。1 个星期左右就会好的。

李小妹:好的。谢谢医生。请问,会留下瘢痕吗?

王魏娜:不用太担心,这个色素沉着可能性不大。但您不要去抓破它。

李小妹:好的,谢谢。

Wang Weina：please sit down. What's the matter with you?

Li Xiaomei：Doctor, I have a lot of small pimples, they are red and itchy.

Wang Weina：Let me see…Oh, I suspect this is skin allergy. Have you had any allergies before?

Li Xiaomei：I'm allergic to too much seafood, but I haven't eaten seafood or high-protein food these days.

Wang Weina：So you think about it, have you eaten or touched anything special recently?

Li Xiaomei：No.

Wang Weina：There are many kinds of allergens that can cause skin allergies, and the general allergens include inhaled allergens, such as pollen, dust, and animal dander. Ingestive allergens, such as seafood, medicine, some fruits. Contactive allergens, such as UV, cosmetics. Injected allergens, such as penicillin, streptomycin. Sometimes too much stress can cause self tissue antigens. Please think these well, do you have any situation above?

Li Xiaomei：Oh, I remember. Yesterday my mother bought me a new pack of facial masks. I used the mask before I went to bed last night.

Wang Weina：That may be the allergic rash caused by the mask, you do not use that facial masks again. I'll give you some anti-allergy medicine and remember to drink plenty of water. It'll be all right in a week.

Li Xiaomei：OK. Thank you, doctor. Excuse me, will it leave a scar?

Wang Weina：Don't worry too much. This pigmentation is unlikely. But you don't scratch them.

Li Xiaomei：OK, thanks.

对话二

场景简介：

人物：医生——林军（男，40 岁）

　　　实习医生——哈桑（男，20 岁，印度人）

地点：皮肤科住院部医生办公室

生词

序号	词语	词性	拼音	词义
1	黄豆	名	huángdòu	soybean
2	丘疹	名	qiūzhěn	papula
3	疱壁	名	pàobì	blister wall
4	澄清	形	chéngqīng	clear
5	皮损（皮肤损伤）	名	písǔn（pífū sǔnshāng）	skin injury
6	排列	动	páiliè	to arrange
7	灼痛感	名	zhuótònggǎn	burning sensation；burning pain

林　军：哈桑，你说一下 17 床的情况吧。

哈　桑：林老师，我仔细看过这个患者的病历了。17 床患者是昨天从内科转过来的。刘美艳，女，37 岁，有胆囊结石病史，无过敏史。因最近比较劳累，感觉腰背、腹部疼痛到医院检查，内科初步诊断是胆囊炎，但用药后病情没有好转。昨天患者发现腰背部出现一些黄豆大小的红色丘疹，转到皮肤科来了。

林　军：哟，不错啊，了解挺详细的。那我再考考你，你觉得17床患者得了什么病？

哈　桑：我昨天下午和今天早上都去看过这个患者，一直处于低热状况，体温37.8 ℃。右腰背部的丘疹明显增多，而且部分已经发展成水疱，疱壁紧张发亮，疱液澄清，周围有红晕，皮损沿某一周围神经呈带状排列。患者还告诉我，这些水疱有灼痛感。所以，我初步诊断应该是带状疱疹。

林　军：刚才我也去看过这个患者了，我的诊断和你一样，看来你最近进步不少啊。

哈　桑：谢谢老师，这都是因为我有一位好老师。哈哈……

Lin Jun：Hassan，tell me about the 17th bed patient.

Hassan：Teacher Lin，I've studied the patient's medical records carefully. The patient was transferred from the internal medicine department yesterday. Liu Meiyan，female，37 years old，has a history of gallbladder stones，no history of allergies. Due to the recent fatigue，She felt painful in the back，waist and abdominal，so she came to the hospital. The initial diagnosis of the internal medicine department is cholecystitis，but the condition did not improve after the medication. Yesterday，the patient found some of the red papules with the size of soybean on her back and waist，and transferred to the dermatology department.

Lin Jun：Oh，you did a good job. It's very detailed. I'll test you again. What do you think of the 17th bed patients？

Hassan：I went to see the patient yesterday afternoon and this morning，and she was in a low fever，with a temperature of 37.8 ℃. The papules on the right side of her back were significantly increased，and some of papules had developed into vesicles，the walls of the vesicles are bright and tense，the vesicles were clear，and there was a red halo around vesicles，and the skin lesions were arranged in a band along a peripheral nerve. The patient also told me that these blisters had a burning sensation. So，my initial diagnosis was herpes zoster.

Lin Jun：I went to see this patient just now. My diagnosis is the same as yours. I think you've made a lot of progress recently.

Hassan：Thank you，teacher. It's all because I have a good teacher. Ha ha…

【短文】

生词

序号	词语	词性	拼音	词义
1	水痘	名	shuǐdòu	chicken pox
2	抵抗力	名	dǐkànglì	immunity
3	繁殖	动	fánzhí	to breed；to grown
4	神经纤维	名	shénjīng xiānwéi	nerve fiber
5	受	动	shòu	to accept；to suffer
6	侵犯	名/动	qīnfàn	invasion；to violate；to invade

带状疱疹

带状疱疹是由水痘-带状疱疹病毒引起的急性感染性皮肤病。因儿童对此病毒无免疫力，感染该病毒后会产生水痘。成人感染该病毒后会产生带状疱疹，部分患者被感染后成为带病毒者而不发生症状，当抵抗力低下或劳累、感染、感冒时，病毒可再次生长繁殖，并沿神经纤维移至皮肤，使受侵犯的神经和皮肤产生强烈的炎症。

带状疱疹的一般症状为乏力、低热,患处出现米粒至黄豆大小的丘疹,之后迅速发展成为水疱,疱壁紧张发亮,疱液澄清,周围有红晕,皮损沿某一周围神经呈带状排列。病程一般 2～3 周,本病愈后可获得较持久的免疫,故一般不会再发。

Herpes zoster

Herpes zoster is an acute infectious skin disease caused by varicella zoster virus. Because children have no immunity to this virus, the virus will cause chicken pox. Adults will produce herpes zoster after the virus infection. Some patients become viral carrier after infected with the virus without symptoms. When they are in low resistance, overworked, infected, or caught cold, the virus can grow again, along the nerve fibers to the skin, makes the infringement of nerve and skin cause intense inflammation.

There are some general symptoms of herpes zoster, such as fatigue, a low grade fever, pimples size of rice or soybean in affected area, and soon become vesicles, vesicles wall is tense, vesicles fluid is clear, and there was a red halo around vesicles. Lesions zonation arranged along the peripheral nerve. The duration of the disease is usually 2–3 weeks. After recovery, the patient can obtain a persistent immunity, so it is usually will not happen again.

【汉字知识】

部首"气"

部首"气"字头的意思为"气体",一般出现在汉字的右上侧。以"气"为部首的汉字多与气体有关,如"氢""氯""氧""氮""氨""氙"等。此类汉字多为半包围结构,右上侧的部首为形旁,内部的部件为声旁,代表字音。

例如:氧——氧气　氧化　臭氧

　　　氮——氮气　氮肥　固氮

构词

——素　表示"在医学中该结构常表示构成物质的基本成分,即元素"。

例如:尿素、毒素、氯霉素、青霉素、红霉素、链霉素。

——品　表示"物品,物件"。

例如:食品、学习用品、药品、商品、化妆品。

【练习】

一、选择听到的词语。

1. (　　　)A. 表皮　　　B. 真皮　　　C. 下皮　　　D. 皮肤

2. (　　　)A. 疙瘩　　　B. 水疱　　　C. 疱疹　　　D. 溃疡

3. (　　　)A. 皮屑　　　B. 皮鞋　　　C. 皮肤　　　D. 皮靴

4. (　　　)A. 青霉素　　B. 氯霉素　　C. 链霉素　　D. 红霉素

5. (　　　)A. 承情　　　B. 陈清　　　C. 澄清　　　D. 成亲

二、根据听到的句子排列词语和短语。

1. 患者　昨天　转　的　从　17 床　内科　过来　　是

2. 排列　皮肤　呈　带状　沿　周围　损伤　神经

3. 皮肤病　带状疱疹　引起　水痘-带状疱疹病毒　是　急性　的　感染性　由

4.再次 低下 病毒 当 可 抵抗力 或 感冒 感染 生长 时 繁殖 劳累

三、选词填空。

痒 变应原 感染 排列 繁殖 抵抗力

1.疱疹引起的皮肤损伤往往沿某一周围神经呈带状_____,所以我们称其为带状疱疹。

2.医生,我的脸上出现了很多丘疹,又红又_____。

3.在清理伤口时,要注意消毒,避免伤口的二次_____。

4.这种病毒的生长_____能力非常强。

5.造成皮肤过敏的_____有很多种。

6.小儿的_____不强,短期内可有重大病情变化,且易发生各种并发症。

四、完成下面的对话和句子。

(一)

患者:医生,从昨天开始我的脸上_____。

医生:我看看,应该是皮肤过敏。_____?

患者:我吃了很多海鲜。

医生:您应该是由海鲜_____的皮肤过敏。

(二)

医生:20 床的情况怎么样?

实习医生:20 床患者是昨天_____内科转过来的。患者一直_____,体温37.6 ℃,腰背部_____,疱壁_____,疱液_____,周围有_____,皮肤损伤_____。

医生:那你认为他的诊断是什么?

实习医生:_____。

(三)

1._____是由水痘-带状疱疹病毒引起的_____皮肤病。

2._____对水痘-带状疱疹病毒无免疫力,感染该病毒后会产生_____,成人感染该病毒后则常会产生_____。

3.带状疱疹的一般症状有_____、_____,患处出现米粒至黄豆大小的_____,之后迅速发展成为_____,疱壁_____,疱液_____,周围有_____,皮损沿某一周围神经呈_____排列。

五、用下列词语造句。

1.抵抗力

2.灼痛感

3.繁殖

六、根据对话和短文内容回答问题。

1.造成皮肤过敏的过敏源有哪几种?

2.李小妹为什么会皮肤过敏?

3.17 床患者为什么转到皮肤科?

4.为什么哈桑诊断 17 床患者得了带状疱疹?

5.什么是带状疱疹?

6.带状疱疹有哪些常见症状?

七、根据课文内容补充病历信息。

姓名：＿＿＿＿＿＿＿　　　性别：＿＿＿＿＿＿

年龄：＿＿＿＿＿＿＿　　　婚姻状况：＿＿＿已婚＿＿＿

职业：＿＿教师＿＿　　　入院时间：2019 年 3 月 20 日 11：00

主诉:腰背、腹部疼痛,腰背右侧出现＿＿＿＿＿＿＿＿＿＿2 天。

现病史:2 天前患者因＿＿＿＿＿＿＿＿＿疼痛到医院就诊,因患者曾患＿＿＿＿＿＿＿＿＿,我院门诊以＿＿＿＿＿＿＿收治,用药后未见好转。1 天前患者腰背右侧出现黄豆大小红色＿＿＿＿＿＿＿＿,转到皮肤科治疗。

既往史:有胆囊结石病史,无过敏史。

体格检查:T ＿＿＿＿＿,R 22 次/分,P 80 次/分,BP 120/80 mmHg。发育正常,营养良好,神志清醒,呈痛苦病容。低热。＿＿＿＿＿＿＿出现一些黄豆大小的＿＿＿＿＿丘疹,有＿＿＿＿＿感。之后丘疹明显＿＿＿＿＿,而且部分已经发展成＿＿＿＿＿＿＿,＿＿＿＿＿＿＿紧张发亮,疱液＿＿＿＿＿＿＿,周围有＿＿＿＿＿,疱皮损沿某一周围神经呈＿＿＿＿＿排列。

辅助检查:血常规示 RBC $4.43×10^{12}$/L,WBC $7.4×10^{9}$/L,Hb 137 g/L,PLT $248×10^{9}$/L。心电图示窦性心律,心电轴正常。腹部彩超示胆囊大小正常,胆囊壁不厚,内见一强光团,大小约 2 mm×3 mm,伴声影,可随体位改变移动。

初步诊断:＿＿＿＿＿＿＿＿＿＿＿＿＿＿＿＿＿

医生签名:林军

（改编自医院病历）

八、交际练习。

患者 A 因背部出现红色丘疹到医院门诊就诊。皮肤科医生 B 和实习医生 C 为其做了病情询问和初步检查。

三人一组,分别扮演角色 A、B、C,组织一段 5 分钟左右的对话展现上文场景。

【补充医学词汇】

序号	词语	拼音	词义
1	湿疹	shīzhěn	eczema
2	牛皮癣	niúpíxuǎn	psoriasis
3	毛囊炎	máonángyán	folliculitis
4	脚气	jiǎoqì	Athlete's foot
5	白癜风	báidiànfēng	vitiligo
6	皮肤瘙痒	pífū sàoyǎng	Itchy skin
7	狐臭	húchòu	body odor
8	皮炎	píyán	dermatitis

（张　勇）

第二十九单元

传染科——乙型病毒性肝炎

最近看到油腻的食物想吐

【学习目的】

1. 学会用汉语表述病毒性肝炎的类型。
2. 学会用汉语问诊典型乙型病毒性肝炎病例。
3. 用汉语了解乙型病毒性肝炎的相关医学常识。

【热身】

一、写出下面图片对应的症状。

　　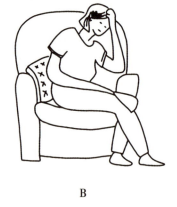　　

　　　A　　　　　　　　　　　B　　　　　　　　　　C

A. _____　　B. _____　　C. _____

二、根据英文写汉字。

1. hepatitis A _____
2. hepatitis B _____
3. hepatitis C _____
4. hepatitis D _____
5. hepatitis E _____

【会话】

场景简介：
人物：患者——李中（男，45 岁）
　　　医生——王美（女，40 岁）
　　　实习医生——穆汗默德（男，20 岁，巴基斯坦人）
地点：肝病科门诊

对话一

生词

序号	词语	词性	拼音	词义
1	油腻	形	yóunì	oily
2	浓	形	nóng	dark；thick
3	胆囊触诊	动	dǎnnáng chùzhěn	gallbladder palpation
4	乏力	形	fálì	weak；feeble
5	乙型肝炎病毒	名	yǐxíng gānyán bìngdú	hepatitis B virus
6	携带	动	xiédài	detect
7	减退	动	jiǎntuì	slack up
8	肝区	名	gānqū	liver area
9	乙型病毒性肝炎	名	yǐxíng bìngdúxìng gānyán	B-type viral hepatitis
10	乙肝五项	名	yǐgān wǔxiàng	hepatitis B five anti-bodies test
11	病毒含量	名	bìngdú hánliàng	virus content

穆汗默德：您哪儿不舒服？
李　　中：我肚子胀，全身无力。
穆汗默德：多长时间了？有没有恶心、呕吐？
李　　中：已经 1 个月了。最近看到油腻的食物想吐，但又吐不出来。
穆汗默德：尿的颜色深吗？
李　　中：像浓茶一样的颜色。
穆汗默德：您先躺下来，我给您检查一下。（进行胆囊触诊）这里痛不痛？
李　　中：有点儿痛。
穆汗默德：以前体检有查出来是乙型肝炎病毒携带么？
李　　中：是的。
穆汗默德：王医生，我觉得他全身乏力，食欲减退，尿色变深，肝区胀痛，有乙型肝炎病毒携带病史，应该是得了乙型病毒性肝炎。您觉得呢？
王　　美：是的，但是还是要做一次肝功能检查。李中，我给您开单子，请明早空腹来抽血，检查"乙肝五项""肝功能"和"乙型肝炎病毒含量"。
李　　中：好的，谢谢医生。

Muhammed:Where do you feel uncomfortable?

Li Zhong:My liver is swollen,feeling weakness in the whole body.

Muhammed:Since how long? Do you have nausea or vomiting?

Li Zhong:It's been a month. Recently I have seen oily food and wants to vomit,but I can't vomit.

Muhammed:The color of your urine is dark?

Li Zhong:Urine color is like a color of a tea.

Muhammed:Please lie down first,I want to do a physical examination. (For gallbladder palpation) Does it hurt here?

Li Zhong:A little pain.

Muhammed:Did the previous lab examinations detect hepatitis B virus?

Li Zhong:Yes.

Muhammed:Doctor Wang,I think he feels fatigue in the whole body,loss of appetite,dark color urine, pain in the liver area,and a history of hepatitis B virus,it should be a B-type viral hepatitis. What do you think?

Wang Mei:Yes,but still we have to do a liver function test. Li Zhong,I will give you a prescription,tomorrow morning take blood on empty stomach,to examine "hepatitis B five anti-bodies test" "liver function test" and "hepatitis B virus content".

Li Zhong:OK,thank you,doctor.

对话二

生词

序号	词语	词性	拼音	词义
1	总胆红素	名	zǒng dǎnhóngsù	total bilirubin
2	谷丙转氨酶	名	gǔbǐngzhuǎnānméi	alanine aminotransferase
3	抗病毒	动	kàng bìngdú	anti-viral
4	抗感染	动	kàng gǎnrǎn	anti-infective
5	消炎	动	xiāoyán	anti-inflammatory
6	人工肝血浆置换	动	réngōng gān xuèjiāng zhìhuàn	artificial liver plasma replacement therapy

李　中:医生,这是我的化验单,您看一下。

王　美:您的总胆红素是220 μmol/L,谷丙转氨酶1 100 U/L,病毒含量高,比较严重,需要马上进行抗病毒、抗感染治疗。

李　中:好的,我会积极配合治疗的。

王　美:我马上给您安排住院,今天先输液消炎,明天进行人工肝血浆置换治疗。

李　中:要治疗多长时间?

王　美:要根据您恢复的情况而定。

(1个星期后,医生查房)

王　美:您现在感觉怎么样? 还腹胀吗?

李　中:好多了,已经不胀了。

王　美:尿黄和乏力好点儿了吗?

李　中:比之前好多了。

王　美：您现在的总胆红素已经下降到 120 μmol/L 了,谷丙转氨酶是 440 U/L,病毒含量还是比较高,需要继续进行当前的治疗。

李　中：好的,我还需要注意什么吗?

王　美：平常注意休息,预防感冒,清淡饮食,不能抽烟和喝酒。

李　中：我会注意的,谢谢医生。

Li Zhong：Doctor,this is my lab examination report,please have a look.

Wang Mei：Your total bilirubin is 220 μmol/L,alanine aminotransferase is 1 100 U/L,virus content is high,condition is very serious,it needs anti-viral and anti-infective treatment immediately.

Li Zhong：OK,I will actively cooperate with the treatment.

Wang Mei：I will immediately arrange hospitalization for you,today first we will infuse anti-inflammatory treatment,tomorrow I will perform artificial liver plasma replacement therapy.

Li Zhong：How long does it take to treat?

Wang Mei：It is based according to your recovery situation.

(After one week,doctor check patient's room)

Wang Mei：How do you feel now? Is there still abdominal distension?

Li Zhong：It's much better,no abdominal distension.

Wang Mei：Is your urine yellow color and fatigue are better?

Li Zhong：It's much better than before.

Wang Mei：Now your total bilirubin is reduced to 120 μmol/L,and alanine aminotransferase is 440 U/L,the virus content is still relatively high,you need to continue the current treatment.

Li Zhong：OK,what else should I pay attention to?

Wang Mei：Always pay attention to have a good rest,prevent common cold,simple diet,can not smoke or drink.

Li Zhong：I will pay attention to this,thank you,doctor.

【短文】

生词

序号	词语	词性	拼音	词义
1	传染病	名	chuánrǎnbìng	infectious disease
2	传播	动	chuánbō	transmit
3	传染源	名	chuánrǎnyuán	source of infection
4	肝硬化	名	gānyìnghuà	liver cirrhosis
5	肝癌	名	gānái	liver cancer
6	接种	动	jiēzhòng	inoculate
7	疫苗	名	yìmiáo	vaccine
8	干扰素	名	gānrǎosù	interferon
9	核苷酸类似物	名	hégānsuān lèisì wù	nucleotide analogues
10	维生素	名	wéishēngsù	vitamin
11	纤维素	名	xiānwéisù	cellulose
12	刺激性	形	cìjīxìng	irritating

乙型病毒性肝炎

乙型病毒性肝炎又叫乙肝,在中国是一种常见的传染病。主要通过母婴传播、血液传播和性传播。乙肝病毒携带者一般没有明显的症状,不容易被发现,所以他们也是最主要的传染源。部分患者会发展成肝硬化、肝癌。

一般通过检查乙肝五项、肝功能和病毒含量来确诊乙肝,可以通过接种疫苗来预防。目前世界上还没有彻底根除乙肝病毒的治疗方法,抗病毒治疗很关键。当前的抗病毒治疗无论是干扰素或者核苷酸类似物,多数患者即使治疗好了,肝细胞中还有病毒。因此对于乙肝患者和携带者来说,定期复查很重要。

乙肝患者和携带者在日常生活中,要多吃蔬菜、水果,补充足够的维生素和纤维素。少吃油腻和油炸食品及生冷、刺激性的食品。平时注意休息,避免过度劳累。乙肝患者一定要禁酒,保持愉快的心情,增强身体的免疫功能。

Viral hepatitis B

Viral hepatitis B is know as hepatitis B and is a common infectious disease in China. Hepatitis B is transmitted in three ways: mother to child, blood and sexual contact. Hepatitis B virus carriers generally have no obvious symptoms which is difficult to be found, so they are the most leading infection source. Some patients will develop into cirrhosis of the liver or liver cancer.

We generally confirm hepatitis B through inspecting hepatitis B five anti-bodies test, liver function and virus. It also can be prevented by getting vaccinated. There is no treatment to eradicate hepatitis B virus so far, so anti-virus therapy is very important. Neither interferon nor nucleotide analogues of present anti-virus therapy can remove the virus even though the patient is cured. Therefore regular re-examination is very important for hepatitis B patients and carriers.

Hepatitis B patients and carriers should eat more vegetables, fruits and have enough supplementary of vitamin and fiber. They also should eat less greasy, fried food and cold, excitant food. Have a good rest and avoid overwork. Hepatitis B patients must against alcoholic drinks and stay in a good mood to enhance the body's immune function.

【汉字知识】

部首"广"

部首"广"的意思为"房屋",一般出现在汉字的左上侧。以"广"为部首的汉字多与房屋有关,也有阔大的意思。如"店""府""庭""麻""康"等。此类汉字多为半包围结构,左上侧的部首为形旁,内部的部件为声旁,代表字音。

例如:麻——麻烦　手麻　麻醉
　　　康——健康　安康　康复

构词

抗——表示"阻止"。

例如:抗病毒、抗感染、抗体、抗癌、抗生素、抗药性。

——型　表示"类型"。

例如:乙型病毒性肝炎、甲型、新型、大型、中型、体型、句型、类型。

【练习】

一、选择听到的词语。

1. （　　）A. 肝炎　　　B. 肺炎　　　C. 脑炎　　　D. 胆汁

2. （　　）A. 腹胀　　　B. 腹部　　　C. 腹痛　　　D. 下腹

3. （　　）A. 乏力　　　B. 发力　　　C. 法力　　　D. 华丽

4. （　　）A. 肝功能　　B. 胆红素　　C. 肝病毒　　D. 肿大

5. （　　）A. 感染　　　B. 传染　　　C. 干扰　　　D. 打扰

二、根据听到的句子排列词语和短语。

1. 最近　看到　我　食物　油腻的　想吐　但　吐不出来　又

2. 减退　他　食欲　全身乏力　胀痛　肝区　得了　应该　是　乙型病毒性肝炎

3. 注意　平常　感冒　休息　预防　清淡　饮食　抽烟　和　喝酒　不能

4. 检查　一般　通过　肝功能　乙肝五项　病毒含量　和　来　确诊　乙肝

三、选词填空。

油腻　尿黄　肝功能　血浆置换　干扰素

1. ＿＿＿＿＿＿＿＿和乏力好点儿了吗?

2. 最近看到＿＿＿＿＿＿＿＿的食物想吐,但又吐不出来。

3. 我给您做一次＿＿＿＿＿＿＿＿检查。

4. 今天先输液消炎,明天进行＿＿＿＿＿＿＿＿治疗。

5. 当前的抗病毒治疗无论是＿＿＿＿＿＿＿＿或者核苷酸类似物,只有很少数患者能根治。

四、完成下面的对话和句子。

（一）

王美:您现在感觉怎么样? 还＿＿＿＿＿＿＿＿吗?

李中:好多了,已经不胀了。

王美:＿＿＿＿＿＿＿＿好点儿了吗?

李中:比之前好多了。

王美:您现在的＿＿＿＿＿＿＿＿已经下降了,＿＿＿＿＿＿＿＿是440 U/L,病毒含量还是比较高,需要继续进行当前的治疗。

李中:好的,我还需要注意什么吗?

王美:平常注意休息,＿＿＿＿＿＿＿＿,不能抽烟和喝酒。

李中:我会注意的,谢谢医生。

（二）

1. 部分患者会发展成＿＿＿＿＿＿＿＿、＿＿＿＿＿＿＿＿。

2. 乙肝传播途径主要是＿＿＿＿＿＿＿＿、＿＿＿＿＿＿＿＿和＿＿＿＿＿＿＿＿。

3. 一般通过检查乙肝五项、＿＿＿＿＿＿＿＿和病毒含量来确诊乙肝。

4. 乙肝患者一定要禁酒,保持愉快的心情,增强身体的＿＿＿＿＿＿＿＿。

5. 目前世界上还没有彻底_____乙肝病毒的治疗方法,_____治疗很关键。

五、用下列词语造句。

1. 油腻

2. 减退

3. 抗感染

六、根据对话和短文内容回答问题。

1. 李中有恶心、呕吐吗?

2. 王美让李中做什么检查?

3. 王美给李中安排了什么治疗?

4. 李中平时要注意什么?

5. 乙肝最主要的传播源是什么?

6. 乙肝患者和携带者日常生活中要注意什么?

七、根据课文内容补充病历信息。

姓名:___李中___　　　　性别:___男___

年龄:___45 岁___　　　　就诊时间:___2017 年 12 月 11 日___

主诉:肚子_____,全身_____,尿_____,食欲减退 1 个月。

现病史:乙型肝炎病毒携带。

既往史:无。

辅助检查:_____、_____、_____;总胆红素_____μmol/L,谷丙转

氨酶_____U/L。

初步诊断:乙型病毒性肝炎

医生签名:王美

（改编自医院病历）

八、交际练习。

　　患者 A 因尿黄、乏力到医院传染病门诊就诊。医生 B 向患者 A 询问了症状,给他做了体格检查、肝功能检查。检查结果显示为乙型病毒性肝炎,医生 B 要给患者 A 先进行抗病毒、抗感染输液,然后马上进行血浆置换治疗。

　　三人一组,分别扮演角色 A、B、C,组织一段 5 分钟左右的对话展现上文场景。

【补充医学词汇】

序号	词语	拼音	词义
1	肝腹水	gān fùshuǐ	liver ascites
2	血氨	xuè ān	blood ammonia
3	血清蛋白	xuèqīng dànbái	serum protein
4	肝衰竭	gān shuāijié	hepatic failure

（张均智　代　晶）

第三十单元

麻醉科——右胫腓骨骨折

第三十单元
生词、对话、短文

因为麻醉药的作用,所以您是不会感到疼痛的

【学习目的】

1.学会用汉语表述麻醉工作流程。

2.学会用汉语完成麻醉手术前访视、谈话及准备。

3.了解麻醉的相关医学常识。

【热身】

一、请选择与下面的短语对应的字母。

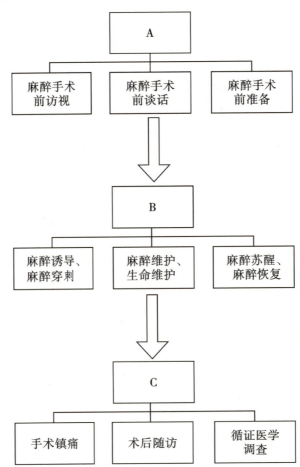

1.麻醉手术中_____ 2.麻醉手术前_____ 3.麻醉手术后_____

二、选出以下麻醉工作属于麻醉工作流程的哪个阶段。

1.麻醉手术前( )

2.麻醉手术中( )

3.麻醉手术后( )

A.麻醉手术前准备

B.麻醉诱导、麻醉穿刺

C.麻醉苏醒、麻醉恢复

D.循证医学调查

E.麻醉手术前访视

F.麻醉维护、生命维护

G.麻醉手术前谈话

H.手术镇痛

I.术后随访

【会话】

场景简介：

人物：患者——李站（男，34 岁）

　　　医生——王柱（男，43 岁）

　　　实习医生——马克（男，21 岁，黎巴嫩人）

　　　护士——刘杰（女，21 岁）

地点：骨科病房、手术室

对话一

生词

序号	词语	词性	拼音	词义
1	胫腓骨	名	jìngféigǔ	tibiofibula
2	硬膜外麻醉	名	yìngmówài mázuì	epidural anesthesia
3	不良反应	名	búliáng fǎnyìng	untoward reaction
4	紧张	形	jǐnzhāng	nervous

（患者李站，因车祸致右胫腓骨骨折入院，计划于明天进行手术。马克到骨科病房访视）

马　克：您好！请问您是右胫腓骨骨折入院的吗？

李　站：是的！

马　克：根据您的骨折情况，我的带教医生王医生，给您选择的麻醉方式是硬膜外麻醉。请问您以前有过什么病史吗？

李　站：没有！

马　克：是否接受过手术和麻醉？有无不良反应？

李　站：医生，都没有！就是有点紧张。

马　克：不要紧张，全身放松！现在我告诉您一些术前注意事项：术前 6 小时禁饮食，排空大小便；取下戒指、手机等物品；术前半小时会有工作人员前来接您，请提前做好准备。

李　站：好的！我会注意的。谢谢医生。

（The patient, Li Zhan, was admitted to the hospital with the right tibiofibula fracture due to a traffic accident, and was scheduled to undergo the surgery tomorrow. Mark visits the orthopedic ward）

Mark：Hello! Then, excuse me, was you admitted to the hospital with the right tibiofibula fracture?

Li Zhan：Yes!

Mark：According to your fracture condition, my instructor, Doctor Wang, has chosen the epidural anesthesia for you. Have you had any medical history before?

Li Zhan：No!

Mark：Have you had any surgery or anesthesia? Have you had any untoward reactions?

Li Zhan：Neither, doctor! Just a little nervous.

Mark：Don't be nervous! Just relax! Now I'm going to tell you some preoperative precautions: forbid the diet for six hours before surgery, and empty the urine; remove the ring, cell phone and other items; the staff will come to pick you up in half an hour before the operation, and please be prepared in advance.

Li Zhan：OK! I'll pay attention. Thank you, doctor.

对话二

生词

序号	词语	词性	拼音	词义
1	核对	动	héduì	check
2	建立	名	jiànlì	set up
3	静脉通道	名	jìngmài tōngdào	passage of vein
4	隐私	名	yǐnsī	privacy
5	监护仪	名	jiānhùyí	monitor

（患者李站被接进手术室，其家属签署麻醉同意书后，即将进行右胫腓骨骨折手术。刘杰辅助王柱实施麻醉）

刘　杰：您好！我先核对您的信息，请问您叫什么名字？

李　站：护士，您好！我叫李站。

刘　杰：您哪里不舒服？

李　站：我右小腿骨折了。

刘　杰：好的。现在，给您打个针，建立静脉通道。

李　站：好紧张啊！

刘　杰：不要紧张，有什么不舒服就及时告诉我。

李　站：好的，谢谢您。

刘　杰：接下来，为您褪去裤子。但是，请您放心，我们会做好隐私保护的。

王　柱：您好！请问您是李站先生吗？

李　站：是的。

王　柱：现在，我给您连接监护仪。

李　站：好的。

王　柱：您的麻醉方式是硬膜外麻醉，手术过程中您是清醒的。

李　站：医生，会很痛吗？

　　王　柱:不要紧张! 因为麻醉药的作用,所以您是不会感到疼痛的。若有什么不舒服,请及时告诉我。

　　(The patient, Li Zhan, has been taken into the operating room, and the family member has signed an anesthetic agreement form. He is about to perform the right tibiofibula fracture surgery. Liu Jie assists Wang Zhu in performing the anesthesia)

Liu Jie:Hello! Let me check your information firstly. May I have your name, please?

Li Zhan:Hello, nurse! My name is Li Zhan.

Liu Jie:What's wrong with you?

Li Zhan:I broke my right shank.

Liu Jie:OK. Now, give you a needle to set up the passage of vein.

Li Zhan:How nervous!

Liu Jie:Don't be nervous. Just let me know if you have any discomfort.

Li Zhan:OK, thank you.

Liu Jie:Next, I will remove your pants. But please rest assured that we will protect your privacy.

Wang Zhu:Hello! Excuse me, Sir, are you Li Zhan?

Li Zhan:Yes.

Wang Zhu:Now, I'll connect you to the monitor.

Li Zhan:OK.

Wang Zhu:Your anesthesia method is the epidural anesthesia. You are conscious during the operation.

Li Zhan:Will it be very painful, doctor?

Wang Zhu:Don't be nervous! You won't feel any pain because of the anesthetic influence. If you have any discomfort, please tell me in time.

【短文】

生词

序号	词语	词性	拼音	词义
1	全身麻醉	名	quánshēn mázuì	general anesthesia
2	局部麻醉	名	júbù mázuì	local anesthesia
3	复合麻醉	名	fùhé mázuì	compound anesthesia
4	麻醉史	名	mázuìshǐ	history of anesthesia
5	病情	名	bìngqíng	state of an illness
6	适应证	名	shìyìngzhèng	adaptation symptom
7	禁忌证	名	jìnjìzhèng	incompatibility symptom
8	保障	动	bǎozhàng	assure
9	技术	名	jìshù	technique
10	生命功能	名	shēngmìng gōngnéng	vital function

临床麻醉

临床麻醉方法主要包括全身麻醉、局部麻醉和复合麻醉。

为了患者的安全,麻醉医生在手术前需要了解患者病史、手术史及麻醉史等。麻醉医生应根据病情和手术需要、麻醉方法的适应证和禁忌证来选择麻醉方案。同时向患者及家属解释有关的麻醉注意事项,回答患者提出的问题等。

麻醉医生的工作不仅仅是术中让患者不痛,还包括保障患者生命安全,手术前后的治疗等。麻醉医生不但熟练各种麻醉操作技术,确保患者手术无痛、手术顺利进行,而且利用先进的仪器随时监测患者的生命功能。如果发现由于手术、麻醉或患者的原有疾病产生威胁患者生命的问题,麻醉医生就要采取各种治疗措施,维持患者生命功能的稳定,保证患者的安全。所以,麻醉医生也被称为"生命守护神"。

Clinical anesthesia

The clinical anesthesia methods mainly include general anesthesia, local anesthesia and compound anesthesia.

For the patient's safety, before surgery anesthesiologists need to know the patients' medical history, surgery history and anesthesia history, etc. Anesthesiologists should choose the anesthesia scheme based on the state of an illness and the surgical needs, indications and contraindications of the anesthesia method. Meanwhile, they should explain relevant anesthesia precautions to the patients and their family members, and answer the questions raised by the patients or something.

The jobs of anesthesiologists are not only to make patients painless during the operation, but also to ensure the patients' life safety, the treatment before and after the operation and so on. Not only are anesthesiologists skilled in various anesthetic techniques, but also ensure that patients have no pain during the operation, and are operated smoothly. Moreover, they use advanced instruments to monitor the patient's life function at any time. If operations, anesthesia, or original diseases of patients threaten patients' lives, anesthesiologists must take a variety of therapeutic measures to maintain the stability of the patients' life function, ensure the safety of patients. Therefore, anesthesiologists are also known as "Life Guardians".

【汉字知识】

部首"酉"

部首"酉"的意思为"酒",一般出现在汉字的左侧。以"酉"为部首的汉字多与酒或因发酵而制成的食物有关。如"醉""醇""酸""醋""醒"等。此类汉字多为形声结构,左侧的部首为形旁,右侧的部件为声旁,代表字音。

例如:醉——麻醉　喝醉　醉痴

酸——胃酸　盐酸　酸痹

构词

——麻醉　表示"用药物或针刺使全身或局部暂时失去知觉或运动的障碍"。

例如:全身麻醉、局部麻醉、复合麻醉。

——神经　表示"由许多神经纤维构成的组织"。

例如:脑神经、脊神经、视神经。

【练习】

一、选择听到的词语。

1.（　　）A.麻花　　B.麻醉　　C.麻木　　D.麻痹
2.（　　）A.同意　　B.同志　　C.同样　　D.同学
3.（　　）A.骨头　　B.骨骼　　C.骨折　　D.骨科
4.（　　）A.隐私　　B.隐藏　　C.自私　　D.私下
5.（　　）A.清澈　　B.清晰　　C.清楚　　D.清醒

二、根据听到的句子排列词语和短语。

1.麻醉　不良反应　无　手术　有　接受过　和　是否

2.我们　请　会　放心　隐私　做好　的　但是　您　保护

3.核对　的　您　请问　叫　信息　我　什么　先　您　名字

4.因为　所以　疼痛的　不会　作用　的　您　麻醉药　是　感到

三、选词填空。

技术　威胁　生命功能　稳定　麻醉史　保障

1.为了患者的安全，麻醉医生在手术前需要了解患者病史、手术史及_____等。

2.麻醉医生的工作不仅仅是术中让患者不痛，还包括_____患者生命安全，手术前后的治疗等。

3.麻醉医生不但熟练各种麻醉操作_____，确保患者手术无痛、手术顺利进行，而且利用先进的仪器随时监测患者_____。

4.如果发现由于手术、麻醉或患者的原有疾病产生_____患者生命的问题，就要采取各种治疗措施，维持患者生命功能的_____，保证患者的安全。

四、完成下面的对话和句子。

（一）

实习医生：根据您的骨折情况，我的带教医生王医生，给您选择的麻醉方式是_____。请问您以前有过什么病史吗？

患　　者：没有！

实习医生：是否接受过_____？有无不良反应？

患　　者：医生，都没有！就是_____。

实习医生：不要紧张，全身放松！现在我告诉您有关麻醉的注意事项：术前_____。

患　　者：好的！我会注意的。谢谢医生。

（二）

1.临床麻醉方法主要包括_____、_____和_____。

2.麻醉医生应根据病情和手术需要、麻醉方法的_____和_____来选择麻醉方案。

3.麻醉医生的工作不仅仅是术中让患者不痛，还包括保障患者生命安全，_____的治疗等。

4.麻醉医生也被称为"_____"。

五、用下列词语造句。

1. 麻醉

2. 清醒

3. 威胁

六、根据对话和短文内容回答问题。

1. 麻醉医生给李站选择的麻醉方式是什么?

2. 手术前,李站应该注意些什么?

3. 临床麻醉方法主要包括哪几种?

4. 简述麻醉医生的工作内容和重要性。

七、根据课文内容补充麻醉知情同意书。

麻醉知情同意书

　　患者_____于 2017 年 10 月 10 日拟行_____手术治疗,交代病情及麻醉有关事项如下。

　　一、根据患者病情及手术需要拟行_____麻醉。

　　二、目前患者存在如下问题。

　　1. 术前意识及精神状态:_____。

　　2. 创伤严重。

　　3. 手术复杂。

　　三、随着麻醉学进展及监测技术的日益完善,麻醉水平和安全性都有了很大提高,但无论何种麻醉方法与技术操作都会对患者生理功能产生不同程度的影响,难免发生一些并发症或意外,如:

　　1. 麻醉药过敏、中毒等不良反应,导致休克、心跳呼吸骤停、严重脏器功能损害。

　　2. 反流、误吸、喉头水肿、喉痉挛、支气管痉挛、缺氧、窒息等。

　　……

　　以上情况严重时均可致死亡。

　　对上述并发症和意外死亡,麻醉医生将本着救死扶伤精神尽力积极救治,但不能绝对避免。

　　患者或代理人意见:对上述交代的问题是否理解:_____

　　　　　　　　是否同意麻醉:_____

　　　　患者签字:_____　　　　　　　　　　代理人签字:王芳

　　　　　　　　　　　　　　　　　　　　　代理人与患者关系:夫妻

　　　　　　　　　　　　　　　　　　　　　　　　麻醉医生:王柱

（改编自医院麻醉知情同意书）

八、交际练习。

　　患者 A 因车祸致右小腿胫腓骨骨折入院,计划于明天进行手术。现在,实习医生 B 前来访视。带教医生决定给患者 A 选择了硬膜外麻醉这种麻醉方式,实习医生 B 向患者 A 询问了病史、手术史及麻醉史。患者 A 说有点紧张。实习医生 B 让患者 A 放松,并告诉他一些术前注意事项。

　　两人一组,分别扮演角色 A、B,组织一段 5 分钟左右的对话展现上文场景。

【补充医学词汇】

序号	词语	拼音	词义
1	吸入麻醉	xīrù mázuì	inhalation anesthesia
2	静脉麻醉	jìngmài mázuì	intravenous anesthesia
3	基础麻醉	jīchǔ mázuì	basis anesthesia
4	麻醉介入	mázuì jièrù	anesthesia intervention
5	麻醉辅助脱毒	mázuì fǔzhù tuōdú	assist detoxification with anesthesia
6	全脊麻性休克	quánjǐ máxìng xiūkè	total spinal anaesthetic shock

（马　平）

第三十一单元

康复科——右侧偏瘫

第三十一单元
生词、对话、短文

您的主要问题是下肢无力呀

【学习目的】

1. 学会用汉语表述偏瘫患者上下肢典型的痉挛模式。
2. 学会用汉语问诊典型偏瘫病例。
3. 了解右侧偏瘫患者在康复治疗过程中的注意事项。

【热身】

一、给下面的词语选择对应的字母。

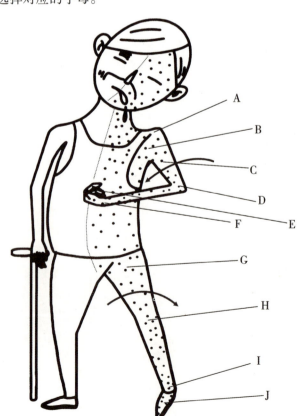

1.肩胛骨内收(回缩)、上提_____　　2.肘关节屈曲_____

3.肩关节后伸、外展、外旋_____　　4.髋关节内收、内旋_____

5.膝关节伸展_____　　6.前臂旋后_____

7.腕和手指屈曲_____　　8.踝趾屈曲、内翻_____

二、连线题。

1.肩胛骨内收(回缩)、上提　　　　　A. qiánbì xuánhòu

2.肩关节后伸、外展、外旋　　　　　B. huáizhǐ qūqū、nèifān

3.肘关节屈曲　　　　　　　　　　　C. jiānjiǎgǔ nèishōu（huísuō）、shàngtí

4.前臂旋后　　　　　　　　　　　　D. zhǒuguānjié qūqū

5.腕和手指屈曲　　　　　　　　　　E. xīguānjié shēnzhǎn

6.髋关节内收、内旋　　　　　　　　F. wàn hé shǒuzhǐ qūqū

7.膝关节伸展　　　　　　　　　　　G. kuānguānjié nèishōu、nèixuán

8.踝趾屈曲、内翻　　　　　　　　　H. jiānguānjié hòushēn、wàizhǎn、wàixuán

【会话】

场景简介:

人物:患者——王醒(男,54 岁)

　　　医生——朱爽(男,35 岁)

地点:康复科住院部

对话一

生词

序号	词语	词性	拼音	词义
1	左脑桥梗死	名	zuǒnǎoqiáo gěngsǐ	left pontine infarction
2	右侧偏瘫	名	yòucè piāntān	right hemiplegia
3	清晰	副	qīngxī	clearly
4	测量	动	cèliáng	measure
5	平衡训练	名	pínghéng xùnliàn	balance training

(患者王醒无明显诱因下突发左脑桥梗死引发右侧偏瘫。入院治疗 1 周后,医生朱爽前来询问病情)

朱　爽:您好! 您是因为右侧偏瘫住进来的吧?

王　醒:是的! 大夫。

朱　爽:现在感觉怎么样?

王　醒:通过康复治疗及锻炼,我的右手能举过头了,右腿也能屈伸了。

朱　爽:确实恢复得不错啊。您现在讲话多清晰啊!

王　醒:是啊,是啊。

朱　爽:能自己坐起来吗?

王　醒:可以。

朱　爽:站起来呢?

王　醒：哎哟，痛！哎哟！不行，头晕！

朱　爽：您呀！先测测血压，再量量体温吧。我让护士过会儿给您测量一下吧！

王　醒：好的！谢谢。

朱　爽：不客气！如果检查结果没有异常，就要进行站立位平衡训练了。

王　醒：说实话，我在床上呆够了！

朱　爽：别着急，我们慢慢来吧！

王　醒：好的！谢谢您。

（Without obvious inducement, the patient, Wang Xing, suddenly suffered from the right paralysis caused by the left pontine infarction. After a week of treatment in hospital, the doctor, Zhu Shuang, comes to ask about his illness state）

Zhu Shuang：Hello！Did you come here on account of the right paralysis？

Wang Xing：Yes！Doctor.

Zhu Shuang：How do you feel now？

Wang Xing：Through rehabilitation therapy and exercises, my right hand can be overstretched and my right leg can be bent.

Zhu Shuang：Actually that's a good recovery. How clearly you are speaking now！

Wang Xing：Yes. Yes.

Zhu Shuang：Can you sit up by yourself？

Wang Xing：Yes, I can.

Zhu Shuang：And what about standing up？

Wang Xing：Ouch, painful！Ouch！No, dizzy！

Zhu Shuang：You！Take your blood pressure first, then take your body temperature. I'll ask the nurse to measure them for you later.

Wang Xing：OK！Thank you.

Zhu Shuang：You're welcome！If there is no abnormality in the test results, the standing balance training will be required.

Wang Xing：To be honest, I don't want to stay in bed any longer！

Zhu Shuang：Don't worry, take your time！

Wang Xing：OK！Thank you.

对话二

生词

序号	词语	词性	拼音	词义
1	细心	形	xìxīn	careful
2	下肢	名	xiàzhī	lower limb
3	行走训练	名	xíngzǒu xùnliàn	walking training
4	陪同	动	péitóng	accompany
5	多亏	形	duōkuī	thank to

（5周后）

朱　爽：您好！王先生！看上去精神不错啊！今天感觉怎么样？

王　醒：挺好啊！睡眠、饮食、二便都正常。您瞧！（缓慢地下床）我能站起来，头已经不晕了，两腿也有劲了。

朱　爽：不错啊！听护士说，您能自己走几步了？

王　醒：（慢慢地走了几步，仍走路不稳）是啊！多亏你们的细心治疗。但是，只能在支撑架的帮助下缓慢行走，独立行走还是坚持不了多少时间呀！

朱　爽：康复地挺快的！还是不能太急！您的主要问题是下肢无力呀！

王　醒：（坐在床上）医生，接下来，我该怎么治疗呢？

朱　爽：还是要加强行走训练，增强下肢力量啊！记得家属必须陪同辅助训练啊！

王　醒：好的！医生！

朱　爽：配合有效治疗，过一段时间，您回去工作还是希望很大的！

王　醒：太好了！真是谢谢您了！

(Five weeks later)

Zhu Shuang：Hello！Mr. Wang！You look great！How are you feeling today？

Wang Xing：Very good！Sleep，diet，urine and stool are all normal. Look！（Gets out of bed slowly）I can stand up，my head is not faint，and my legs are stronger.

Zhu Shuang：Not bad！The nurse said you could take a few steps by yourself？

Wang Xing：(Slowly takes a few steps，still walks unsteadily）Yeah！Thanks to your careful treatment. But I can only walk slowly with the support frame，and still can't hold out much time by myself！

Zhu Shuang：How fast your rehabilitation is！Still not too hurry！Your main problem is the weakness of the lower limbs！

Wang Xing：(Sits on the bed）Doctor？How should I be treated next？

Zhu Shuang：You still need to increase walking training，in order to enhance your lower limb strength！Remember your family members must accompany and aid you to take the training！

Wang Xing：OK！Doctor！

Zhu Shuang：Cooperating with the effective treatment，you are still greatly hopeful to return to work after a period of time！

Wang Xing：Great！Thank you very much！

【短文】

生词

序号	词语	词性	拼音	词义
1	轻瘫	名	qīngtān	paresis
2	不完全性瘫	名	bùwánquánxìngtān	incomplete hemiplegia
3	全瘫	名	quántān	complete hemiplegia
4	血流	名	xuèliú	blood flow
5	肢体功能	名	zhītǐ gōngnéng	limb function
6	患肢	名	huànzhī	affected limb
7	被动运动	动	bèidòng yùndòng	passive movement

序号	词语	词性	拼音	词义
8	锻炼	名	duànliàn	exercise
9	肢体训练	名	zhītǐ xùnliàn	limb training
10	楼梯	名	lóutī	stair

右侧偏瘫

偏瘫是指一侧上下肢、面肌和舌肌下部的运动障碍,是急性脑血管病的常见症状之一。偏瘫患者轻者尚能活动,但走路时常上肢屈曲、下肢伸直;重者常卧床不起,丧失生活能力。按照程度,偏瘫可分为轻瘫、不完全性瘫和全瘫。左脑桥梗死引起右侧偏瘫最为常见,主要表现为头晕、眩晕、偏瘫、语言表达不清等。

右侧偏瘫是康复科治疗的典型病例之一。为了促进神经早期恢复,右侧偏瘫患者应卧床休息,平卧为好,以保证脑血流供给、减轻脑组织缺血状况;同时,保持瘫痪肢体功能位置,做患肢及关节的被动运动。病情稳定后,患者要主动锻炼,尽早下床活动,并进行起床、患肢平衡、站立、行走等肢体训练;并且,逐步增加活动范围和次数,最后由他人协助进行上下楼梯训练,以便患肢得到运动,利于功能的恢复。

Right hemiparesis

Hemiplegia is the dyskinesia in one side of the upper and lower limbs, facial muscles and the lower part of the tongue. It is one of the common symptoms of acute cerebrovascular disease. The mild patients with hemiplegia are still movable, but often buckle upper limbs and straighten lower limbs while walking. And the severe ones are often bedridden and lose life ability. According to the degree, hemiplegia can be divided into hemiparesis, incomplete hemiplegia and complete hemiplegia. The right hemiplegia caused by the left pontine infarction is the most common, mainly manifested as dizziness, vertigo, hemiplegia, unclear language and so on.

Right hemiplegia is one of the typical cases of rehabilitation therapy. In order to promote the early recovery of the nerve, patients with right hemiplegia should rest in bed and had better lie on the back, so that ensure the supply of cerebral blood flow and reduction in the ischemia of cerebral tissue. At the same time, they should maintain the limb function position of paralysis, and do the passive movements of affected limbs and joints as well. After the condition is stable, patients should take active exercise, get out of bed as early as possible, and get up, balance limbs, stand, walk and other limb trainings. In addition, the scope and frequency of the activity should be increased gradually. Finally patients should need to take the training of up and down stairs with the help of others, so that to affected limbs can get movements, which is beneficial to the recovery of functions.

【汉字知识】

部首"纟"

部首"纟"的意思为"丝线、细丝",一般出现在汉字的左侧。以"纟"为部首的汉字大都跟丝线、纺织、布匹有关。如"细""绞""红""绿""绀"等。此类汉字多为形声结构,左侧的部首为形旁,右侧的部件为声旁,代表字音。

例如:细——细线　细胞　细菌

织——组织　纺织　织布

构词

——瘫　表示"偏瘫"。

例如:轻瘫、不完全性瘫、全瘫、面瘫、截瘫。

——卧　表示"睡倒,躺或趴"。

例如:平卧、仰卧、侧卧、俯卧。

【练习】

一、选择听到的词语。

1. (　　　)A.感觉　　B.感情　　C.感触　　D.感想

2. (　　　)A.康盛　　B.康泰　　C.康复　　D.小康

3. (　　　)A.血液　　B.血压　　C.血脉　　D.血型

4. (　　　)A.站立　　B.坐立　　C.行走　　D.迈步

5. (　　　)A.上肢　　B.下肢　　C.四肢　　D.肢体

二、根据听到的句子排列词语和短语。

1. 通过　头　了　及　锻炼　我　举过　的　右手　能　了　屈伸　右腿　也　康复　能　治疗

2. 吧　测测　量量　先　再　体温　血压

3. 增强　要　还是　训练　力量　下肢　啊　行走　加强

4. 陪同　啊　家属　辅助　训练　必须　记得

三、选词填空。

平卧　患肢　楼梯　血流　锻炼　常见

1. 左脑桥梗死引起右侧瘫最为＿＿＿＿＿＿＿。

2. 右侧偏瘫患者应卧床休息,＿＿＿＿＿＿＿为好,以保证脑＿＿＿＿＿＿＿供给、减轻脑组织缺血状况。

3. 保持瘫痪肢体功能位置,做＿＿＿＿＿＿＿及关节的被动运动。

4. 病情稳定后,患者要主动＿＿＿＿＿＿＿,尽早下床活动,并进行起床、患肢平衡、站立、行走等肢体训练。

5. 由他人协助进行上下＿＿＿＿＿＿＿训练,让患肢得到运动,利于功能的恢复。

四、完成下面的对话和句子。

(一)

医　生:您好! 王先生! 看上去精神不错啊! 今天感觉怎么样?

患　者:挺好啊! 睡眠、饮食、二便一切正常。您瞧!(缓慢地下床)我能站起来,＿＿＿＿＿。

医　生:不错啊! 听护士说,您能自己走几步了?

患　者:(慢慢地走了几步,仍走路不稳)是啊! 多亏你们的细心治疗。但是,＿＿＿＿＿＿＿!

医　生:康复地挺快的! 还是不能太急! 您的主要问题是＿＿＿＿＿＿＿!

患　者:(坐在床上)医生,接下来,我该怎么治疗呢?

医　生:还是要＿＿＿＿＿＿! 记得家属必须陪同辅助训练啊!

（二）

1．偏瘫是指一侧上下肢、面肌和舌肌下部的_____，是_____的常见症状之一。

2．按照程度，偏瘫可分为_____、_____和_____。

3．左脑桥梗死引起_____最为常见，主要表现为头晕、眩晕、偏瘫、语言表达不清等。

4．保持瘫痪_____位置，做患肢及关节的_____。

五、用下列词语造句。

1．清晰

2．偏瘫

3．行走训练

六、根据对话和短文内容回答问题。

1．王醒患了什么病？其症状如何？

2．医生要王醒以后如何加强康复训练？

3．偏瘫的定义是什么？

4．右侧偏瘫患者应该如何康复治疗？

七、根据课文内容补充病历信息。

姓名：_____　　　　　　性别：_____

年龄：_____　　　　　　就诊时间：2017－10－11

主诉：_____肢体活动不利1个半月。

现病史：患者无明显诱因下突然出现头晕，_____肢体麻木无力且无法自主活动，吐字含糊。治疗后，患者神志转清，吐字_____，头晕和_____肢体乏力较前好转，仍有_____，可在_____帮助下缓慢行走，精神尚可，睡眠、饮食、二便正常。

既往史：平素体健。

辅助检查：头颅 MRI 及 MRA 示"左侧脑桥梗死灶，颅内大血管未见明显狭窄"。

初步诊断：_____恢复期

医生签名：_____

（改编自医院病历）

八、交际练习。

患者 A 因左脑桥梗死引起右侧偏瘫，由救护车送至医院康复科，医生 B 接待了患者 A。1 周后，医生 B 向患者 A 询问了症状。患者 A 说右侧上下肢恢复明显。医生 B 提议患者 A 尝试站立，患者 A 感觉头晕。医生 B 要求他测血压，量体温。如检查结果无异常，医生 B 建议患者 A 以后要加强站立及行走训练。

两人一组，分别扮演角色 A、B，组织一段 3 分钟左右的对话展现上文场景。

【补充医学词汇】

序号	词语	拼音	词义
1	综合性康复	zōnghé xìng kāngfù	comprehensive rehabilitation
2	社会康复	shèhuì kāngfù	social rehabilitation
3	治疗性训练	zhìliáo xìng xùnliàn	therapeutic training
4	手法肌力测试	shóufǎ jīlì cèshì	manual muscle testing
5	语言治疗	yǔyán zhìliáo	speech and language therapy

（马　平）

附录一

参考答案

【第一单元】

【热身】

一、1. A　2. C　3. B　4. F　5. E　6. D　7. G

二、1. cardia　2. pyloric antrum　3. duodenum　4. esophagus　5. pylorus

【练习】

一、1. B　2. A　3. D　4. D　5. A

二、1. 最主要的病因是幽门螺杆菌感染。

2. 我考虑您得的是慢性胃炎。

3. 我肚子痛得厉害。

4. 还需要做胃镜检查才能进一步明确诊断。

三、略

四、1. 上腹部　2. 复查　3. 诊断　4. 胃炎　5. 呕吐物

五、(一) 略

(二) 1. 胃黏膜炎性　2. 病因　3. 无症状　4. 胃镜　活检　幽门螺杆菌

六、略

七、略

【第二单元】

【热身】

一、1. A　2. E　3. C　4. F　5. B　6. D　7. G　8. H

二、D

【练习】

一、1. A　2. B　3. A　4. D　5. B

二、1. 初步诊断您得的是消化性溃疡。

2. 您需要做胃镜检查才能进一步确定。

3. 您现在麻醉作用还没有消失。

4. 一般男性更容易患这种病。

三、略

四、1. 胃镜　2. 消化性溃疡　3. 血生化　4. 溃疡灶　5. 麻醉

五、(一)略

(二)1.消化作用　2.嗳气　恶心　呕吐　3.戒烟戒酒　4.消化性溃疡　慢性溃疡　5.长期性　周期性　节律性

六、略

七、略

【第三单元】

【热身】

一、1.F　2.C　3.G　4.D　5.B　6.E　7.A

二、1.左肺　2.肺组织　3.肺泡　4.细支气管　5.右肺　6.气管　7.支气管

【练习】

一、1.D　2.B　3.A　4.A　5.B

二、1.我最近咳嗽咳得厉害。

2.应该是支气管炎或者肺炎的可能性大。

3.他的右下肺胸片显示有一个斑片状浸润影。

4.肺是人体器官中最容易被感染的器官。

三、略

四、1.青霉素　2.湿啰音　3.痰培养　4.抗生素　5.免疫力

五、(一)略

(二)1.病原体　2.威胁　3.忽视　导致　4.受凉　5.免疫力　感染

六、略

七、略

【第四单元】

【热身】

一、1.D　2.C　3.B　4.E　5.A　6.F

二、1.桶状胸　2.慢性支气管炎　3.肺气肿　4.肺泡

【练习】

一、1.C　2.B　3.A　4.B　5.A

二、1.冬天或者天气冷的时候咳嗽、气喘得更厉害。

2.慢性阻塞性肺疾病对肺的损坏是不可逆转的。

3.他的胸廓前后径几乎与左右径相等，像个木桶。

4.身体中产生的二氧化碳经过毛细血管进入肺泡。

三、略

四、1.有效的　2.胸廓　3.胸闷　4.桶状胸

五、(一)略

(二)1.气管　支气管　细支气管　肺泡　2.扩张　收缩　3.二氧化碳　4.有效的

六、略

七、略

【第五单元】

【热身】

一、1.A　2.B　3.C　4.D　5.E　6.F　7.G　8.H　9.I

二、1.C　2.D　3.B　4.A

【练习】

一、1. C 2. B 3. A 4. B 5. A

二、1. 这些应该是癫痫的一些症状。

2. 最好让赵医生再给您诊断一下。

3. 第一次犯病时我在县医院做了头颅CT。

4. 癫痫的患病率仅次于脑卒中。

5. 继发性癫痫是由脑内外各种疾病所引起。

三、略

四、1. 持续 2. 抽搐 3. 确诊 4. 痉挛 5. 诱发

五、(一)略

(二)1. 羊角风 2. 原发性 继发性 3. 脑炎 脑膜炎 脑寄生虫病 脑瘤 脑外伤 脑缺氧 铅汞引起的脑中毒

六、略

七、略

【第六单元】

【热身】

一、1. A 2. E 3. F 4. H 5. B 6. C 7. D 8. G

二、1. 高血压 2. 低血压 3. 冠心病 4. 心律 5. 心肌

【练习】

一、1. B 2. C 3. A 4. D 5. C

二、1. 持续 2. 病史 3. 窦性心律 4. 频繁 5. 高血压

三、略

四、1. 急性 2. 频繁 3. 硝酸甘油 4. 血液循环 5. 坚持 6. 毫米汞柱

五、(一)略

(二)1. 心脏 血管 2. 完成血液循环 保证身体功能 3. 左心房 左心室 右心房 右心室 4. 动脉 静脉 毛细血管 静脉 动脉

六、略

七、略

【第七单元】

【热身】

一、1. F 2. E 3. C 4. D 5. B 6. A 7. G 8. H

二、1. 肺动脉 2. 毛细血管 3. 主动脉 4. 静脉 5. 下腔静脉

【练习】

一、1. B 2. C 3. B 4. A 5. C

二、1. 我们考虑您得的是贫血。

2. 我们会给您制定系统的治疗方案。

3. 贫血指人体外周血红细胞容量减少。

4. 溶血性贫血采用糖皮质激素或脾切除术治疗。

三、略

四、1. 心悸 2. 叶酸 3. 风湿病 4. 红细胞

五、(一)略

(二)1. 疼痛 2. 检查 3. 诊断 4. 有时候 5. 详细

六、略

七、略

【第八单元】

【热身】

一、1．D K　2．C J　3．F M　4．B I　5．E L　6．N　7．G　8．A H　9．O

二、1．D　2．J　3．G　4．C　5．I　6．A　7．B　8．H　9．E　10．F

【练习】

一、1．D　2．A　3．B　4．C　5．C

二、1．家人的身体状况都怎么样？

2．糖尿病的诊断由血糖水平确定。

3．每年查一次有无并发症。

4．您需要住院接受进一步的治疗。

三、略。

四、1．制定　2．控制　3．空腹血糖　4．并发症　5．配合

五、（一）略

（二）1.1 型　2 型　其他特殊类型　妊娠糖尿病　2．饮　食　尿　体重减轻

六、略

七、略

【第九单元】

【热身】

一、1．E　2．F　3．D　4．C　5．A　6．B　7．H　8．G

二、1．乙状结肠　2．直肠　3．肛门　4．阑尾　5．盲肠　6．升结肠　7．横结肠　8．降结肠

【练习】

一、1．C　2．D　3．A　4．B　5．A

二、1．他已经两天没有排气、排便了。

2．医生叮嘱他多吃清淡、易消化、有营养的食物。

3．肠梗阻是外科常见的急腹症之一。

4．肠梗阻的典型症状是"痛、吐、胀、闭"。

三、略

四、1．半流质　2．叮嘱　3．内容物　4．采集　5．蔓延

五、（一）略

（二）1．急腹症　2．痛　吐　胀　闭　3．清淡　易消化　富含蛋白质　铁质的

六、略

七、略

【第十单元】

【热身】

一、1．E　2．B　3．A　4．C　5．F　6．D

二、1．盲肠　2．回盲瓣　3．阑尾　4．阑尾口　5．回肠　6．回肠口

【练习】

一、1．A　2．A　3．A　4．C　5．D

二、1．我昨晚开始肚子痛得厉害。

2．您的检查结果除了血常规提示有炎症的表现，其他检查都没有问题。

3．典型的急性阑尾炎初期有腹部的中上部位置或肚脐周围疼痛。

4.外科医生通常根据患者右下腹麦氏点的固定压痛和实验室检查来确诊阑尾炎。

三、略

四、1.体格 2.胀痛 3.提示 4.扭曲 5.盲管

五、(一)略

(二)1.盲管 2.扭曲 压迫 3.腹痛 4.转移性 麦氏点 反跳痛 5.粪块 寄生虫

六、略

七、略

【第十一单元】

【热身】

一、1.C 2.B 3.A 4.D 5.E

二、1.A 2.E 3.G 4.D 5.B 6.F 7.C 8.I 9.H

【练习】

一、1.B 2.A 3.C 4.B 5.D

二、1.我就去当地医院拍了个胸部CT。

2.根据检查结果才能决定治疗方案。

3.血常规各相关指标也下降明显。

4.其他各系统据目前检查还未见异常。

5.您现在要避免剧烈活动,特别是胸部不能随意扭动。

三、略

四、1.稳定 2.明显 3.保守 4.沟通 5.评估 6.初步

五、(一)略

(二)1.车祸 挤压伤 摔伤 锐器伤 2.钝性伤 穿透伤 开放伤 闭合伤 3.穿透伤

六、略

七、略

【第十二单元】

【热身】

一、1.C 2.F 3.A 4.D 5.E 6.B 7.G

二、B

【练习】

一、1.A 2.C 3.B 4.A 5.A

二、1.患者因打篮球摔了一跤,左臂剧烈疼痛、活动受限前来就诊。

2.您是左侧肱骨外科颈骨折,需要复位和石膏固定。

3.肱骨骨折是一种常见的上肢骨折。

三、略

四、1.肱骨外科颈 复位 2.康复 3.失用性萎缩 4.畸形 骨擦音 骨擦感 5.错位 6.麻醉药 7.愈合

五、(一)略

(二)1.完整性 连续性 2.完全性 不完全性 3.肩部疼痛 肿胀 瘀斑

六、略

七、略

【第十三单元】

【热身】

一、1. B 2. D 3. A 4. C 5. E

二、1. 颈椎 2. 胸椎 3. 骶椎 4. 尾椎 5. 腰椎

【练习】

一、1. A 2. B 3. B 4. A 5. B

二、1. 您需要拍 X 射线片和磁共振成像检查背部的情况。

2. 看了您的检查结果之后,我能确定您得了腰椎间盘突出症。

3. 他们安排一些运动帮您解决这个问题,让您行动更自如。

4. 在打喷嚏或咳嗽的情况下,疼痛会加剧。

三、略

四、1. 复发 2. 蹲 3. 恶化 4. 理疗 5. 姿势

五、(一)略

(二)1. 症状 腰痛 2. 卧床 佩戴 3. 靠背 硬板床 4. 姿势 弯腰 后突

六、略

七、略

【第十四单元】

【热身】

一、1. F 2. D 3. H 4. A 5. E 6. I 7. G 8. B 9. C 10. J

二、1. 肾盏 2. 肾盂 3. 输尿管 4. 肾动脉 5. 肾静脉 6. 肾乳头

【练习】

一、1. B 2. B 3. C 4. B 5. A

二、1. 今天深夜睡觉时被痛醒了。

2. 尿常规提示白细胞和红细胞有轻微升高。

3. 建议您住院并进行手术治疗。

三、略

四、1. 轻微 尿路 2. 输尿管 3. 肾绞痛 4. 尽快

五、(一)略

(二)1. 白细胞 红细胞 升高 尿路 2. 绞痛 血尿 梗阻 3. 解除疼痛 功能 结石复发

六、略

七、略

【第十五单元】

【热身】

一、1. G 2. B 3. E 4. F 5. D 6. C 7. H 8. A

二、1. 肝 2. 胰腺 3. 胰管 4. 胆囊 5. 小肠 6. 肝总管 7. 十二指肠 8. 胆总管

【练习】

一、1. C 2. C 3. B 4. B 5. C

二、1. 我感觉右肩和右腰部也有一阵一阵的疼痛。

2. 但是呕吐之后腹痛稍微缓解了一些。

3. 血胆红素也明显升高了。

4. 胆总管结石一般分为原发性胆总管结石和继发性胆总管结石。

三、略

四、1.忍受　2.结石　3.缓解　4.紧急　5.黄疸

五、(一)略

(二)1.原发性胆总管结石　继发性胆总管结石　2.上腹部绞痛　寒战　黄疸　3.取净结石

解除梗阻

六、略

七、略

【第十六单元】

【热身】

一、1.B　2.A

二、1.卵巢上皮性肿瘤　2.卵巢浆液性肿瘤

【练习】

一、1.C　2.C　3.B　4.A　5.D

二、1.上皮性肿瘤是最常见的卵巢恶性肿瘤,包括浆液性和黏液性两种。

2.最近3个月,我感觉左下腹一直有一个包块。

3.卵巢肿瘤增长速度相当快,而且很容易发生病变。

三、略

四、1.稳定性　2.直径　3.病房　4.超声　5.妇科

五、(一)略

(二)1.生殖器官　2.良性　恶性　3.诊断　治疗　4.肿块　症状

六、略

七、略

【第十七单元】

【热身】

一、1.E　2.D　3.A　4.C　5.B　6.G　7.F

二、1.uterus　2.cervix　3.ovary　4.subserous myoma

【练习】

一、1.B　2.A　3.A　4.B　5.C

二、1.最常见的临床表现为月经过多或经期失血过多。

2.子宫肌瘤是常见的肿瘤,发病率可达25%。

3.我们发现您的子宫里有一些纤维状的肿块。

4.两次经期之间及同房之后您有没有阴道出血的情况?

三、略

四、1.明确　2.恶变　3.生育　4.折磨　5.同房

五、(一)略

(二)1.临床症状　监控观察　2.骨盆　膀胱　压迫　3.不规则　居骨盆中位　质硬　宫颈

4.大小　临床症状　生育要求

六、略

七、略

【第十八单元】

【热身】

一、1.H　2.A　3.G　4.C　5.E　6.B　7.D　8.F

二、1.B　2.C　3.G　4.A　5.D　6.F　7.E

【练习】

一、1. A　2. C　3. B　4. A　5. D

二、1. 初次产检非常重要,内容也很详细,通常在妊娠12周之前预约。

2. 我最近胃口不太好,前2个月饭后经常恶心想吐。

3. 我有个双胞胎妹妹,她是因为生孩子大出血去世的。

三、略

四、1. 预产期　2. 怀孕　3. 营养　4. 胎儿　分娩　5. 双胞胎

五、(一)略

(二)1. 病史询问　月经　避孕　用药　盆腔及腹部手术　孕产　家族病　糖尿病　高血压　多胎妊娠　血栓病　2. 腹部超声　心肺　体重　宫颈涂片　3. 孕妇　胎儿

六、略

七、略

【第十九单元】

【热身】

一、1. D　2. E　3. A　4. C　5. B

二、1. 前置胎盘　2. 部分性前置胎盘　3. 完全性前置胎盘　4. 低置胎盘　5. 边缘性前置胎盘 6. 正常胎盘

【练习】

一、1. C　2. D　3. A　4. B　5. C

二、1. 正常的胎盘位于子宫前后壁、两侧壁和宫底。

2. 我以为一会儿能停,但还是一直流。

3. 我先给您初步检查下,再和其他医生讨论怎么处理。

4. 您有过流产或者剖宫产的经历吗?

三、略

四、1. 精确　定位　2. 剖宫产　3. 胎动　4. 边缘性　5. 耽误

五、(一)略

(二)1. 完全性　覆盖　宫颈内口　2. 低置胎盘　附着　3. 典型　妊娠晚　先兆　阴道出血 4. 剖宫产　终止

六、略

七、略

【第二十单元】

【热身】

一、1. C　2. A　3. D　4. B　5. E

二、1. 双顶径　2. 股骨长　3. 头围　4. 腹围　5. 枕额径

【练习】

一、1. A　2. D　3. A　4. B　5. A

二、1. 您的孩子出生时体重极低,需要入院治疗。

2. 早产儿常常需要采取措施帮助他们调节呼吸、体温等。

3. 阿氏评分是评价新生儿出生时有无窒息及窒息严重程度的一种方法。

4. 必要时我们会采用呼吸机辅助早产儿通气。

三、略

四、1. 调节　2. 指标　3. 浅促　4. 窒息　5. 辅助

五、(一)略

(二)1.胎龄小于37周的新生儿 2.胎龄小 体重低 适应能力 3.薄嫩 稀疏 柔软 趾端 4.并发症

六、略

七、略

【第二十一单元】

【热身】

一、1.D 2.C 3.E 4.A 5.B

二、1.肝细胞性黄疸 2.阻塞性黄疸 3.母乳性黄疸 4.溶血性黄疸 5.生理性黄疸 6.病理性黄疸

【练习】

一、1.C 2.D 3.A 4.B 5.A

二、1.昨晚从产科转来的患者安排在15床。

2.新生儿黄疸可分为生理性黄疸和病理性黄疸。

3.新生儿的肝发育不完善,胆红素代谢能力差。

4.生理性黄疸是新生儿的正常生理现象,常常不需要特殊治疗。

三、略

四、1.抽搐 2.黄疸 3.重度 4.烦躁 5.进展

五、(一)略

(二)1.肝 胆红素 浓度 2.60% 80% 3.过高 4.1周内

六、略

七、

姓名:李少芳	性别:女
年龄:1 天	就诊时间:2017 年 4 月 1 日

主诉:母孕38^{+4}周,生后1天,皮肤黄染1天。

现病史:母孕38^{+4}周,2017年3月31日在我院产科顺产出生。出生时1分钟、5分钟阿氏评分均正常。生后当天开奶,吸吮有力。1天前出现脸部皮肤黄染,向胸腹部、四肢蔓延,伴黄色大便及黄色尿。皮肤黄染进行加重。

既往史:无。

辅助检查:经皮测胆红素值249.66 μmol/L,277.02 μmol/L,225.72 μmol/L。

初步诊断:新生儿高胆红素血症

医生签名:张明

(改编自医院病历)

八、略

【第二十二单元】

【热身】

一、1. E　2. D　3. F　4. A　5. B　6. C

二、1. 手足口病　2. 高热惊厥　3. 新生儿肺炎　4. 注意缺陷多动障碍

【练习】

一、1. B　2. C　3. A　4. A　5. C

二、1. 我想跟您详细了解一下患者的病情。

2. 患者精神和食欲都不太好,伴有咳嗽、呕吐、惊厥和抽搐。

3. 儿科是全面研究小儿时期身心发育、保健及疾病防治的综合医学科学。

4. 小儿免疫力低下,调节和适应能力差。

三、略

四、1. 复杂　2. 红晕　3. 溃疡　流质食物　4. 详细　5. 发绀

五、(一)略

(二)略

(三)1. 身体特征　生理生化正常值　年龄　2. 比较大　先天性　遗传性　感染性　3. 年龄因素　治疗效果

六、略

七、

姓名:王晓红	性别:女
年龄:2 岁零 6 个月	婚姻状况:否
职业:无	就诊时间:2019 年 7 月 3 日 02:15
病史陈述者:患者母亲,李晓雨	

主诉:(患者母亲代述)纳差,流口水,发热,口腔溃疡,手足皮肤有疱疹。

现病史:患者母亲述患者 1 天前食欲差,流口水,口腔黏膜有少量溃疡,手部皮肤有少量红疹,无瘙痒和疼痛,半夜发热不退到我院就诊。

既往史:患者既往体健,为第 1 胎第 1 产,足月顺产。无外伤、输血及手术史,无药物过敏史。预防接种按国际计划进行。

体格检查:T 38.8 ℃,R 24 次/分,P:110 次/分,BP 90/50 mmHg ,W 14.15 kg。发育正常,营养中等;神志清醒。精神差,食欲差,伴有咳嗽、呕吐、惊厥和抽搐。手、脚、臀部出现散在的红色斑点和疱疹,疱疹周围有炎性红晕。舌头和口腔黏膜上也有散在疱疹。双肺呼吸音浅促,有湿啰音。

辅助检查:血常规示 WBC $11.84×10^9$/L,N 0.30,Hb 107 g/L,PLT $178×10^9$/L。

入院诊断:手足口病

医生签名:张琪

(改编自医院病历)

八、略

【第二十三单元】

【热身】

一、1. B　2. C　3. E　4. A　5. D

二、1. 耳蜗　2. 半规管　3. 外耳道　4. 内耳　5. 鼓膜　6. 中耳　7. 咽鼓管

【练习】

一、1. D　2. C　3. A　4. A　5. B

二、1. 听声音的时候,好像自己被关在一个密封的小舱里似的。

2. 这是一种中耳的非化脓性感染,有黏液但是没有化脓。

3. 分泌性中耳炎患者最先感觉到的就是耳闷和听力下降。

三、略

四、1. 分泌性　2. 鼓室腔　3. 咽鼓管　4. 鼓膜　5. 嚼嚼

五、(一)略

(二)1. 聚集　2. 蒙　鼓　3. 肿瘤　抗　4. 口香糖　捏　5. 促进　康复

六、略

七、

姓名:张伟	性别:男
年龄:23 岁	就诊时间:2017 年 10 月 09 日

主诉:因双耳闷堵,听力下降 3 天前来就诊。

现病史:3 天前出现双耳闷堵,听力下降,间歇性耳鸣。

既往史:平素体健。

体格检查:透过鼓膜可见液体阴影。

辅助检查:无。

初步诊断:分泌性中耳炎

医生签名:陈丽

(改编自医院病历)

八、略

【第二十四单元】

【热身】

一、1. B　2. A　3. G　4. H　5. I　6. D　7. F　8. E　9. C

二、1. 角膜　2. 瞳孔　3. 视网膜　4. 视神经　5. 巩膜　6. 晶状体　7. 脉络膜　8. 玻璃体

9. 虹膜

【练习】

一、1. C　2. D　3. A　4. B　5. A

二、1. 您需要先在这边做个手术再转到住院部去。

2. 门诊检查结果显示她的左眼被击伤。

3. 青光眼是我国主要致盲原因之一。

4.急性青光眼患者会突然出现眼睛痛,同时伴有头痛、恶心、呕吐、视力急剧下降等症状。

三、略

四、1.处理 2.骤降 3.致盲 4.推测 5.摘除术 6.预防 7.畏光

五、(一)略

(二)1.青白眼 2.急性青光眼 慢性青光眼 3.家族史 眼压 血压 血糖 年龄

六、略

七、

门诊病历

姓名:吴琼艳   性别:女

年龄:57 岁   婚姻状况:已婚

职业:农民   就诊时间:2017 年 12 月 8 日

主诉:左眼被木材击伤后视力下降伴胀痛 1 天。

现病史:患者 1 天前砍树时左眼被木材击伤,视力下降,仅有手动,伴畏光、流泪、眼红、眼痛等不适。

既往史:体健。

专科检查:

	右眼	左眼
视力	远0.6	手动/眼前
眼压	16.0 mmHg	28.0 mmHg
角膜	透明	3:00～5:00 有裂伤
瞳孔	3.0 mm×3.0 mm,对光反射灵敏	4.5 mm×4.0 mm,对光反射迟钝
晶状体	较透明	混浊

初步诊断:左眼角膜穿通伤,左眼继发性青光眼,左眼外伤性白内障

医生签名:陈雪

(改编自医院病历)

八、略

【第二十五单元】

【热身】

一、1.E 2.A 3.C 4.B 5.D

二、1.初发期 2.未成熟期 3.成熟期 4.过熟期

【练习】

一、1.C 2.D 3.A 4.B

二、1.需要先把病变的晶状体取出来,再植入人工晶状体。

2.人体眼球前部有一个双凸面透明的组织,叫作晶状体。

3.老年性白内障是最常见的一种白内障。

4.白内障是目前全球范围内第一大致盲眼病,与年龄、日晒、遗传、外伤等因素有关。

三、略

四、1. 范围　2. 逐年　3. 会聚　4. 过滤　5. 挡住

五、(一)略

(二)1. 屈光　会聚　视网膜　2. 老年性白内障　3. 手术　4. 混浊　不透明　人工晶状体

六、略

七、

<table>
<tr><td colspan="2">姓名:吴朝阳</td><td colspan="2">性别:男</td></tr>
</table>

姓名:吴朝阳		性别:男	
年龄:65 岁		婚姻状况:已婚	
职业:农民		就诊时间:2017 年 12 月 11 日	

主诉:双眼渐进性视力下降 3 年余,左眼加重 2 个月余。

现病史:患者于 3 年前无明显诱因双眼视力下降,呈渐进性发展,2 个月前左眼视力下降加重。

既往史:体健。

专科检查:

	右眼	左眼
视力	远 0.2	远 0.02
眼压	12.0 mmHg	13.0 mmHg
巩膜	正常,无黄染	正常,无黄染
瞳孔	3 mm×3 mm,对光反射灵敏	3 mm×3 mm,对光反射灵敏
晶状体	乳白色,混浊	乳白色,混浊

初步诊断:双眼老年性白内障

医生签名:陈雪

（改编自医院病历）

八、略

【第二十六单元】

【热身】

一、1. A　2. B　3. C　4. D

二、1. B　2. D　3. A　4. C

【练习】

一、1. C　2. A　3. A　4. D　5. C

二、1. 多喝水,多吃水果、蔬菜,保持大便畅通。

2. 在季节气候变换的时候要注意预防感冒。

3. 中医是一门研究人体生命、健康、疾病的科学。

4. 中医通过"望闻问切"四诊合参的方法来检查病情,诊断疾病。

三、1. 打喷嚏　2. 舌苔　3. 增强　4. 视觉　5. 嗅觉

四、(一)略

(二)1. 生命　健康　疾病　2. 望闻问切　3. 家属　症状　4. 动脉

五、略

六、略

七、

姓名:李华	性别:男
年龄:24 岁	就诊时间:2017 年 12 月 20 日

主诉:流鼻涕,打喷嚏,咳嗽4 天。

现病史:患者一直流鼻涕,打喷嚏,还有点咳嗽。不发烧。大便比较干,一两天 1 次。舌头偏红、舌苔偏厚。

既往史:平素体健。

辅助检查:无。

初步诊断:感冒。

医生签名:王桂香

(改编自医院病历)

八、略

【第二十七单元】

【热身】

一、1. D　2. A　3. C　4. B

二、1. B　2. C　3. A　4. D

【练习】

一、1. A　2. B　3. B　4. D　5. B

二、1. 平时不要有过度紧张、急躁、忧郁、愤怒等负面情绪,要保持精神舒畅。

2. 失眠常伴随头痛、健忘、缺乏精力、多梦等症状。

3. 阴阳和五行都是中国古代哲学的范畴。

4. 五行,指金、木、水、火、土这5 种物质及其运动方式。

三、1. 五行　2. 古代　3. 对立　4. 湿润　5. 颈椎病

四、(一)略

(二)1. 中药　针灸　推拿　拔罐　2. 阳　3. 阴　4. 五行　5. 高血压

五、略

六、略

七、

姓名:张真	性别:女
年龄:50 岁	就诊时间:2017 年 12 月 25 日

主诉:入睡困难1 个月。

现病史:患者晚上入睡困难,半夜易醒,醒后再睡困难。倦怠乏力,情绪急躁,吃饭没有胃口。大便比较干,舌头偏红,舌苔偏少。

既往史:有高血压病史。

辅助检查:无。

初步诊断:失眠。

医生签名:王桂香

(改编自医院病历)

八、略

【第二十八单元】

【热身】

一、1. E　2. I　3. D　4. H　5. A　6. B　7. F　8. C　9. G　10. J

二、1. √　2. ×　3. √　4. ×　5. √

【练习】

一、1. B　2. C　3. A　4. A　5. C

二、1. 17 床患者是昨天从内科转过来的。

2. 皮肤损伤沿周围神经呈带状排列。

3. 带状疱疹是由水痘-带状疱疹病毒引起的急性感染性皮肤病。

4. 当抵抗力低下或劳累、感染、感冒时,病毒可再次生长繁殖。

三、1. 排列　2. 痒　3. 感染　4. 繁殖　5. 变应原　6. 抵抗力

四、(一)略

(二)略

(三)1. 带状疱疹　急性感染性　2. 儿童　水痘　带状疱疹　3. 乏力　低热　丘疹　水疱　紧张发亮　澄清　红晕　带状

五、略

六、略

七、

姓名:刘美艳	性别:女
年龄:37 岁	婚姻状况:已婚
职业:教师	就诊时间:2019 年 3 月 20 日 11:00

主诉:腰背、腹部疼痛,腰背右侧出现疱疹 2 天。

现病史:2 天前患者因腰背及腹部疼痛到医院就诊,因患者曾患胆囊结石,我院门诊以胆囊炎收治,用药后未见好转。1 天前患者腰背右侧出现黄豆大小红色丘疹,转到皮肤科治疗。

既往史:有胆囊结石病史,无过敏史。

体格检查:T 37.8 ℃,R 22 次/,P 80 次/分,BP 120/80 mmHg。发育正常,营养良好,神志清醒,呈痛苦病容。低热。腰背部出现一些黄豆大小的红色丘疹,有灼痛感。之后丘疹明显增多,而且部分已经发展成水疱,疱壁紧张发亮,疱液澄清,周围有红晕,疱皮损沿某一周围神经呈带状排列。

辅助检查:血常规示:RBC 4.43×10^{12}/L, WBC 7.4×10^9/L, Hb 137 g/L, PLT 248×10^9/L。

心电图示:窦性心律,心电轴正常。腹部彩超示:胆囊大小正常,胆囊壁不厚,内见一强光团,大小约 2 mm×3 mm,伴声影,可随体位改变移动。

入院诊断:带状疱疹

医生签名:林军

八、略

【第二十九单元】

【热身】

一、1.食欲减退　2.乏力　3.肝区胀痛

二、1.甲型肝炎　2.乙型肝炎　3.丙型肝炎　4.丁型肝炎　5.戊型肝炎

【练习】

一、1.A　2.A　3.A　4.B　5.A

二、1.我最近看到油腻的食物想吐,但又吐不出来。

2.他全身乏力,食欲减退,肝区胀痛,应该是得了乙型病毒性肝炎。

3.平常注意休息,预防感冒,清淡饮食,不能抽烟和喝酒。

4.一般通过检查乙肝五项、肝功能和病毒含量来确诊乙肝。

三、1.尿黄　2.油腻　3.肝功能　4.血浆置换　5.干扰素

四、(一)略

(二)1.肝硬化　肝癌　2.母婴传播　血液传播　性传播　3.肝功能　4.免疫功能　5.根除抗病毒

五、略

六、略

七、

姓名:李中　　　　　　　　性别:男 年龄:45 岁　　　　　　　就诊时间:2017 年 12 月 11 日   主诉:腹胀,全身无力,尿黄,食欲减退 1 个月。 现病史:乙型肝炎病毒携带。 既往史:无。 辅助检查:乙肝五项、肝功能、乙肝病毒含量示:总胆红素 120 μmol/L,谷丙转氨酶 440 U/L。 初步诊断:乙型病毒性肝炎 　　　　　　　　　　　　　　　　　　　　医生签名:王美

(改编自医院病历)

八、略

【第三十单元】

【热身】

一、1.B　2.A　3.C

二、1.A E G　2.B C F　3.D H I

【练习】

一、1.B　2.A　3.C　4.A　5.D

二、1.是否接受过手术和麻醉? 有无不良反应?

2.但是,请您放心,我们会做好隐私保护的。

3. 我先核对您的信息,请问您叫什么名字?

4. 因为麻醉药的作用,所以您是不会感到疼痛的。

三、1. 麻醉史　2. 保障　3. 技术　生命功能　4. 威胁　稳定

四、(一)略

(二)1. 全身麻醉　局部麻醉　复合麻醉　2. 适应证　禁忌证　3. 手术前后　4. 生命守护神

五、略

六、略

七、

麻醉知情同意书

　　患者李站于 2017 年 10 月 10 日拟行右胫腓骨骨折手术治疗,交代病情及麻醉有关事项如下。

一、根据患者病情及手术需要拟行硬膜外麻醉。

二、目前患者存在如下问题。

1. 术前意识及精神状态:清醒。

2. 创伤严重。

3. 手术复杂。

三、随着麻醉学进展及监测技术的日益完善,麻醉水平和安全性都有了很大提高,但无论何种麻醉方法与技术操作都会对患者生理功能产生不同程度的影响,难免发生一些并发症或意外,如:

1. 麻醉药过敏、中毒等不良反应,导致休克、心跳呼吸骤停、严重脏器功能损害。

2. 反流、误吸、喉头水肿、喉痉挛、支气管痉挛、缺氧、窒息等。

……

以上情况严重时均可致死亡。

对上述并发症和意外死亡,麻醉医生将本着救死扶伤精神尽力积极救治,但不能绝对避免。

患者或代理人意见:对上述交代的问题是否理解:理解

　　　　　　　　是否同意麻醉:同意

患者签字:李站　　　　　　　　　　　　　　代理人签字:王芳

　　　　　　　　　　　　　　　　　　　　代理人与患者关系:夫妻

　　　　　　　　　　　　　　　　　　　　麻醉医生:王柱

(改编自医院麻醉知情同意书)

八、略

【第三十一单元】

【热身】

一、1. B　2. D　3. A　4. G　5. H　6. C　7. E F　8. I J

二、1. C　2. H　3. D　4. A　5. F　6. G　7. E　8. B

【练习】

一、1. A　2. C　3. B　4. D　5. B

二、1. 通过康复治疗及锻炼,我的右手能举过头了,右腿也能屈伸了。

2. 先测测血压,再量量体温吧。

3. 还是要加强行走训练,增强下肢力量啊!

4. 记得家属必须陪同辅助训练啊!

三、1. 常见　2. 平卧　血流　3. 患肢　4. 锻炼　5. 楼梯

四、(一)略

(二)1. 运动障碍　急性脑血管病　2. 轻瘫　不完全性瘫　全瘫　3. 右侧偏瘫　4. 肢体功能被动运动

五、略

六、略

七、略

姓名:王醒	性别:男
年龄:54 岁	就诊时间:2017 年 10 月 11 日

主诉:右侧肢体活动不利 1 个半月。

现病史:患者无明显诱因下突然出现头晕,右侧肢体麻木无力且无法自主活动,吐字含糊。治疗后,患者神志转清,吐字尚清,头晕和右侧肢体乏力较前好转,仍有走路不稳,可在支撑架帮助下缓慢行走,精神尚可,睡眠、饮食、二便正常。

既往史:平素体健。

辅助检查:头颅 MRI 及 MRA 示:左侧脑桥梗死灶,颅内大血管未见明显狭窄。

初步诊断:左脑桥梗死恢复期

医生签名:朱爽

(改编自医院病历)

八、略

附录二

词汇表

词性对照表

词性	英文简称	词性	英文简称	词性	英文简称
名词	n.	量词	m.	形容词	adj.
动词	v.	助词	part.	代词	pron.
能愿动词	mod.	叹词	int.	数词	num.
副词	adv.	拟声词	onom.		
介词	prep.	连词	conj.		

生词表（一）

序号	词语	词性	拼音	词义	单元
A					
1	阿氏评分	名	āshìpíngfēn	Apgar scores	20
2	癌变	动	áibiàn	canceration	1
3	嗳气	名	àiqì	belching	1
4	癌症	名	áizhèng	cancer	17
5	阿莫西林	名	āmòxīlín	amoxicillin	3
B					
6	拔罐	名	báguàn	cupping	27
7	百分数	名	bǎifēnshù	percentage	21
8	白细胞	名	báixìbāo	leukocytosis	3
9	把脉	动	bǎmài	feel the pulse	26
10	伴	动	bàn	and	15
11	伴发	动	bànfā	concomitant	8
12	斑片状浸润影	-	bānpiànzhuàng jìnrùnyǐng	patchy infiltrating shadow	3
13	半流质	形	bàn liúzhì	semi-liquid	9

序号	词语	词性	拼音	词义	单元
14	伴随	动	bànsuí	accompany；follow	27
15	薄	形	báo	thin	20
16	包块	名	bāo kuài	enclosed mass	16
17	保持	动	bǎochí	maintain	26
18	保健	名	bǎojiàn	health and fitness	22
19	保守	形	báoshǒu	conservative	11
20	保温	动	bǎowēn	insulation	20
21	保养	动	báoyǎng	maintenance	23
22	保障	动	bǎozhàng	assure	30
23	背	名	bèi	human back	13
24	钡餐	名	bèicān	barium meal	2
25	被动运动	动	bèidòng yùndòng	passive movement	31
26	绷带	名	bēngdài	bandage	12
27	本质	名	běnzhì	essence	26
28	闭	动	bì	closure	9
29	变应原	名	biànyìngyuán	allergen	28
30	边缘	名	biānyuán	edge	11
31	边缘性	名	biānyuánxìng	marginality	19
32	表现	名	biǎoxiàn	manifestation	16
33	比例	名	bǐlì	proportion	3
34	避免	动	bìmiǎn	avoid	11
35	病变	动	bìngbiàn	lesion	1
36	病毒	名	bìngdú	virus	26
37	病毒含量	名	bìngdú hánliàng	virus content	29
38	病房	名	bìngfáng	ward	16
39	并发症	名	bìngfāzhèng	complication	8
40	病理性	形	bìnglǐxìng	pathological	21
41	病情	名	bìngqíng	state of an illness	30
42	病原体	名	bìngyuántǐ	causative agent	3
43	病灶	名	bìngzào	focus of primary lesion	5
44	鼻腔	名	bíqiāng	nasal cavity	3
45	鼻塞	名	bísè	nasal obstruction	26
46	鼻涕	名	bítì	rhinorrhea	26
47	不完全性瘫	名	bùwánquánxìngtān	incomplete hemiplegia	31
48	部分性	名	bùfenxìng	partial seizures	19
49	不良反应	名	bùliáng fǎnyìng	untoward reaction	30

序号	词语	词性	拼音	词义	单元
			C		
50	彩超	名	cǎichāo	color ultrasound	19
51	采集	动	cǎijí	collect	9
52	采取	动	cǎiqǔ	take	20
53	舱	名	cāng	cabin	23
54	残疾	名	cánjí	disability	8
55	嘈杂	形	cáozá	noisy	23
56	测量	动	cèliáng	measure	31
57	肠道	名	chángdào	intestine	10
58	肠梗阻	名	chánggěngzǔ	intestinal obstruction	9
59	肠鸣音	名	chángmíngyīn	bowel sound	9
60	畅通	形	chàngtōng	unobstructed	26
61	产前检查	名	chǎnqián jiǎnchá	antenatal examination	18
62	超	副	chāo	ultra	20
63	超声	名	chāoshēng	ultrasound	16
64	车把	名	chēbǎ	handlebar	11
65	车祸	名	chēhuò	accident	11
66	程度	名	chéngdù	degree	8
67	成分	名	chéngfèn	ingredient	14
68	澄清	形	chéngqīng	clear	28
69	迟钝	形	chídùn	slow	24
70	持续	动	chíxù	continue	5
71	重影	名	chóngyǐng	double image	8
72	抽	动	chōu	take out	23
73	抽搐	动	chōuchù	convulsion	5
74	抽烟	动	chōuyān	smoking	4
75	触按	动	chùàn	touch and press	26
76	传播	动	chuánbō	transmit	29
77	穿刺	动	chuāncì	puncture	23
78	穿孔	动	chuānkǒng	perforation	23
79	传染病	名	chuánrǎnbìng	infectious disease	29
80	传染源	名	chuánrǎnyuán	source of infection	29
81	穿透伤	名	chuāntòu shāng	penetrating injury	11
82	初步	形	chūbù	initial	11
83	处理	动	chǔlǐ	deal with	19
84	触诊	名	chùzhěn	palpation	9

序号	词语	词性	拼音	词义	单元
85	磁共振成像	名	cígòngzhèn chéngxiàng	magnetic resonance imaging	13
86	刺激性	形	cìjīxìng	irritating	29
87	脆弱	形	cuìruò	fragile	9
88	促进	动	cùjìn	promote	18
89	挫伤	动	cuòshāng	contuse	11
90	措施	名	cuòshī	measure	16
91	错位	动	cuòwèi	dislocate	12
			D		
92	打嗝	动	dǎgé	hiccup	2
93	代谢	动	dàixiè	metabolic	5
94	代谢紊乱	名	dàixiè wěnluàn	metabolic disorder	8
95	胆固醇	名	dǎngùchún	cholesterol	15
96	挡住	动	dǎngzhù	block	25
97	胆红素	名	dǎnhóngsù	bilirubin	15
98	胆囊	名	dǎnnáng	gall bladder	15
99	胆囊触诊	动	dǎnnáng chùzhěn	gallbladder palpation	29
100	胆囊结石	名	dǎnnáng jiéshí	gallstone	15
101	胆囊炎	名	dǎnnángyán	cholecystitis	15
102	胆色素	名	dǎnsèsù	bile pigment	15
103	耽误	动	dānwu	delay	19
104	胆汁淤积	名	dǎnzhī yūjī	cholestasis	15
105	导致	动	dǎozhì	result in	3
106	打喷嚏	动	dǎ pēntì	sneeze	26
107	低色素	名	dī sèsù	hypochromic	7
108	低置	动	dīzhì	locate in a low position	19
109	垫	动	diàn	pad	4
110	癫痫	名	diānxián	epilepsy	5
111	典型	形	diǎnxíng	typical	8
112	抵抗力	名	dǐkànglì	immunity	28
113	定位	动	dìngwèi	orient	19
114	叮嘱	动	dīngzhǔ	advise；warn	9
115	动力	名	dònglì	power	6
116	动脉	名	dòngmài	artery	6
117	动脉硬化	名	dòngmài yìnghuà	arteriosclerosis	1
118	动态脑电图	名	dòngtài nǎodiàntú	electroencephalogram（EEG）	5
119	窦性心律	名	dòuxìng xīnlù	sinus rhythm	6

序号	词语	词性	拼音	词义	单元
120	端	名	duān	end	20
121	断断续续	形	duànduànxùxù	off and on	13
122	锻炼	名	duànliàn	exercise	31
123	对立	动	duìlì	oppose	27
124	蹲	动	dūn	kneel down	13
125	钝性伤	名	dùn xìng shāng	blunt trauma	11
126	多亏	形	duōkuī	thank to	31
127	多胎妊娠	名	duōtāi rènshēn	multiple pregnancy	18
E					
128	恶变	动	èbiàn	degenerate	17
129	恶化	动	èhuà	get worse	13
130	耳鸣	动	ěrmíng	tinnitus	23
131	二氧化碳	名	èryǎnghuàtàn	carbon dioxide	4
132	恶心	形	ěxin	nausea	2
133	恶性	形	èxìng	malignant	16
F					
134	发病率	名	fābìnglǜ	incidentce rate	25
135	发绀	名	fāgàn	cyanosis	22
136	乏力	形	fálì	weak；feeble	29
137	发闷	动	fāmen	stuffy	23
138	犯病	动	fànbìng	fall ill	5
139	范畴	名	fànchóu	category	27
140	反复	副	fǎnfù	repeatedly	19
141	房间隔	名	fáng jiàngé	interatrial septum	6
142	方案	名	fāng'àn	scheme	8
143	方式	名	fāngshì	way；pattern	27
144	反射	动	fǎnshè	reflection	24
145	反酸	动	fǎnsuān	sour regurgitation	2
146	反跳痛	名	fǎntiàotòng	rebound symptoms	10
147	范围	名	fànwéi	scope	22
148	反胃	形	fǎnwèi	regurgitation	2
149	烦躁	形	fánzào	irritability	21
150	繁殖	动	fánzhí	to breed；to grown	28
151	发育	名/动	fāyù	growth；grow	22
152	肥大	形	féidà	hypertrophy	23
153	肺泡	名	fèipào	alveoli	4

序号	词语	词性	拼音	词义	单元
154	肺气肿	名	fèiqìzhǒng	emphysema	4
155	肺炎	名	fèiyán	pneumonia	3
156	肺炎链球菌	名	fèiyán liànqiújūn	streptococcus bacteria	3
157	粪	名	fèn	feces	10
158	分型	名	fēn xíng	type	8
159	粉尘	名	fěnchén	dust	28
160	分割点	名	fēngē diǎn	break point	8
161	风湿性心脏病	名	fēngshī xìng xīnzàngbìng	rheumatic heart disease（RHD）	6
162	风湿病	名	fēngshībìng	rheumatism	7
163	分泌	动	fēnmì	secrete	8
164	分娩	动	fēnmiǎn	childbirth；delivery	18
165	分泌物	名	fēnmìwù	secretions	23
166	分泌性	形	fēnmìxìng	secretory	23
167	愤怒	形	fènnù	wrathful	27
168	服（药）	动	fú（yào）	to take（medicine）	6
169	腹围	名	fùwéi	abdominal perimeter	18
170	腹部	名	fùbù	abdomen	16
171	腹部 X 射线	名	fùbù X shèxiàn	abdominal X-ray	10
172	复查	动	fùchá	recheck	1
173	复发率	名	fùfālǜ	recurrence rate	16
174	覆盖	动	fùgài	cover	19
175	富含	动	fù hán	be rich in	9
176	复合麻醉	名	fùhé mázuì	compound anesthesia	30
177	妇科	名	fùkē	gynecology department	16
178	复位	名	fùwèi	restoration	12
179	复诊	名	fùzhěn	further consultation（with a doctor）	26
180	辅助	形	fǔzhù	aid	20
181	附着	动	fùzhuó	adhere to	19
			G		
182	概率	名	gàilǜ	probability	13
183	改善	动	gǎishàn	ameliorate	18
184	肝区	名	gānqū	liver area	29
185	干湿啰音	名	gānshī luóyīn	dry and moist rale	4
186	肝癌	名	gānái	liver cancer	29
187	肝功能	名	gāngōngnéng	liver function	15
188	感染	动	gǎnrǎn	infect	1

序号	词语	词性	拼音	词义	单元
189	感染性	形	gǎnrǎnxìng	infectious	22
190	干扰素	名	gānrǎosù	interferon	29
191	肝硬化	名	gānyìnghuà	liver cirrhosis	29
192	高蛋白	形	gāo dànbái	high protein	9
193	高血压	名	gāoxuèyā	hypertension	6
194	疙瘩	名	gēda	pimple；knot	28
195	根除	动	gēnchú	eradicate	2
196	根治	动	gēnzhì	radical cure	4
197	汞	名	gǒng	mercury	5
198	宫高	名	gōnggāo	fundal height	18
199	肱骨干	名	gōnggǔ gàn	shaft of humerus	12
200	肱骨外科颈	名	gōnggǔ wàikē jǐng	surgical neck of humerus	12
201	宫颈	名	gōngjǐng	cervix	17
202	宫颈口	名	gōngjǐngkǒu	cervix	19
203	巩膜	名	gǒngmó	sclera	21
204	功能	名	gōngnéng	function	6
205	恭喜	动	gōngxǐ	congratulations	20
206	沟通	动	gōutōng	communicate	11
207	鼓	名	gǔ	drum	23
208	谷丙转氨酶	名	gǔbǐngzhuǎnānméi	alanine aminotransferase	29
209	骨擦感	名	gǔcāgǎn	bone abrasion	12
210	骨擦音	名	gǔcāyīn	bone crepitus	12
211	管道	名	guǎndào	pipeline	6
212	冠心病	名	guānxīnbìng	coronary heart disease	8
213	冠状窦	名	guānzhuàngdòu	coronary sinus	6
214	古代	形	gǔdài	ancient	27
215	规律	名	guīlǜ	regular	16
216	规则	形	guīzé	regular	17
217	鼓膜	名	gǔmó	tympanic membrane	23
218	过度	形	guòdù	excessive	27
219	过滤	动	guòlǜ	filter	3
220	过敏	动	guòmǐn	allergy	3
221	骨盆	名	gǔpén	pelvis	17
222	鼓气	动	gǔqì	blow air	23
223	鼓室腔	名	gǔshìqiāng	tympanic cavity	23
224	骨髓	名	gǔsuǐ	marrow	7

序号	词语	词性	拼音	词义	单元
			H		
225	寒战	名	hánzhàn	shivering	15
226	毫米汞柱	量	háomǐgǒngzhù	mmHg	6
227	好转	动	hǎozhuǎn	be better	9
228	核对	动	héduì	check	30
229	核苷酸类似物	名	hégānsuān lèisì wù	nucleotide analogues	29
230	黑便	名	hēibiàn	dark stools；melena	2
231	虹膜	名	hóngmó	iris	24
232	红细胞	名	hóngxìbāo	red blood cell	7
233	红晕	名	hóngyùn	flush	22
234	喉反射	名	hóufǎnshè	laryngeal reflex	20
235	花粉	名	huāfěn	pollen	28
236	怀孕	动	huáiyùn	be pregnant	18
237	换	动	huàn	change	25
238	患肢	名	huànzhī	affected limb	31
239	黄染	形	huángrǎn	yellow dye	21
240	黄疸	名	huángdǎn	jaundice	15
241	黄豆	名	huángdòu	soybean	28
242	缓解	动	huǎnjiě	ease	4
243	化脓性	形	huànóngxìng	purulent infection	23
244	化验	动	huàyàn	test	18
245	互不	–	hù bù	be not…each other	6
246	蛔虫	名	huíchóng	ascarid	15
247	恢复	动	huīfù	get well	23
248	会聚	动	huìjù	converge	25
249	会阴	名	huìyīn	perineum	14
250	浑身	副	húnshēn	from head to foot	19
251	混浊	形	húnzhuó	turbid	24
252	火锅	名	huǒguō	hot pot	15
253	活检	动	huójiǎn	biopsies	2
254	忽视	动	hūshì	neglect	3
255	呼吸	动	hūxī	breath	3
256	呼吸窘迫综合征	名	hūxī jiǒngpò zōnghézhēng	respiratory distress syndrome	20
			J		
257	极	副	jí	pole	20
258	脊	名	jǐ	costolumbar	14

序号	词语	词性	拼音	词义	单元
259	疾病史	名	jíbìngshǐ	disease history	3
260	肌张力	名	jīzhānglì	muscle tension	20
261	佳	形	jiā	fine	8
262	加剧	动	jiājù	aggravat	13
263	监测	动	jiāncè	monitor	18
264	降压药	名	jiàngyāyào	hypotensor	27
265	浆液性	形	jiāngyèxìng	serous	16
266	监护仪	名	jiānhùyí	monitor	30
267	监控	动	jiānkòng	monitor	17
268	建立	名	jiànlì	set up	30
269	减弱	动	jiǎnruò	weaken	4
270	减退	动	jiǎntuì	slack up	29
271	嚼	动	jiáo	chew	23
272	角膜	名	jiǎomó	cornea	24
273	角膜穿通伤	名	jiǎomó chuāntōngshāng	corneal penetrating injury	24
274	绞痛	动	jiǎotòng	colic pain	10
275	加重期	名	jiāzhòng qī	aggravating period	4
276	家族病	名	jiāzúbìng	hereditary disease	18
277	急促	形	jícù	tachypnea	11
278	戒	动	jiè	quit	2
279	节律性	形	jiélǜxìng	rhythmic	2
280	解除	动	jiěchú	get rid of	14
281	解除梗阻	–	jiěchú gěngzǔ	relieve the obstruction	15
282	结合	动	jiéhé	combine	3
283	接近	动	jiējìn	be close to	19
284	解开	动	jiěkāi	unclasp	3
285	接种	动	jiēzhòng	inoculate	29
286	继发性	形	jìfāxìng	secondary	5
287	继发性青光眼	名	jìfāxìng qīngguāngyǎn	secondary glaucoma	24
288	肌肤	名	jīfū	skin	26
289	急腹症	名	jífùzhèng	acute abdomen diseases	9
290	急剧	形	jíjù	sudden drop	24
291	肌瘤	名	jīliú	leiomyomata	17
292	进行性血胸	名	jìnxíngxìng xuèxiōng	progressive hemothorax	11
293	径	名	jìng	path	4
294	胫腓骨	名	jìngféigǔ	tibiofibula	30

序号	词语	词性	拼音	词义	单元
295	惊厥	名	jīngjué	convulsions	22
296	精力	名	jīnglì	energy；vigour	27
297	痉挛	动	jìngluán	spasm	5
298	静脉	名	jìngmài	vein	6
299	静脉通道	名	jìngmài tōngdào	passage of vein	30
300	精确	形	jīngquè	precise	19
301	镜头	名	jìngtóu	lens	25
302	晶状体	名	jīngzhuàngtǐ	lens	24
303	颈椎病	名	jǐngzhuībìng	cervical spondylosis	27
304	紧急	形	jǐnjí	urgent	15
305	禁忌证	名	jìnjìzhèng	incompatibility symptom	30
306	禁食	动	jìnshí	fast	9
307	进展	动	jìnzhǎn	progress	21
308	紧张	形	jǐnzhāng	nervous	30
309	寄生虫	名	jìshēngchóng	parasites	10
310	技术	名	jìshù	technique	30
311	积水	名	jīshuǐ	hydrops	14
312	就医	动	jiùyī	see the doctor	10
313	急性	形	jíxìng	acute	6
314	畸形	名	jīxíng	malformation	12
315	积液	名	jīyè	effusion	23
316	急躁	形	jízào	irritable；impatient	27
317	巨幼细胞贫血	名	jù yòu xìbāo pínxuè	megaloblastic anemia	7
318	局部麻醉	名	júbù mázuì	local anesthesia	30
319	绝对	副	juéduì	absolute	13
320	聚集	动	jùjí	accumulate	23
321	剧烈	形	jùliè	strenuous	11
			K		
322	抗	动	kàng	anti-	23
323	抗病毒	动	kàng bìngdú	anti-viral	29
324	康复	动	kāngfù	rehabilitate	12
325	抗感染	动	kàng gǎnrǎn	anti-infective	29
326	抗菌	动	kàngjūn	antibiotic	3
327	抗生素	名	kàngshēngsù	antibiotics	3
328	靠背	名	kàobèi	backrest of chair	13
329	咳痰	动	kétán	cough with phlegm	3

序号	词语	词性	拼音	词义	单元
330	空腹血糖	名	kōngfù xuètáng	fasting blood-glucose（FBG）	8
331	控制	动	kòngzhì	control	8
332	叩击痛	名	kòujī tòng	percussive pain	14
333	口腔黏膜	名	kǒuqiāng niánmó	mucous membrane of mouth	22
334	口吐白沫	–	kǒu tǔ báimò	foam started coming out of mouth	5
335	口香糖	名	kǒuxiāngtáng	chewing gum	23
336	溃疡灶	名	kuìyáng zào	ulcer lesion	2
			L		
337	拉肚子	动	lādùzi	diarrhea	10
338	阑尾腔	名	lánwěi qiāng	appendix	10
339	肋	名	lèi	rib	14
340	类	名	lèi	kind；category	19
341	类（似）	形	lèi（sì）	similar	14
342	肋骨	名	lèigǔ	rib	11
343	良性	形	liángxìng	benign	16
344	链霉素	名	liànméisù	streptomycin	28
345	裂伤	名	lièshāng	laceration	24
346	裂隙灯显微镜检查	名	lièxìdēng xiǎnwēijìng jiǎnchá	slit lamp microscope test	25
347	厉害	形	lìhai	powerful	4
348	理疗	名	lǐliáo	physiotherapy	13
349	淋巴细胞	名	línbā xìbāo	lymphocyte	21
350	临床表现	–	línchuáng biǎoxiàn	general clinic manifestation	1
351	凌晨	名	língchén	before dawn	14
352	灵敏	形	língmǐn	sensitivity	24
353	流	动	liú	flow	19
354	流产	名	liúchǎn	abortion	19
355	流动	动	liúdòng	flow	23
356	流通	动	liútōng	circulate	26
357	楼梯	名	lóutī	stair	31
358	卵巢囊肿	名	luǎncháo nángzhǒng	ovarian cyst	16
			M		
359	吗丁啉	名	Mǎdīnglín	Domperidone	1
360	麦氏点	名	Màishì diǎn	McBurney point	10
361	脉搏	名	màibó	pulse	26
362	脉象	名	màixiàng	pulse condition	26

序号	词语	词性	拼音	词义	单元
363	盲管	名	mángguǎn	blind tube	10
364	慢性	形	mànxìng	chronic	1
365	慢性支气管炎	名	mànxìng zhīqìguǎnyán	chronic bronchitis	4
366	慢性阻塞性肺疾病	名	mànxìng zǔsèxìng fèijíbìng	chronic obstructive pulmonary disease	4
367	蔓延	动	mànyán	spread	9
368	满月	名	mǎnyuè	a baby's completion of its first month of life	21
369	毛细血管	名	máoxì xuèguǎn	capillaries	4
370	麻醉	动	mázuì	anesthetic	2
371	麻醉史	名	mázuìshǐ	history of anesthesia	30
372	麻醉药	名	mázuìyào	anesthetics	12
373	蒙	动	méng	imprison	23
374	免疫力	名	miǎnyìlì	immune capacity	3
375	密封	形	mìfēng	sealed	23
376	明确	形	míngquè	explicite	17
377	目前	形	mùqián	at present	18
378	木桶	名	mùtǒng	barrel	4
379	木屑	名	mùxiè	sawdust	24
			N		
380	耐受	动	nàishòu	tolerate	11
381	脑梗死	名	nǎogěngsǐ	cerebral infarction	8
382	脑卒中	名	nǎocùzhòng	stroke	5
383	脑脊液	名	nǎojǐyè	cerebrospinal fluid	5
384	脑膜炎	名	nǎomóyán	meningitis	5
385	内口	名	nèikǒu	internal opening	19
386	内容物	名	nèiróng wù	content	9
387	黏液	名	niányè	mucus	23
388	黏液促排剂	名	niányè cùpáijì	mucus promoting agents	23
389	黏液性	形	niányèxìng	mucinous	16
390	尿路感染	–	niàolù gǎnrǎn	urinary tract infection	14
391	尿常规	名	niàochángguī	urine routine	10
392	尿糖	名	niàotáng	urine glucose (UGLU)	8
393	捏	动	niē	hold between fingers	23
394	扭曲	动	niǔqū	twist	10
395	浓	形	nóng	dark;thick	29
396	浓度	名	nóngdù	concentration	21

序号	词语	词性	拼音	词义	单元
397	暖箱	名	nuǎnxiāng	warm box	20
O					
398	呕吐	动	ǒutù	vomit	1
P					
399	排出物	名	páichūwù	discharge	26
400	排列	动	páiliè	to arrange	28
401	排气	动	páiqì	fart	9
402	膀胱	名	pángguāng	bladder	17
403	疱壁	名	pàobì	blister wall	28
404	疱疹	名	pàozhěn	herpes	22
405	佩戴	动	pèidài	wear	13
406	配合	名	pèihé	cooperation	8
407	陪同	动	péitóng	accompany	31
408	盆腔	名	pénqiāng	pelvis	18
409	脾	名	pí	spleen	7
410	脾胃病	名	píwèibìng	spleen and stomach diseases	27
411	频繁	副	pínfán	often；frequently	6
412	评估	动	pínggū	evaluate	11
413	平衡训练	名	pínghéng xùnliàn	balance training	31
414	平衡	名	pínghéng	balance	27
415	皮损（皮肤损伤）	名	písǔn（pífū sǔnshāng）	skin injury	28
416	皮屑	名	píxiè	scuff；dander	28
417	破裂	动	pòliè	rupture	11
418	剖宫产	名	pōugōngchǎn	caesarean section	19
419	葡萄糖耐量	名	pútaotáng nàiliàng	glucose tolerance	8
Q					
420	脐	名	qí	funicle	22
421	铅	名	qiān	plumbum	5
422	前后壁	名	qián hòu bì	anterior posterior wall	19
423	浅促	形	qiǎn cù	shortness of breath	20
424	腔	名	qiāng	cavity；antrum	6
425	强力	形	qiánglì	strong	13
426	前置胎盘	名	qiánzhì tāipán	placenta previa	19
427	气喘	动	qìchuǎn	asthma	4
428	器官	名	qìguān	organ	3
429	侵犯	名/动	qīnfàn	invasion；to violate；to invade	28

序号	词语	词性	拼音	词义	单元
430	轻瘫	名	qīng tān	paresis	31
431	清淡	形	qīngdàn	light	9
432	青霉素	名	qīngméisù	penicillin	3
433	请示	动	qǐngshì	consult	25
434	轻微	形	qīngwēi	slightly	14
435	清晰	副	qīngxī	clearly	31
436	清醒	形	qīngxǐng	sober	5
437	丘疹	名	qiūzhěn	papula	28
438	气味	名	qìwèi	smell；odour；flavour	26
439	气血	名	qìxuè	vital energy and blood	27
440	全瘫	名	quán tān	complete hemiplegia	31
441	全面	形	quánmiàn	comprehensive	22
442	全球	形	quánqiú	global	25
443	全身麻醉	名	quánshēn mázuì	general anesthesia	30
444	缺乏	动	quēfá	be short of；lack	27
445	确切	形	quèqiè	definite	17
446	缺铁性贫血	名	quētiěxìng pínxuè	iron deficiency anemia	7
447	缺陷	名	quēxiàn	defect	8
448	缺氧	动	quēyǎng	hypoxia	20
449	确诊	动	quèzhěn	make definite diagnosis	5
450	屈光的	形	qūguāngde	refractive	25
451	去世	动	qùshì	die	18
			R		
452	人工	名	réngōng	artificial	25
453	人工肝血浆置换	动	réngōng gān xuèjiāng zhìhuàn	artificial liver plasma replacement therapy	29
454	妊娠	名	rènshēn	pregnancy	8
455	忍受	动	rěnshòu	tolerate；endure	15
456	人为	形	rénwéi	man-made；artificial	8
457	日晒	名	rìshài	exposure to the sun	25
458	容量	名	róngliàng	capacity	7
459	溶血	名	róngxuè	hemolytic	7
460	乳白色	名	rǔbáisè	milky	25
461	锐器	名	ruìqì	sharp	11
462	入院单	名	rùyuàn dān	admission list	16
			S		
463	丧失	动	sàngshī	loss	5

序号	词语	词性	拼音	词义	单元
464	扫描	动	sǎomiáo	scan	13
465	上腹部	名	shàng fùbù	upper abdomen	1
466	上呼吸道	名	shànghūxīdào	upper respiratory tract	3
467	上皮性	形	shàngpíxìng	epithelial	16
468	稍微	副	shāowēi	slightly	15
469	肾绞痛	名	shèn jiǎotòng	renal colic	14
470	生理性	形	shēnglǐxìng	physiological	21
471	生命功能	名	shēngmìng gōngnéng	vital function	30
472	生育	名	shēngyù	bearing	17
473	生殖	名	shēngzhí	reproduction	16
474	肾结石	名	shènjiéshí	renal calculus	14
475	神经纤维	名	shénjīng xiānwéi	nerve fiber	28
476	神经系统	名	shénjīng xìtǒng	nervous system	5
477	肾上盏结石	名	shèn shàng zhǎn jiéshí	upper calyceal calculus	14
478	神态	名	shéntài	expression;manner	26
479	身心	名	shēnxīn	mind and body	22
480	深夜	名	shēnyè	late at night	14
481	舌苔	名	shétāi	coating on the tongue	26
482	舌头	名	shétou	tongue	26
483	式	名	shì	type;style;mode	28
484	室间隔	名	shì jiàngé	interventricular septum	6
485	湿啰音	名	shī luóyīn	moist rales	3
486	失用性萎缩	动	shīyòngxìng wěisuō	disuse atrophy	12
487	似的	助	shìde	rather like	23
488	十二指肠	名	shí'èrzhǐcháng	duodenum	2
489	视觉	名	shìjué	sense of sight	26
490	视力	名	shìlì	vision	24
491	失眠	名	shīmián	insomnia;sleeplessness	27
492	湿润	形	shīrùn	moist	27
493	适应	动	shìyìng	adapt	20
494	适应证	名	shìyìngzhèng	adaptation symptom	30
495	食欲	名	shíyù	appetite	1
496	受	动	shòu	to accept;to suffer	28
497	手段	名	shǒuduàn	means	8
498	手法	名	shóufǎ	method	13
499	受凉	动	shòuliáng	catch cold	3

序号	词语	词性	拼音	词义	单元
500	受限	动	shòuxiàn	be limitted	12
501	手足口病	名	shǒuzúkǒubìng	hand-foot-and-mouth disease	22
502	舒缩	动	shū suō	systolic and diastolic	12
503	双胞胎	名	shuāngbāotāi	twins	18
504	蔬菜	名	shūcài	vegetables	26
505	舒畅	形	shūchàng	entirely free from worry	27
506	水痘	名	shuǐdòu	chicken pox	28
507	水疱	名	shuǐpào	blister	22
508	顺产	名	shùnchǎn	natural labor	21
509	输尿管镜	名	shūniàoguǎn jìng	ureteroscope	14
510	输液	动	shūyè	infusion	5
511	属于	动	shǔyú	be belong to	19
512	四诊合参	名	sìzhěn hécān	comprehensive analysis by the four examination methods	26
513	酸性	形	suānxìng	acidic	2
514	随意	副	suíyì	arbitrarily	11
515	随着	动	suízhe	along with	22
516	损害	名	sǔnhài	damage	8
517	损坏	动	sǔnhuài	damage	4
518	损伤	动	sǔnshāng	injury	11
519	素质	名	sùzhì	quality	26
			T		
520	胎龄	名	tāilíng	gestational age	20
521	胎动	名	tāidòng	fetal movement	19
522	胎儿	名	tāi'ér	fetal	18
523	痰	名	tán	sputum	4
524	痰鸣音	名	tánmíngyīn	spittle sound	20
525	痰培养	动	tán péiyǎng	sputum culture	3
526	糖钳石膏	名	tángqián shígāo	forcep	12
527	糖化血红蛋白	名	tánghuà xuèhóng dànbái	glycosylated hemoglobin	8
528	探索	动	tànsuǒ	explore；probe	27
529	特殊	形	tèshū	special	3
530	调节	动	tiáojié	adjust	20
531	铁蛋白	名	tiě dànbái	ferritin	7
532	体格	名	tǐgé	physigue	10
533	听觉	名	tīngjué	sense of hearing	26
534	听诊	动	tīngzhěn	auscultate	3

序号	词语	词性	拼音	词义	单元
535	提示	动	tíshì	indicate	10
536	体征	名	tǐzhēng	sign	3
537	体重	名	tǐzhòng	body weight	18
538	通过	动	tōngguò	pass	9
539	通畅	形	tōngchàng	unobstructed	15
540	同房	动	tóngfáng	intercourse	17
541	痛经	名	tòngjīng	dysmenorrhea	17
542	瞳孔	名	tóngkǒng	pupil	24
543	通气	动	tōngqì	ventilate	20
544	桶状胸	名	tǒngzhuàng xiōng	barrel chest	4
545	头颅 CT	名	tóulú CT	head CT scan	5
546	透明	形	tòumíng	transparent	24
547	推测	动	tuīcè	speculated	24
548	推拿	动	tuīná	massage	13
549	凸面	名	tūmiàn	convex	25
550	臀部	名	túnbù	hip	13
551	唾液	名	tuòyè	saliva	2
			W		
552	外感	形	wàigǎn	exogenous	26
553	外界	名	wàijiè	outside	25
554	外伤性白内障	名	wàishāngxìng báinèizhàng	traumatic cataract	24
555	网织红细胞	名	wǎngzhī hóngxìbāo	reticulocyte	7
556	望闻问切	动	wàng-wén-wèn-qiè	inspect，listen-smell，question and take the pulse	26
557	完善	形	wánshàn	perfect	20
558	弯腰	动	wānyāo	stoop	13
559	胃纳	名	wèinà	appetite	1
560	胃黏膜	名	wèi niánmó	gastric mucosa	1
561	萎缩性	形	wěisuōxìng	atrophic	1
562	胃窦	名	wèidòu	antrum of stomach	2
563	畏光	形	wèiguāng	photophobia	24
564	危害	动	wēihài	harm	8
565	胃镜	名	wèijìng	gastroscope	1
566	胃口	名	wèikǒu	appetite	18
567	胃溃疡	名	wèikuìyáng	gastric ulcer（GU）	2
568	卫生巾	名	wèishēngjīn	sanitary towel	19
569	维生素	名	wéishēngsù	vitamin	29

序号	词语	词性	拼音	词义	单元
570	胃炎	名	wèiyán	gastritis	1
571	威胁	动	wēixié	threat	3
572	位于	动	wèiyú	locate	19
573	胃灼热	形	wèizhuórè	heartburn	2
574	温的	形	wēnde	warm	22
575	稳定	形	wěndìng	stable	11
576	稳定性	名	wěndìngxìng	stability	16
577	纹理	名	wénlǐ	texture	24
578	卧床	名	wòchuáng	lie on the bed	13
579	五行	名	wǔxíng	the five elements (metal, wood, water, fire and earth, held by the ancients to compose the physical universe and later used in traditional Chinese medicine to explain various physiological and pathological phenomena)	27
580	物质	名	wùzhì	material	27
			X		
581	细支气管	名	xì zhīqìguǎn	bronchiole	4
582	下腰部	名	xià yāobù	back bend	13
583	下降	动	xiàjiàng	fall	24
584	腺样体	名	xiànyàngtǐ	adenoid	23
585	响	动	xiǎng	loud	23
586	详细	形/副	xiángxì	particular; in detail	22
587	先天性	形	xiāntiānxìng	congenital	22
588	纤维	名	xiānwéi	fibrous	17
589	纤维素	名	xiānwéisù	cellulose	29
590	先兆	名	xiānzhào	foreboding	19
591	消化性溃疡	名	xiāohuàxìng kuìyáng	peptic ulcer	2
592	硝酸甘油	名	xiāosuān gānyóu	nitroglycerin	6
593	消炎	动	xiāoyán	anti-inflammatory	29
594	下肢	名	xiàzhī	lower limb	31
595	携带	动	xiédài	detect	29
596	膝盖	名	xīgài	knee	13
597	细菌	名	xìjūn	bacteria	3
598	细菌性	形	xìjūnxìng	baterial	3
599	型	名	xíng	type	8
600	心前区	名	xīnqiánqū	pericardial region	6

序号	词语	词性	拼音	词义	单元
601	心电图	名	xīndiàntú	electrocardiogram	2
602	行走训练	名	xíngzǒu xùnliàn	walking training	31
603	心悸	动	xīnjì	palpitation	7
604	心肌梗死	动	xīnjī gěngsǐ	myocardial infarction（MI）	6
605	心肌坏死	动	xīnjī huàisǐ	myocardial necrosis	6
606	心肌缺血	动	xīnjī quēxuè	myocardial ischemia	6
607	心绞痛	名	xīnjiǎotòng	angina	6
608	心肌炎	名	xīnjīyán	myocarditis	6
609	辛辣	形	xīnlà	spicy	23
610	新生儿高胆红素血症	名	xīnshēng'ér gāo dǎnhóngsù xuèzhèng	neonatal hyperbilirubinemia	21
611	胸带	名	xiōng dài	chest strap	11
612	胸廓	名	xiōngkuò	thorax	4
613	胸闷	形	xiōngmèn	chest tightness	4
614	胸壁	名	xiōngbì	chest wall	11
615	胸膜腔	名	xiōngmóqiāng	pleural cavity	11
616	胸片	名	xiōngpiàn	chest X-ray	3
617	胸腔闭式引流	动	xiōngqiāng bìshì yǐnliú	closed thoracic drainage	11
618	吸吮	动	xīshǔn	sucking	21
619	嗅觉	名	xiùjué	sense of smell	26
620	细心	形	xìxīn	careful	31
621	虚	形	xū	deficient	19
622	悬挂	动	xuánguà	hang	12
623	血生化	名	xuè shēnghuà	blood biochemistry	2
624	血常规	名	xuèchángguī	blood routine	3
625	血块	名	xuèkuài	blood clot	17
626	血流	名	xuèliú	blood flow	31
627	血尿	名	xuèniào	hematuria	14
628	血清生物标志物	名	xuèqīng shēngwù biāozhìwù	serum biomarker	6
629	血清胃泌素	名	xuèqīng wèimìsù	serum gastric	2
630	血气胸	名	xuè qì xiōng	blood pneumothorax	11
631	血栓病	名	xuèshuānbìng	thrombus	18
632	血液循环	名	xuèyè xúnhuán	blood circulation	6
633	询问	动	xúnwèn	inquire	18
634	寻找	动	xúnzhǎo	seek；look for	27
Y					
635	压痛感	名	yātònggǎn	tenderness	9

序号	词语	词性	拼音	词义	单元
636	咽鼓管吹张	动	yāngǔguǎn chuīzhāng	eustachian tube insufflation	23
637	咽腔	名	yānqiāng	trachea	3
638	痒	形	yǎng	itching	28
639	阳性	形	yángxìng	positive	13
640	眼球	名	yǎnqiú	eyeball	25
641	烟雾	名	yānwù	smoke	4
642	验血	动	yànxuè	blood test	2
643	眼压	名	yǎnyā	intraocular pressure	24
644	炎症	名	yánzhèng	inflammation	10
645	腰椎间盘突出症	名	yāozhuījiānpán tūchū zhèng	lumbar disc herniation	13
646	腰围保护	名	yāowéi bǎohù	waist protection	13
647	压迫	动	yāpò	oppress	10
648	叶酸	名	yèsuān	folic acid	7
649	液体	名	yètǐ	liquid	11
650	异常	形	yìcháng	abnormal	4
651	一旦	副	yīdàn	once	17
652	胰岛素释放试验	名	yídǎosù shìfàng shìyàn	insulin release test	8
653	乙肝五项	名	yǐgān wǔxiàng	hepatitis B five anti-bodies test	29
654	依据	动	yījù	according to	8
655	依赖	动	yīlài	rely on	27
656	疫苗	名	yìmiáo	vaccine	29
657	阴道	名	yīndào	vagina	17
658	硬板床	名	yìngbǎnchuáng	hard bed	13
659	婴儿	名	yīng'ér	infant	16
660	硬膜外麻醉	名	yìngmówài mázuì	epidural anesthesia	30
661	影像学	名	yǐngxiàng xué	Imaging	5
662	营养	名	yíngyǎng	nutrition	18
663	隐私	名	yǐnsī	privacy	30
664	阴阳	名	yīnyáng	(in Chinese philosophy, medicine, etc) yin and yang, the two opposing principles in nature, the former feminine and negative, the latter masculine and positive	27
665	阴影	名	yīnyǐng	shadow	11
666	意识	名	yìshí	consciousness	5
667	异物	名	yìwù	foreign bodies	10

序号	词语	词性	拼音	词义	单元
668	乙型病毒性肝炎	名	yǐxíng bìngdúxìng gānyán	B-type viral hepatitis	29
669	乙型肝炎病毒	名	yǐxíng gānyán bìngdú	hepatitis B virus	29
670	抑制	动	yìzhì	inhibit	2
671	由……组成	–	yóu……zǔchéng	be made up of；consist of	6
672	右侧偏瘫	名	yòucè piāntān	right hemiplegia	31
673	诱发	动	yòufā	induce	5
674	幽门螺杆菌	名	yōumén luógǎnjūn	*Helicobacter pylori*	1
675	油腻	形	yóunì	oily	29
676	右下肺	名	yòuxiàfèi	lower right lung	3
677	有效的	形	yǒuxiàode	effective	4
678	忧郁	形	yōuyù	gloomy	27
679	原发性	形	yuánfāxìng	primary	5
680	瘀斑	名	yūbān	ecchymosis	12
681	预产期	名	yùchǎnqī	expected date of confinement	18
682	月经	名	yuèjīng	menstruation	16
683	预防	动	yùfáng	prevent	13
684	愈合	动	yùhé	heal	12
685	淤血	名	yūxuè	clotted blood	11
686	预约	动	yùyuē	make an appoinment	13
687	宇宙	名	yǔzhòu	universe；cosmos	27
Z					
688	增大	动	zēngdà	enlarge	4
689	增强	动	zēngqiáng	strengthen；enhance	26
690	摘除术	名	zhāichúshù	excision	24
691	胀	形	zhàng	bloating	9
692	胀痛	动	zhàngtòng	swelling pain	10
693	障碍	名	zhàng'ài	obstruction	9
694	折磨	动	zhémó	torment	17
695	诊断	动	zhěnduàn	diagnose	1
696	针对性	名	zhēnduìxìng	pertinence	8
697	整个	形	zhěnggè	whole	19
698	针灸	名	zhēnjiǔ	acupuncture and moxibustion	27
699	诊疗室	名	zhěnliáoshì	clinic	23
700	阵痛	动	zhèntòng	labour pain	10
701	枕头	名	zhěntou	pillow	4
702	疹子	名	zhěnzi	measles	22

序号	词语	词性	拼音	词义	单元
703	哲学	名	zhéxué	philosophy	27
704	致盲	动	zhìmáng	cause of blindness	24
705	直腿抬高	动	zhí tuǐ táigāo	straight leg raise	13
706	指标	名	zhǐbiāo	indicator	11
707	致病	形	zhìbìng	pathogenic	3
708	直肠	名	zhícháng	rectum	17
709	支撑	动	zhīchēng	support	11
710	制定	动	zhìdìng	formulate	8
711	趾甲	名	zhǐjiǎ	nail	20
712	直径	名	zhíjìng	diameter	16
713	之前	副	zhīqián	before	19
714	支气管炎	名	zhīqìguǎnyán	bronchitis	3
715	植入	动	zhírù	implant	24
716	肢体功能	名	zhītǐ gōngnéng	limb function	31
717	肢体训练	名	zhītǐ xùnliàn	limb training	31
718	窒息	动	zhìxī	apnea	11
719	重度	形	zhòngdù	severe	21
720	中耳腔	名	zhōng'ěrqiāng	middle ear cavity	23
721	中耳炎	名	zhōng'ěryán	otitis media	23
722	肿瘤	名	zhǒngliú	tumor	16
723	中性粒细胞	名	zhōngxìng lìxìbāo	neutrophil	3
724	中药	名	zhōngyào	traditional Chinese herb	26
725	终止	动	zhōngzhǐ	end	19
726	骤降	动	zhòujiàng	sudden drop	24
727	周期	名	zhōuqī	period	16
728	周期性	形	zhōuqīxìng	periodic	2
729	转移	动	zhuǎnyí	transfer	10
730	逐年	副	zhúnián	year by year	25
731	灼痛感	名	zhuótònggǎn	burning sensation；burning pain	28
732	子宫	名	zǐgōng	uterus	16
733	自然	形	zìrán	natural	21
734	自如	形	zìrú	free	13
735	自身组织抗原	名	zìshēn zǔzhī kàngyuán	self tissue antigens	28
736	姿势	名	zīshì	posture	13
737	紫外线	名	zǐwàixiàn	ultraviolet	25
738	总胆红素	名	zǒng dǎnhóngsù	total bilirubin	29

序号	词语	词性	拼音	词义	单元
739	综合	动	zōnghé	synthesize	8
740	左脑桥梗死	名	zuǒnǎoqiáo gěngsǐ	left pontine infarction	31
741	阻塞	动	zǔsè	block	10

生词表（二）

序号	词语	词性	拼音	词义
		第一单元		
1	癌变	动	áibiàn	canceration
2	嗳气	名	àiqì	belching
3	病变	动	bìngbiàn	lesion
4	动脉硬化	名	dòngmài yìnghuà	arteriosclerosis
5	复查	动	fùchá	recheck
6	感染	动	gǎnrǎn	infect
7	临床表现	–	línchuáng biǎoxiàn	general clinic manifestation
8	吗丁啉	名	Mǎdīnglín	Domperidone
9	慢性	形	mànxìng	chronic
10	呕吐	动	ǒutù	vomit
11	上腹部	名	shàng fùbù	upper abdomen
12	食欲	名	shíyù	appetite
13	胃黏膜	名	wèi niánmó	gastric mucosa
14	胃镜	名	wèijìng	gastroscope
15	胃纳	名	wèinà	appetite
16	萎缩性	形	wěisuōxìng	atrophic
17	胃炎	名	wèiyán	gastritis
18	幽门螺杆菌	名	yōumén luógǎnjūn	*Helicobacter pylori*
19	诊断	动	zhěnduàn	diagnose
		第二单元		
20	钡餐	名	bèicān	barium meal
21	打嗝	动	dǎgé	hiccup
22	恶心	形	ěxin	nausea
23	反酸	动	fǎnsuān	sour regurgitation
24	反胃	形	fǎnwèi	regurgitation
25	根除	动	gēnchú	eradicate
26	黑便	名	hēibiàn	dark stools；melena
27	活检	动	huójiǎn	biopsies
28	节律性	形	jiélùxìng	rhythmic

序号	词语	词性	拼音	词义
29	戒	动	jiè	quit
30	溃疡灶	名	kuìyáng zào	ulcer lesion
31	麻醉	动	mázuì	anesthetic
32	胃灼热	形	wèizhuórè	heartburn
33	十二指肠	名	shí'èrzhǐcháng	duodenum
34	酸性	形	suānxìng	acidic
35	唾液	名	tuòyè	saliva
36	胃窦	名	wèidòu	antrum of stomach
37	胃溃疡	名	wèikuìyáng	gastric ulcer（GU）
38	消化性溃疡	名	xiāohuàxìng kuìyáng	peptic ulcer
39	心电图	名	xīndiàntú	electrocardiogram
40	血清胃泌素	名	xuèqīng wèimìsù	serum gastric
41	血生化	名	xuè shēnghuà	blood biochemistry
42	验血	动	yànxuè	blood test
43	抑制	动	yìzhì	inhibit
44	周期性	形	zhōuqīxìng	periodic
			第三单元	
45	阿莫西林	名	āmòxīlín	amoxicillin
46	病原体	名	bìngyuántǐ	causative agent
47	肺炎	名	fèiyán	pneumonia
48	肺炎链球菌	名	fèiyán liànqiújūn	streptococcus bacteria
49	咳痰	动	kétán	cough with phlegm
50	右下肺	名	yòuxiàfèi	lower right lung
51	支气管炎	名	zhīqìguǎnyán	bronchitis
52	结合	动	jiéhé	combine
53	青霉素	名	qīngméisù	penicillin
54	白细胞	名	báixìbāo	leukocytosis
55	斑片状浸润影	–	bānpiànzhuàng jìnrùnyǐng	patchy infiltrating shadow
56	鼻腔	名	bíqiāng	nasal cavity
57	比例	名	bǐlì	proportion
58	导致	动	dǎozhì	result in
59	过滤	动	guòlǜ	filter
60	过敏	动	guòmǐn	allergy
61	呼吸	动	hūxī	breath
62	忽视	动	hūshì	neglect
63	疾病史	名	jíbìngshǐ	disease history

序号	词语	词性	拼音	词义
64	解开	动	jiěkāi	unclasp
65	抗菌	动	kàngjūn	antibiotic
66	抗生素	名	kàngshēngsù	antibiotics
67	免疫力	名	miǎnyìlì	immune capacity
68	器官	名	qìguān	organ
69	上呼吸道	名	shànghūxīdào	upper respiratory tract
70	湿啰音	名	shī luóyīn	moist rales
71	受凉	动	shòuliáng	catch cold
72	痰培养	动	tán péiyǎng	sputum culture
73	特殊	形	tèshū	special
74	体征	名	tǐzhēng	sign
75	听诊	动	tīngzhěn	auscultate
76	威胁	动	wēixié	threat
77	细菌	名	xìjūn	bacteria
78	细菌性	形	xìjūnxìng	baterial
79	胸片	名	xiōngpiàn	chest X-ray
80	血常规	名	xuèchángguī	blood routine
81	咽腔	名	yānqiāng	trachea
82	致病	形	zhìbìng	pathogenic
83	中性粒细胞	名	zhōngxìng lìxìbāo	neutrophil
第四单元				
84	抽烟	动	chōuyān	smoking
85	垫	动	diàn	pad
86	二氧化碳	名	èryǎnghuàtàn	carbon dioxide
87	肺泡	名	fèipào	alveoli
88	肺气肿	名	fèiqìzhǒng	emphysema
89	干湿啰音	名	gānshī luóyīn	dry and moist rale
90	根治	动	gēnzhì	radical cure
91	缓解	动	huǎnjiě	ease
92	加重期	名	jiāzhòng qī	aggravating period
93	减弱	动	jiǎnruò	weaken
94	径	名	jìng	path
95	厉害	形	lìhai	powerful
96	慢性支气管炎	名	mànxìng zhīqìguǎnyán	chronic bronchitis
97	慢性阻塞性肺疾病	名	mànxìng zǔsèxìng fèijíbìng	chronic obstructive pulmonary disease
98	毛细血管	名	máoxì xuèguǎn	capillaries

序号	词语	词性	拼音	词义
99	木桶	名	mùtǒng	barrel
100	气喘	动	qìchuǎn	asthma
101	损坏	动	sǔnhuài	damage
102	痰	名	tán	sputum
103	桶状胸	名	tǒngzhuàng xiōng	barrel chest
104	细支气管	名	xì zhīqìguǎn	bronchiole
105	胸廓	名	xiōngkuò	thorax
106	胸闷	形	xiōngmèn	chest tightness
107	烟雾	名	yānwù	smoke
108	异常	形	yìcháng	abnormal
109	有效的	形	yǒuxiàode	effective
110	增大	动	zēngdà	enlarge
111	枕头	名	zhěntou	pillow
			第五单元	
112	病灶	名	bìngzào	focus of primary lesion
113	持续	动	chíxù	continue
114	抽搐	动	chōuchù	convulsion
115	代谢	动	dàixiè	metabolic
116	癫痫	名	diānxián	epilepsy
117	动态脑电图	名	dòngtài nǎodiàntú	electroencephalogram（EEG）
118	犯病	动	fànbìng	fall ill
119	汞	名	gǒng	mercury
120	继发性	形	jìfāxìng	secondary
121	痉挛	动	jìngluán	spasm
122	口吐白沫	–	kǒu tǔ báimò	foam started coming out of mouth
123	脑脊液	名	nǎojǐyè	cerebrospinal fluid
124	脑膜炎	名	nǎomóyán	meningitis
125	脑卒中	名	nǎocùzhòng	stroke
126	铅	名	qiān	plumbum
127	清醒	形	qīngxǐng	sober
128	确诊	动	quèzhěn	make definite diagnosis
129	丧失	动	sàngshī	loss
130	神经系统	名	shénjīng xìtǒng	nervous system
131	输液	动	shūyè	infusion
132	头颅CT	名	tóulú CT	head CT scan
133	意识	名	yìshí	consciousness

序号	词语	词性	拼音	词义
134	影像学	名	yǐngxiàng xué	Imaging
135	诱发	动	yòufā	induce
136	原发性	形	yuánfāxìng	primary
			第六单元	
137	动力	名	dònglì	power
138	动脉	名	dòngmài	artery
139	窦性心律	名	dòuxìng xīnlǜ	sinus rhythm
140	房间隔	名	fáng jiàngé	interatrial septum
141	风湿性心脏病	名	fēngshī xìng xīnzàngbìng	rheumatic heart disease（RHD）
142	服（药）	动	fú（yào）	to take（medicine）
143	高血压	名	gāoxuèyā	hypertension
144	管道	名	guǎndào	pipeline
145	冠状窦	名	guānzhuàngdòu	coronary sinus
146	功能	名	gōngnéng	function
147	毫米汞柱	量	háomǐgǒngzhù	mmHg
148	互不	–	hù bù	be not…each other
149	急性	形	jíxìng	acute
150	静脉	名	jìngmài	vein
151	频繁	副	pínfán	often；frequently
152	腔	名	qiāng	cavity；antrum
153	室间隔	名	shì jiàngé	interventricular septum
154	硝酸甘油	名	xiāosuān gānyóu	nitroglycerin
155	心肌梗死	动	xīnjī gěngsǐ	myocardial infarction（MI）
156	心肌坏死	动	xīnjī huàisǐ	myocardial necrosis
157	心肌缺血	动	xīnjī quēxuè	myocardial ischemia
158	心肌炎	名	xīnjīyán	myocarditis
159	心绞痛	名	xīnjiǎotòng	angina
160	心前区	名	xīnqiánqū	pericardial region
161	血清生物标志物	名	xuèqīng shēngwù biāozhìwù	serum biomarker
162	血液循环	名	xuèyè xúnhuán	blood circulation
163	由……组成	–	yóu……zǔchéng	be made up of；consist of
			第七单元	
164	低色素	名	dī sèsù	hypochromic
165	风湿病	名	fēngshībìng	rheumatism
166	骨髓	名	gǔsuǐ	marrow
167	红细胞	名	hóngxìbāo	red blood cell

序号	词语	词性	拼音	词义
168	巨幼细胞贫血	名	jù yòu xìbāo pínxuè	megaloblastic anemia
169	脾	名	pí	spleen
170	缺铁性贫血	名	quētiěxìng pínxuè	iron deficiency anemia
171	容量	名	róngliàng	capacity
172	溶血	名	róngxuè	hemolytic
173	铁蛋白	名	tiě dànbái	ferritin
174	网织红细胞	名	wǎngzhī hóngxìbāo	reticulocyte
175	心悸	动	xīnjì	palpitation
176	叶酸	名	yèsuān	folic acid
	第八单元			
177	型	名	xíng	type
178	伴发	动	bànfā	concomitant
179	并发症	名	bìngfāzhèng	complication
180	残疾	名	cánjí	disability
181	程度	名	chéngdù	degree
182	代谢紊乱	名	dàixiè wěnluàn	metabolic disorder
183	典型	形	diǎnxíng	typical
184	方案	名	fāng'àn	scheme
185	分割点	名	fēngē diǎn	break point
186	分泌	动	fēnmì	secrete
187	分型	名	fēn xíng	type
188	冠心病	名	guānxīnbìng	coronary heart disease
189	佳	形	jiā	fine
190	空腹血糖	名	kōngfù xuètáng	fasting blood-glucose (FBG)
191	控制	动	kòngzhì	control
192	脑梗死	名	nǎogěngsǐ	cerebral infarction
193	尿糖	名	niàotáng	urine glucose (UGLU)
194	配合	名	pèihé	cooperation
195	葡萄糖耐量	名	pútaotáng nàiliàng	glucose tolerance
196	缺陷	名	quēxiàn	defect
197	人为	形	rénwéi	man-made;artificial
198	妊娠	名	rènshēn	pregnancy
199	手段	名	shǒuduàn	means
200	损害	名	sǔnhài	damage
201	糖化血红蛋白	名	tánghuà xuèhóng dànbái	glycosylated hemoglobin
202	危害	动	wēihài	harm

序号	词语	词性	拼音	词义
203	依据	动	yījù	according to
204	胰岛素释放试验	名	yídǎosù shìfàng shìyàn	insulin release test
205	针对性	名	zhēnduìxìng	pertinence
206	制定	动	zhìdìng	formulate
207	重影	名	chóngyǐng	double image
208	综合	动	zōnghé	synthesize
第九单元				
209	半流质	形	bàn liúzhì	semi-liquid
210	闭	动	bì	closure
211	采集	动	cǎijí	collect
212	肠梗阻	名	chánggěngzǔ	intestinal obstruction
213	肠鸣音	名	chángmíngyīn	bowel sound
214	触诊	名	chùzhěn	palpation
215	脆弱	形	cuìruò	fragile
216	叮嘱	动	dīngzhǔ	advise; warn
217	富含	动	fù hán	be rich in
218	禁食	动	jìnshí	fast
219	高蛋白	形	gāo dànbái	high protein
220	好转	动	hǎozhuǎn	be better
221	急腹症	名	jífùzhèng	acute abdomen diseases
222	蔓延	动	mànyán	spread
223	内容物	名	nèiróng wù	content
224	排气	动	páiqì	fart
225	清淡	形	qīngdàn	light
226	通过	动	tōngguò	pass
227	压痛感	名	yātònggǎn	tenderness
228	胀	形	zhàng	bloating
229	障碍	名	zhàng'ài	obstruction
第十单元				
230	肠道	名	chángdào	intestine
231	反跳痛	名	fǎntiàotòng	rebound symptoms
232	粪	名	fèn	feces
233	腹部 X 射线	名	fùbù X shèxiàn	abdominal X-ray
234	寄生虫	名	jìshēngchóng	parasites
235	绞痛	动	jiǎotòng	colic pain
236	就医	动	jiùyī	see the doctor

序号	词语	词性	拼音	词义
237	拉肚子	动	lādùzi	diarrhea
238	阑尾腔	名	lánwěi qiāng	appendix
239	麦氏点	名	Màishì diǎn	McBurney point
240	盲管	名	mángguǎn	blind tube
241	尿常规	名	niàochángguī	urine routine
242	扭曲	动	niǔqū	twist
243	提示	动	tíshì	indicate
244	体格	名	tǐgé	physique
245	压迫	动	yāpò	oppress
246	炎症	名	yánzhèng	inflammation
247	异物	名	yìwù	foreign bodies
248	胀痛	动	zhàngtòng	swelling pain
249	阵痛	动	zhèntòng	labour pain
250	转移	动	zhuǎnyí	transfer
251	阻塞	动	zǔsè	block
			第十一单元	
252	保守	形	bǎoshǒu	conservative
253	避免	动	bìmiǎn	avoid
254	边缘	名	biānyuán	edge
255	车把	名	chēbǎ	handlebar
256	车祸	名	chēhuò	accident
257	穿透伤	名	chuāntòu shāng	penetrating injury
258	初步	形	chūbù	initial
259	挫伤	动	cuòshāng	contuse
260	钝性伤	名	dùn xìng shāng	blunt trauma
261	沟通	动	gōutōng	communicate
262	急促	形	jícù	tachypnea
263	进行性血胸	名	jìnxíngxìng xuèxiōng	progressive hemothorax
264	剧烈	形	jùliè	strenuous
265	肋骨	名	lèigǔ	rib
266	耐受	动	nàishòu	tolerate
267	评估	动	pínggū	evaluate
268	破裂	动	pòliè	rupture
269	锐器	名	ruìqì	sharp
270	随意	副	suíyì	arbitrarily
271	损伤	动	sǔnshāng	injury

序号	词语	词性	拼音	词义
272	稳定	形	wěndìng	stable
273	胸壁	名	xiōngbì	chest wall
274	胸带	名	xiōng dài	chest strap
275	胸膜腔	名	xiōngmóqiāng	pleural cavity
276	胸腔闭式引流	动	xiōngqiāng bìshì yǐnliú	closed thoracic drainage
277	血气胸	名	xuè qì xiōng	blood pneumothorax
278	液体	名	yètǐ	liquid
279	阴影	名	yīnyǐng	shadow
280	淤血	名	yūxuè	clotted blood
281	支撑	动	zhīchēng	support
282	指标	名	zhǐbiāo	indicator
283	窒息	动	zhìxī	apnea
			第十二单元	
284	绷带	名	bēngdài	bandage
285	错位	动	cuòwèi	dislocate
286	复位	名	fùwèi	restoration
287	肱骨干	名	gōnggǔ gàn	shaft of humerus
288	肱骨外科颈	名	gōnggǔ wàikē jǐng	surgical neck of humerus
289	骨擦感	名	gǔcāgǎn	bone abrasion
290	骨擦音	名	gǔcāyīn	bone crepitus
291	畸形	名	jīxíng	malformation
292	康复	动	kāngfù	rehabilitate
293	麻醉药	名	mázuìyào	anesthetics
294	失用性萎缩	动	shīyòngxìng wěisuō	disuse atrophy
295	受限	动	shòuxiàn	be limitted
296	舒缩	动	shū suō	systolic and diastolic
297	糖钳石膏	名	tángqián shígāo	forcep
298	悬挂	动	xuánguà	hang
299	瘀斑	名	yūbān	ecchymosis
300	愈合	动	yùhé	heal
			第十三单元	
301	背	名	bèi	human back
302	磁共振成像	名	cígòngzhèn chéngxiàng	magnetic resonance imaging
303	断断续续	形	duànduànxùxù	off and on
304	蹲	动	dūn	kneel down
305	恶化	动	èhuà	get worse

序号	词语	词性	拼音	词义
306	概率	名	gàilǜ	probability
307	加剧	动	jiājù	aggravat
308	绝对	副	juéduì	absolute
309	靠背	名	kàobèi	backrest of chair
310	理疗	名	lǐliáo	physiotherapy
311	佩戴	动	pèidài	wear
312	强力	形	qiánglì	strong
313	扫描	动	sǎomiáo	scan
314	手法	名	shóufǎ	method
315	推拿	动	tuīná	massage
316	臀部	名	túnbù	hip
317	弯腰	动	wānyāo	stoop
318	卧床	名	wòchuáng	lie on the bed
319	膝盖	名	xīgài	knee
320	下腰部	名	xià yāobù	back bend
321	阳性	形	yángxìng	positive
322	腰围保护	名	yāowéi bǎohù	waist protection
323	腰椎间盘突出症	名	yāozhuījiānpán tūchū zhèng	lumbar disc herniation
324	硬板床	名	yìngbǎnchuáng	hard bed
325	预防	动	yùfáng	prevent
326	预约	动	yùyuē	make an appoinment
327	直腿抬高	动	zhí tuǐ táigāo	straight leg raise
328	姿势	名	zīshì	posture
329	自如	形	zìrú	free
第十四单元				
330	成分	名	chéngfèn	ingredient
331	会阴	名	huìyīn	perineum
332	积水	名	jīshuǐ	hydrops
333	脊	名	jǐ	costolumbar
334	解除	动	jiěchú	get rid of
335	叩击痛	名	kòujī tòng	percussive pain
336	肋	名	lèi	rib
337	类(似)	形	lèi(sì)	similar
338	凌晨	名	língchén	before dawn
339	尿路感染	–	niàolù gǎnrǎn	urinary tract infection
340	轻微	形	qīngwēi	slightly

序号	词语	词性	拼音	词义
341	深夜	名	shēnyè	late at night
342	肾绞痛	名	shèn jiǎotòng	renal colic
343	肾结石	名	shènjiéshí	renal calculus
344	肾上盏结石	名	shèn shàng zhǎn jiéshí	upper calyceal calculus
345	输尿管镜	名	shūniàoguǎn jìng	ureteroscope
346	血尿	名	xuèniào	hematuria
第十五单元				
347	伴	动	bàn	and
348	胆固醇	名	dǎngùchún	cholesterol
349	胆红素	名	dǎnhóngsù	bilirubin
350	胆囊结石	名	dǎnnáng jiéshí	gallstone
351	胆囊炎	名	dǎnnángyán	cholecystitis
352	肝功能	名	gāngōngnéng	liver function
353	黄疸	名	huángdǎn	jaundice
354	紧急	形	jǐnjí	urgent
355	胆囊	名	dǎnnáng	gall bladder
356	胆色素	名	dǎnsèsù	bile pigment
357	胆汁淤积	名	dǎnzhī yūjī	cholestasis
358	寒战	名	hánzhàn	shivering
359	蛔虫	名	huíchóng	ascarid
360	火锅	名	huǒguō	hot pot
361	解除梗阻	–	jiěchú gěngzǔ	relieve the obstruction
362	忍受	动	rěnshòu	tolerate；endure
363	稍微	副	shāowēi	slightly
364	通畅	形	tōngchàng	unobstructed
第十六单元				
365	包块	名	bāo kuài	enclosed mass
366	表现	名	biǎoxiàn	manifestation
367	病房	名	bìngfáng	ward
368	超声	名	chāoshēng	ultrasound
369	措施	名	cuòshī	measure
370	恶性	形	èxìng	malignant
371	妇科	名	fùkē	gynecology department
372	复发率	名	fùfālǜ	recurrence rate
373	腹部	名	fùbù	abdomen
374	规律	名	guīlǜ	regular

序号	词语	词性	拼音	词义
375	浆液性	形	jiāngyèxìng	serous
376	良性	形	liángxìng	benign
377	卵巢囊肿	名	luǎncháo nángzhǒng	ovarian cyst
378	黏液性	形	niányèxìng	mucinous
379	入院单	名	rùyuàn dān	admission list
380	上皮性	形	shàngpíxìng	epithelial
381	生殖	名	shēngzhí	reproduction
382	稳定性	名	wěndìngxìng	stability
383	婴儿	名	yīng'ér	infant
384	月经	名	yuèjīng	menstruation
385	直径	名	zhíjìng	diameter
386	肿瘤	名	zhǒngliú	tumor
387	周期	名	zhōuqī	period
388	子宫	名	zǐgōng	uterus
第十七单元				
389	癌症	名	áizhèng	cancer
390	恶变	动	èbiàn	degenerate
391	宫颈	名	gōngjǐng	cervix
392	骨盆	名	gǔpén	pelvis
393	规则	形	guīzé	regular
394	肌瘤	名	jīliú	leiomyomata
395	监控	动	jiānkòng	monitor
396	明确	形	míngquè	explicite
397	膀胱	名	pángguāng	bladder
398	确切	形	quèqiè	definite
399	生育	名	shēngyù	bearing
400	同房	动	tóngfáng	intercourse
401	痛经	名	tòngjīng	dysmenorrhea
402	纤维	名	xiānwéi	fibrous
403	血块	名	xuèkuài	blood clot
404	一旦	副	yīdàn	once
405	阴道	名	yīndào	vagina
406	折磨	动	zhémó	torment
407	直肠	名	zhícháng	rectum
第十八单元				
408	产前检查	名	chǎnqián jiǎnchá	antenatal examination

序号	词语	词性	拼音	词义
409	促进	动	cùjìn	promote
410	多胎妊娠	名	duōtāi rènshēn	multiple pregnancy
411	分娩	动	fēnmiǎn	childbirth；delivery
412	腹围	名	fùwéi	abdominal perimeter
413	改善	动	gǎishàn	ameliorate
414	宫高	名	gōnggāo	fundal height
415	化验	动	huàyàn	test
416	怀孕	动	huáiyùn	be pregnant
417	家族病	名	jiāzúbìng	hereditary disease
418	监测	动	jiāncè	monitor
419	目前	形	mùqián	at present
420	盆腔	名	pénqiāng	pelvis
421	去世	动	qùshì	die
422	双胞胎	名	shuāngbāotāi	twins
423	胎儿	名	tāi'ér	fetal
424	体重	名	tǐzhòng	body weight
425	胃口	名	wèikǒu	appetite
426	血栓病	名	xuèshuānbìng	thrombus
427	询问	动	xúnwèn	inquire
428	营养	名	yíngyǎng	nutrition
429	预产期	名	yùchǎnqī	expected date of confinement
第十九单元				
430	边缘性	名	biānyuánxìng	marginality
431	部分性	名	bùfenxìng	partial seizures
432	彩超	名	cǎichāo	color ultrasound
433	处理	动	chǔlǐ	deal with
434	耽误	动	dānwu	delay
435	低置	动	dīzhì	locate in a low position
436	定位	动	dìngwèi	orient
437	反复	副	fǎnfù	repeatedly
438	附着	动	fùzhuó	adhere to
439	覆盖	动	fùgài	cover
440	宫颈口	名	gōngjǐngkǒu	cervix
441	浑身	副	húnshēn	from head to foot
442	接近	动	jiējìn	be close to
443	精确	形	jīngquè	precise

序号	词语	词性	拼音	词义
444	类	名	lèi	kind；category
445	流	动	liú	flow
446	流产	名	liúchǎn	abortion
447	内口	名	nèikǒu	internal opening
448	剖宫产	名	pōugōngchǎn	caesarean section
449	前后壁	名	qián hòu bì	anterior posterior wall
450	前置胎盘	名	qiánzhì tāipán	placenta previa
451	属于	动	shǔyú	be belong to
452	胎动	名	tāidòng	fetal movement
453	卫生巾	名	wèishēngjīn	sanitary towel
454	位于	动	wèiyú	locate
455	先兆	名	xiānzhào	foreboding
456	虚	形	xū	deficient
457	整个	形	zhěnggè	whole
458	之前	副	zhīqián	before
459	终止	动	zhōngzhǐ	end
	第二十单元			
460	阿氏评分	名	āshìpíngfēn	Apgar scores
461	薄	形	báo	thin
462	保温	动	bǎowēn	insulation
463	采取	动	cǎiqǔ	take
464	超	副	chāo	ultra
465	端	名	duān	end
466	辅助	形	fǔzhù	aid
467	恭喜	动	gōngxǐ	congratulations
468	喉反射	名	hóufǎnshè	laryngeal reflex
469	呼吸窘迫综合征	名	hūxī jiǒngpò zōnghézhēng	respiratory distress syndrome
470	肌张力	名	jīzhānglì	muscle tension
471	极	副	jí	pole
472	暖箱	名	nuǎnxiāng	warm box
473	浅促	形	qiǎncù	shortness of breath
474	缺氧	动	quēyǎng	hypoxia
475	适应	动	shìyìng	adapt
476	胎龄	名	tāilíng	gestational age
477	痰鸣音	名	tánmíngyīn	spittle sound
478	调节	动	tiáojié	adjust

序号	词语	词性	拼音	词义
479	通气	动	tōngqì	ventilate
480	完善	形	wánshàn	perfect
481	趾甲	名	zhǐjiǎ	nail
第二十一单元				
482	百分数	名	bǎifēnshù	percentage
483	病理性	形	bìnglǐxìng	pathological
484	烦躁	形	fánzào	irritability
485	巩膜	名	gǒngmó	sclera
486	黄染	形	huángrǎn	yellow dye
487	进展	动	jìnzhǎn	progress
488	淋巴细胞	名	línbā xìbāo	lymphocyte
489	满月	名	mǎnyuè	a baby's completion of its first month of life
490	浓度	名	nóngdù	concentration
491	生理性	形	shēnglǐxìng	physiological
492	顺产	名	shùnchǎn	natural labor
493	吸吮	动	xīshǔn	sucking
494	新生儿高胆红素血症	名	xīnshēng'ér gāo dǎnhóngsù xuèzhèng	neonatal hyperbilirubinemia
495	重度	形	zhòngdù	severe
496	自然	形	zìrán	natural
第二十二单元				
497	保健	名	bǎojiàn	health and fitness
498	发绀	名	fāgàn	cyanosis
499	发育	名/动	fāyù	growth；grow
500	范围	名	fànwéi	scope
501	感染性	形	gǎnrǎnxìng	infectious
502	红晕	名	hóngyùn	flush
503	惊厥	名	jīngjué	convulsions
504	口腔黏膜	名	kǒuqiāng niánmó	mucous membrane of mouth
505	温的	形	wēnde	warm
506	疱疹	名	pàozhěn	herpes
507	脐	名	qí	funicle
508	全面	形	quánmiàn	comprehensive
509	身心	名	shēnxīn	mind and body
510	手足口病	名	shǒuzúkǒubìng	hand-foot-and-mouth disease
511	水疱	名	shuǐpào	blister
512	随着	动	suízhe	along with

序号	词语	词性	拼音	词义
513	先天性	形	xiāntiānxìng	congenital
514	详细	形/副	xiángxì	particular; in detail
515	疹子	名	zhěnzi	measles
第二十三单元				
516	保养	动	bǎoyǎng	maintenance
517	舱	名	cāng	cabin
518	嘈杂	形	cáozá	noisy
519	抽	动	chōu	take out
520	穿刺	动	chuāncì	puncture
521	穿孔	动	chuānkǒng	perforation
522	耳鸣	动	ěrmíng	tinnitus
523	发闷	动	fāmen	stuffy
524	肥大	形	féidà	hypertrophy
525	分泌物	名	fēnmìwù	secretions
526	分泌性	形	fēnmìxìng	secretory
527	鼓	名	gǔ	drum
528	鼓膜	名	gǔmó	tympanic membrane
529	鼓气	动	gǔqì	blow air
530	鼓室腔	名	gǔshìqiāng	tympanic cavity
531	化脓性	形	huànóngxìng	purulent infection
532	恢复	动	huīfù	get well
533	积液	名	jīyè	effusion
534	嚼	动	jiáo	chew
535	聚集	动	jùjí	accumulate
536	抗	动	kàng	anti-
537	口香糖	名	kǒuxiāngtáng	chewing gum
538	流动	动	liúdòng	flow
539	蒙	动	méng	imprison
540	密封	形	mìfēng	sealed
541	黏液	名	niányè	mucus
542	黏液促排剂	名	niányè cùpáijì	mucus promoting agents
543	捏	动	niē	hold between fingers
544	似的	助	shìde	rather like
545	腺样体	名	xiànyàngtǐ	adenoid
546	响	动	xiǎng	loud
547	辛辣	形	xīnlà	spicy

序号	词语	词性	拼音	词义
548	咽鼓管吹张	动	yāngǔguǎn chuīzhāng	eustachian tube insufflation
549	诊疗室	名	zhěnliáoshì	clinic
550	中耳腔	名	zhōng'ěrqiāng	middle ear cavity
551	中耳炎	名	zhōng'ěryán	otitis media
第二十四单元				
552	迟钝	形	chídùn	slow
553	反射	动	fǎnshè	reflection
554	虹膜	名	hóngmó	iris
555	混浊	形	húnzhuó	turbid
556	急剧	形	jíjù	sudden drop
557	继发性青光眼	名	jìfāxìng qīngguāngyǎn	secondary glaucoma
558	角膜	名	jiǎomó	cornea
559	角膜穿通伤	名	jiǎomó chuāntōngshāng	corneal penetrating injury
560	晶状体	名	jīngzhuàngtǐ	lens
561	裂伤	名	lièshāng	laceration
562	灵敏	形	língmǐn	sensitivity
563	木屑	名	mùxiè	sawdust
564	视力	名	shìlì	vision
565	瞳孔	名	tóngkǒng	pupil
566	透明	形	tòumíng	transparent
567	推测	动	tuīcè	speculated
568	外伤性白内障	名	wàishāngxìng báinèizhàng	traumatic cataract
569	畏光	形	wèiguāng	photophobia
570	纹理	名	wénlǐ	texture
571	下降	动	xiàjiàng	fall
572	眼压	名	yǎnyā	intraocular pressure
573	摘除术	名	zhāichúshù	excision
574	植入	动	zhírù	implant
575	致盲	动	zhìmáng	cause of blindness
576	骤降	动	zhòujiàng	sudden drop
第二十五单元				
577	挡住	动	dǎngzhù	block
578	发病率	名	fābìnglǜ	incidentce rate
579	换	动	huàn	change
580	会聚	动	huìjù	converge
581	镜头	名	jìngtóu	lens

序号	词语	词性	拼音	词义
582	裂隙灯显微镜检查	名	lièxìdēng xiǎnwēijìng jiǎnchá	slit lamp microscope test
583	请示	动	qǐngshì	consult
584	屈光的	形	qūguāngde	refractive
585	全球	形	quánqiú	global
586	人工	名	réngōng	artificial
587	日晒	名	rìshài	exposure to the sun
588	乳白色	名	rǔbáisè	milky
589	凸面	名	tūmiàn	convex
590	外界	名	wàijiè	outside
591	眼球	名	yǎnqiú	eyeball
592	逐年	副	zhúnián	year by year
593	紫外线	名	zǐwàixiàn	ultraviolet
第二十六单元				
594	把脉	动	bǎmài	feel the pulse
595	保持	动	bǎochí	maintain
596	本质	名	běnzhì	essence
597	鼻塞	名	bísè	nasal obstruction
598	鼻涕	名	bítì	rhinorrhea
599	病毒	名	bìngdú	virus
600	畅通	形	chàngtōng	unobstructed
601	触按	动	chùàn	touch and press
602	打喷嚏	动	dǎ pēntì	sneeze
603	复诊	名	fùzhěn	further consultation (with a doctor)
604	肌肤	名	jīfū	skin
605	流通	动	liútōng	circulate
606	脉搏	名	màibó	pulse
607	脉象	名	màixiàng	pulse condition
608	排出物	名	páichūwù	discharge
609	气味	名	qìwèi	smell；odour；flavour
610	舌苔	名	shétāi	coating on the tongue
611	舌头	名	shétou	tongue
612	神态	名	shéntài	expression；manner
613	视觉	名	shìjué	sense of sight
614	蔬菜	名	shūcài	vegetables
615	四诊合参	名	sìzhěn hécān	comprehensive analysis by the four examination methods

序号	词语	词性	拼音	词义
616	素质	名	sùzhì	quality
617	听觉	名	tīngjué	sense of hearing
618	外感	形	wàigǎn	exogenous
619	望闻问切	动	wàng-wén-wèn-qiè	inspect, listen-smell, question and take the pulse
620	嗅觉	名	xiùjué	sense of smell
621	增强	动	zēngqiáng	strengthen; enhance
622	中药	名	zhōngyào	traditional Chinese herb
第二十七单元				
623	拔罐	名	báguàn	cupping
624	伴随	动	bànsuí	accompany; follow
625	对立	动	duìlì	oppose
626	范畴	名	fànchóu	category
627	方式	名	fāngshì	way; pattern
628	愤怒	形	fènnù	wrathful
629	古代	形	gǔdài	ancient
630	过度	形	guòdù	excessive
631	急躁	形	jízào	irritable; impatient
632	降压药	名	jiàngyāyào	hypotensor
633	精力	名	jīnglì	energy; vigour
634	颈椎病	名	jǐngzhuībìng	cervical spondylosis
635	脾胃病	名	píwèibìng	spleen and stomach diseases
636	平衡	名	pínghéng	balance
637	气血	名	qìxuè	vital energy and blood
638	缺乏	动	quēfá	be short of; lack
639	失眠	名	shīmián	insomnia; sleeplessness
640	湿润	形	shīrùn	moist
641	舒畅	形	shūchàng	entirely free from worry
642	探索	动	tànsuǒ	explore; probe
643	五行	名	wǔxíng	the five elements (metal, wood, water, fire and earth, held by the ancients to compose the physical universe and later used in traditional Chinese medicine to explain various physiological and pathological phenomena)
644	物质	名	wùzhì	material
645	寻找	动	xúnzhǎo	seek; look for
646	依赖	动	yīlài	rely on

序号	词语	词性	拼音	词义
647	阴阳	名	yīnyáng	（in Chinese philosophy，medicine，etc）yin and yang，the two opposing principles in nature，the former feminine and negative，the latter masculine and positive
648	忧郁	形	yōuyù	gloomy
649	宇宙	名	yǔzhòu	universe；cosmos
650	哲学	名	zhéxué	philosophy
651	针灸	名	zhēnjiǔ	acupuncture and moxibustion
第二十八单元				
652	变应原	名	biànyìngyuán	allergen
653	澄清	形	chéngqīng	clear
654	抵抗力	名	dǐkànglì	immunity
655	繁殖	动	fánzhí	to breed；to grown
656	粉尘	名	fěnchén	dust
657	疙瘩	名	gēda	pimple；knot
658	花粉	名	huāfěn	pollen
659	黄豆	名	huángdòu	soybean
660	链霉素	名	liànméisù	streptomycin
661	排列	动	páiliè	to arrange
662	疱壁	名	pàobì	blister wall
663	皮损（皮肤损伤）	名	písǔn（pífū sǔnshāng）	skin injury
664	皮屑	名	píxiè	scuff；dander
665	侵犯	名/动	qīnfàn	invasion；to violate；to invade
666	丘疹	名	qiūzhěn	papula
667	神经纤维	名	shénjīng xiānwéi	nerve fiber
668	式	名	shì	type；style；mode
669	受	动	shòu	to accept；to suffer
670	水痘	名	shuǐdòu	chicken pox
671	痒	形	yǎng	itching
672	灼痛感	名	zhuótònggǎn	burning sensation；burning pain
673	自身组织抗原	名	zìshēn zǔzhī kàngyuán	self tissue antigens
第二十九单元				
674	病毒含量	名	bìngdú hánliàng	virus content
675	传播	动	chuánbō	transmit
676	传染病	名	chuánrǎnbìng	infectious disease
677	传染源	名	chuánrǎnyuán	source of infection
678	刺激性	形	cìjīxìng	irritating

序号	词语	词性	拼音	词义
679	胆囊触诊	动	dǎnnáng chùzhěn	gallbladder palpation
680	乏力	形	fálì	weak;feeble
681	干扰素	名	gānrǎosù	interferon
682	肝癌	名	gānái	liver cancer
683	肝区	名	gānqū	liver area
684	肝硬化	名	gānyìnghuà	liver cirrhosis
685	谷丙转氨酶	名	gǔbǐngzhuǎnānméi	alanine aminotransferase
686	核苷酸类似物	名	hégānsuān lèisì wù	nucleotide analogues
687	减退	动	jiǎntuì	slack up
688	接种	动	jiēzhòng	inoculate
689	抗病毒	动	kàng bìngdú	anti-viral
690	抗感染	动	kàng gǎnrǎn	anti-infective
691	浓	形	nóng	dark;thick
692	人工肝血浆置换	动	réngōng gān xuèjiāng zhìhuàn	artificial liver plasma replacement therapy
693	维生素	名	wéishēngsù	vitamin
694	纤维素	名	xiānwéisù	cellulose
695	消炎	动	xiāoyán	anti-inflammatory
696	携带	动	xiédài	detect
697	乙肝五项	名	yǐgān wǔxiàng	hepatitis B five anti-bodies test
698	乙型病毒性肝炎	名	yǐxíng bìngdúxìng gānyán	B-type viral hepatitis
699	乙型肝炎病毒	名	yǐxíng gānyán bìngdú	hepatitis B virus
700	疫苗	名	yìmiáo	vaccine
701	油腻	形	yóunì	oily
702	总胆红素	名	zǒng dǎnhóngsù	total bilirubin
第三十单元				
703	保障	动	bǎozhàng	assure
704	病情	名	bìngqíng	state of an illness
705	不良反应	名	bùliáng fǎnyìng	untoward reaction
706	复合麻醉	名	fùhé mázuì	compound anesthesia
707	核对	动	héduì	check
708	技术	名	jìshù	technique
709	监护仪	名	jiānhùyí	monitor
710	建立	名	jiànlì	set up
711	紧张	形	jǐnzhāng	nervous
712	禁忌证	名	jìnjìzhèng	incompatibility symptom
713	胫腓骨	名	jìngféigǔ	tibiofibula

序号	词语	词性	拼音	词义
714	静脉通道	名	jìngmài tōngdào	passage of vein
715	局部麻醉	名	júbù mázuì	local anesthesia
716	麻醉史	名	mázuìshǐ	history of anesthesia
717	全身麻醉	名	quánshēn mázuì	general anesthesia
718	生命功能	名	shēngmìng gōngnéng	vital function
719	适应证	名	shìyìngzhèng	adaptation symptom
720	隐私	名	yǐnsī	privacy
721	硬膜外麻醉	名	yìngmówài mázuì	epidural anesthesia
	第三十一单元			
722	被动运动	动	bèidòng yùndòng	passive movement
723	不完全性瘫	名	búwánquánxìngtān	incomplete hemiplegia
724	测量	动	cèliáng	measure
725	锻炼	名	duànliàn	exercise
726	多亏	形	duōkuī	thank to
727	患肢	名	huànzhī	affected limb
728	楼梯	名	lóutī	stair
729	陪同	动	péitóng	accompany
730	平衡训练	名	pínghéng xùnliàn	balance training
731	轻瘫	名	qīng tān	paresis
732	清晰	副	qīngxī	clearly
733	全瘫	名	quán tān	complete hemiplegia
734	细心	形	xìxīn	careful
735	下肢	名	xiàzhī	lower limb
736	行走训练	名	xíngzǒu xùnliàn	walking training
737	血流	名	xuèliú	blood flow
738	右侧偏瘫	名	yòucè piāntān	right hemiplegia
739	肢体功能	名	zhītǐ gōngnéng	limb function
740	肢体训练	名	zhītǐ xùnliàn	limb training
741	左脑桥梗死	名	zuǒnǎoqiáo gěngsǐ	left pontine infarction

附录三

参考文献

[1]安晓芳.康复医疗评价会对脑出血后左侧瘫伴单侧空间忽略及足内翻、下垂的治疗[J].中国组织工程研究与临床康复,2001,5(8):20-21.

[2]陈丽萍,张哲,孙景辉.实用医学汉语·临床篇[M].北京:外语教学与研究出版社,2010.

[3]陈孝平,汪建平.外科学[M].8版.北京:人民卫生出版社,2013.

[4]葛坚,王宁利.眼科学[M].北京:人民卫生出版社,2015.

[5]葛均波,徐永健.内科学[M].北京:人民卫生出版社,2013.

[6]关骅.临床康复学[M].北京:华夏出版社,2005.

[7]李兰娟,任红.传染病学[M].北京:人民卫生出版社出版,2013.

[8]廖二元.内分泌代谢病学[M].3版.人民卫生出版社,2012.

[9]凌奕,金松.英汉对照妇产科实践指南[M].浙江:浙江大学出版社,2013.

[10]田伟.实用骨科学[M].5版.北京:人民卫生出版社,2008.

[11]田勇泉.耳鼻喉头颈外科学[M].8版.北京:人民卫生出版社,2013.

[12]王卫平.儿科学[M].8版.北京:人民卫生出版社,2013.

[13]徐启明.临床麻醉学[M].2版.北京:人民卫生出版社.2006.

[14]张哲,李彩霞.汉英·英汉:实用医学汉语临床词汇手册[M].北京:外语教学与研究出版社,2010.

[15]周小兵,莫秀英.医学汉语·实习篇[M].北京:北京大学出版社,2007.

[16]周仲英.中医内科学[M].北京:中国中医药出版社,2003.

[17]朱德军,潘国栋.实用医学汉语·基础篇1[M].北京:外语教学与研究出版社,2008.

[18]朱文锋.中医诊断学[M].北京:中国中医药出版社,2002.